Friends Face the World

Some Continuing and Current Quaker Concerns

Leonard S. Kenworthy, Editor

Friends General Conference
Philadelphia, Pennsylvania

Friends United Press
Richmond, Indiana

Quaker Publications
Kennett Square, Pennsylvania

Library of Congress Cataloging-in-Publication Data

Friends face the world.

      1. Church and the world.   2. Society of Friends.
I. Kenworthy, Leonard Stout, 1912—
BR115.W6F75   1987   261   87-8664
ISBN 0-913408-97-2

Published cooperatively by Friends General Conference, Friends United Press,
and Quaker Publications

Dedicated to Olcutt Sanders
who contributed creatively to many Quaker concerns

Contents

FRIENDS FACE THE WORLD

INTRODUCTION

Throughout the more than three hundred years of its existence, members of the Religious Society of Friends have been more concerned with the here and now than with the hereafter. They have sought in many different ways to improve the societies in which they have lived–locally, nationally, and internationally. At their best they have tried to carry out Amos' injunction to "let justice roll down as waters and righteousness as a mighty stream," and Jesus' admonition in the Lord's Prayer that "Thy kingdom come, Thy will be done on earth, as it is in heaven."

At some undetermined point in Friends history those intense desires to bring about needed changes came to be called "concerns." That is a glorious word, but it is one which we use too often for some passing whim or fancy. Douglas Steere has written perceptively on the meaning of that word, as follows:

> In its truest form a concern refers to a costly inner leading to some act that in the course of its fulfillment may take over the very life of the one it engages. At this level it can be said that in a genuine concern a person has been drawn into the living, inward linkage of man and God, of man and man, and of man and creation.

Even in that demanding sense, Quakers have had concerns for centuries. They have felt deeply about many causes or movements and have been willing to expend vast amounts of time and energy to bring about needed changes, often giving sacrificially to those concerns.

Some of those causes have continued from the earliest time to the

1

present (education, women's rights, peace, and the plight of minority groups) even though the emphasis may have changed, depending upon the place and the period of history. Others are more current, such as the movement to designate Quaker Meetinghouses as "sanctuaries" for refugees, or the movement of individuals to withhold a part of their federal income taxes that would be used for military purposes.

As the chapter titles in this book indicate, there are nineteen essays on continuing and current concerns, plus Jack Kirk's essay on the importance of religious motivation for such work. Moreover, several other concerns are subsumed under those comprehensive titles. Of course, there are other movements in which some Friends are interested which have not been included lest this book become too long and too expensive.

Perhaps some readers will be interested in the reasons for this volume and its genesis. In 1952, Jack Kavanaugh edited a book on *The Quaker Approach*, with such distinguished authors as Curtis Bok, Kenneth Boulding, Henry Cadbury, Clarence Pickett, and Elton Trueblood. It served its purpose well, but has long been out of print. Then, in 1972, a group of Quakers in Western Yearly Meeting produced a paperback with the title *Concerns*. It, too, was a useful compendium, but it served a limited audience and has also been out of print for many years.

Aware of the lack of a volume on contemporary Quaker concerns, and convinced of the need for such a publication, I began to plan this book. I approached Olcutt Sanders, the imaginative editor of the *Friends Journal*, and he agreed to co-edit such a volume. Shortly after that, however, Olcutt died. Hence I am very glad to dedicate this book to him as a creative and concerned Quaker.

When I approached the Publications Committee of Friends General Conference and Friends United Press of Friends United Meeting, they agreed to co-publish this book with Quaker Publications.

This volume is based on several key considerations, including the following:

1. We need to be aware of the long history of Quaker concerns and proud of our past. But we need to be even more concerned about various causes today and tomorrow.

2. We need to be certain that our concerns are spritually-based, lest we outrun our "leadings" and became involved in what Quakers have sometimes called "creaturely activities".

3. We need to be well-informed and constantly seeking new light on issues, wherever we can find it. Truth often seems elusive, but it needs to be pursued relentlessly.
4. We need to consider the local, national, and international dimensions of any concern, finding the level where we can contribute most effectively as individuals and/or as groups.
5. We need generalists and specialists on every Quaker concern; individuals and groups must determine how they can function best.
6. We need persons with skills as well as altruistic attitudes.
7. We need long-term and short-term goals.
8. We need to be constantly working on ourselves as individuals, as well as on the causes for which we are struggling.
9. We need to choose our priorities carefully and in most instances to concentrate on one or two concerns rather than spreading ourselves thin on a great variety of them.
10. We need perspective, persistence, and patience— realizing that we may not see the achievement of our goals in our lifetime.

It is my hope that this book will serve a variety of purposes and uses:

1. To be read and studied by individuals.
2. To be used by First Day School or Sunday School classes of young people and adults.
3. To be studied in Friends schools and colleges.
4. To assist various committees at the local, Quarterly, Yearly Meeting, national, and international levels in pursuing their work.
5. To further a sense of common purpose and unity among the various groups of Friends as they examine carefully and prayerfully their priorities in this period of history.
6. To serve as a catalytic agent, reactivating local Quaker groups and stimulating active groups in

the application of their Quaker faith to social, economic, and political issues.

7. To suggest vocational possibilities to some individuals, especially young people.

8. To foster local service projects by Quaker Meetings and Friends Churches.

9. To extend the background of Friends on Quaker concerns through the readings suggested and the organizations cited in this volume.

10. To provide inquirers from outside the Religious Society of Friends with accurate and up-to-date information on Quaker concerns, past and present.

We have been unusually fortunate in enlisting the help of the contributors to this book. They represent individuals well-versed in the concerns about which they have written. Furthermore, they represent Friends from thirteen different Yearly Meetings in the United States and the five major groups of Quakers in our country: Conservative Friends, Evangelical Friends Alliance, Friends General Conference, Friends United Meeting, and independent Yearly Meetings. The writers express here their own views, and they do not necessarily represent the opinions of the volume's sponsors. Each of the authors had complete freedom to express his or her own convictions, and the editing has been minimal. We are grateful to them for their generous contribution of their time, energy, concern, and expertise.

It is my fervent hope that this book will help many Friends to rediscover and to reclaim their Quaker heritage, and to rededicate themselves to the creation of the world not only of peace, but of freedom and justice for all members of the worldwide human family.

Leonard S. Kenworthy
Kendal at Longwood
Kennett Square, Pennsylvania

Chapter 1

Creaturely Activities or Spiritually Based Concerns?

Jack Kirk

Across the years sincere, conscientious Friends, acting on their concerns, have had an impact on society in some highly significant ways. One thinks of some obvious examples: John Woolman's gently persuading his fellow Quakers to renounce the practice of keeping slaves; William and Esther Tuke's giving up their home in York, England, to show that Christian love could make a difference with the mentally disturbed; Elizabeth Fry's venturing into the depths of Newgate Prison, where even the jailers feared to go, and starting the modern prison reform movement; and Lucretia Mott's tirelessly giving impetus to women's rights. There have been hundreds and thousands of others—a few dramatic, but most of them humble, often behind-the-scenes, perhaps hardly noticed—all faithful.

Concerns are the way that God gets our attention and gives us our portions of work to do for the Kingdom. How many times have you heard a Friend stand up in Monthly Meeting for business and say, "I have a concern"? When a sensitive person is listening to the Inward Guide, perceiving the leadings accurately and acting obediently, this is the way the Kingdom goes forward. How does it all begin?

THE FIRST MOTION IS LOVE

"For God so loved the world..." (John 3:16). Most of us have heard it many times. Maybe that is the problem. We have heard the words so often that they have become overly familiar and lost their meaning. They have become just words, or they never became more than just words. Unless those words are accompanied by a deep firsthand

5

experience of the living Christ, they will remain only words. We are loved by the God who created all that is, and because we are loved, we can love. We are loved with a love that knows no height nor depth nor breadth nor any limitations.

Often we mistakenly think that we are the initiators in the spiritual quest, forgetting that all the while God has been intently searching for us. The Bible from Genesis to Jesus tells of a God who searches for humankind. One of the first questions in the Bible has God calling in the Garden, "Adam, where art thou?" (Genesis 3:9). Jesus told a story of a father who waited by the gate and ran to embrace a son who had squandered his heritage in a distant land (Luke 15:11–32). God is like that. The story of the prodigal son should remind us forever of just how much a loving God longs to embrace us. God is the shepherd who goes in search of the sheep. If God seems distant or hard to find, who has really wandered? We are loved with an unconditional love! Responding to that love, we are enabled to love. We come to love the world for which Christ gave Himself.

When John Woolman spoke of his concern to visit the Delaware Indians at the headwaters of the Susquehanna at the height of the tensions of the French-Indian War, he said, "Love was the first motion." When tender Stephen Grellet saw the terrible conditions that the inmates of Newgate prison had to endure, he was moved to tears. Travel demands would not permit him to do anything directly, but before he left England, he went to see his friend Elizabeth Fry and told her of the situation. Thus began what we have already noted as one of the most remarkable careers ever in human undertakings to improve the lot of others. Again, love had proven to be the first motion, and it set off a chain reaction of love which had far-reaching consequences. Elizabeth Fry once wisely observed, "It appears to me that we who desire to be servants of Christ, must expect to do a part of our Master's work...." And so it was given to her.

When as a young man Levi Coffin saw slaves treated cruelly in his native North Carolina, he made a resolution to strike a hard blow at the evil system of slavery if an opportunity should arise. His home in Newport, Indiana (now Fountain City, Indiana) became known as the Grand Union Station on the Underground Railroad through which more than two thousand blacks passed safely on their way to freedom. Again love had been the first motion.

The 1900s saw Friends developing organizations to more effectively carry out our concerns. In 1902, Willis Hotchkiss, Arthur Chilson, and Edgar Hole, sponsored by the recently formed American Friends Board of Missions, landed at Mombassa and journeyed inland to establish a Friends Mission base in Kenya. With four emphases—industrial, educational, medical, and evangelical (church extension)—the work took root, grew, and flourished. Today there are three thriving Friends Yearly Meetings in East Africa with a combined membership of between 80 thousand and 250 thousand—the largest number of Friends in any area in the world. The first motion was the compassionate love of God.

The American Friends Service Committee (AFSC) was organized in 1917 to carry out a "service of love in wartime." Its beginnings were small. In 1918 several Quaker young men and a few women went to Belgium and France to repair farm machinery and prepare the fields for spring planting. In just a few years the AFSC would be administering a daily feeding program to over a million children of the former enemy, Germany. The AFSC and its British counterpart, the Friends Service Council, were awarded the Nobel Peace Prize in 1947 for their work in reconciliation during and following World War II. Once more love was the first motion.

Through the centuries Friends have experienced the invading, overwhelming love of God and then reached out to others to share that love whether in regard to slavery, prison reform, missions, or service. Friends endeavor to minister to the world in a spirit of self-giving love of the One who died on the cross.

CONCERNS SPRING FROM OUR PRAYER LIFE

To pray is to risk change. As we pray, our hearts come into the field of the radiant force of God's infinite caring. Douglas Steere observes that this leads us "...to feel inwardly the terrible pull of the unlimited liability for one another which the New Testament ethic lays upon us."[1]

We marvel at the breadth and intensity of George Fox's concern which was sustained over most of a lifetime. What was his secret? William Penn reveals it very plainly when he says in his Preface to Fox's *Journal,* "But above all he excelled in prayer.... The most awful, living, reverent frame I ever felt or beheld, I must say, was his in prayer."[2]

The seeds of the works that we are to do for the Kingdom are sown in our lives during prayer. Douglas Steere notes:

> In prayer, the seeds of concern have a way of appearing. Often enough a concern begins in a feeling of being liable, personally responsible for someone or some event. With it may come an intimation that one should do some little thing: speak to some person, make an inquiry into a certain situation, write a letter, send some money, send a book. Or it may be a stop in our minds about some pending decision, or a clear directive that now is not the time to rest, or an urge to stay home when we had been meaning to be away. It may be that no more than this will be given us. But his seed is given us to follow, and if we do not follow it, we cannot expect to see what may grow from it. Seeds, not fruit, are given in prayer, but they are given for planting.[3]

The deeper we go into the life of prayer, the more God's perspective becomes ours. A child digs in the sand on the beach by the sea. A bit of the ocean begins to seep into the hole. She keeps on digging and more and more of the ocean fills the hole until eventually she excavates a small pond. The deeper she goes, the more the waters of the sea well up in her little pool. The deeper we go into prayer, the more we are filled with the compassionate Spirit of God.

If we persist in prayer, our hearts will be made tender and pliable. They will be shaped and molded until we can say with Paul, "...it is no longer I who live, but Christ who lives in me; and the life I now live in the flesh I live by faith in the son of God who loved me and gave himself for me" (Gal. 2:20).

CONCERN SPRINGS FROM FRIENDS WORSHIP

In his youth John Woolman entered into an unsettling period of searching for the road he was to travel in life. He wrote in his *Journal*, "I kept steadily to meetings...."[4] As he "kept steadily to meetings" the way began to open to him, and he saw the path that he must take. His inner strength and resolve grew. He states that he was convinced in his mind "...that true religion consisted in an inward life, wherein the heart doth love and reverence God the creator and learns to exercise true justice and goodness not only toward all men, but also toward the brute creatures."[5] Woolman learned the way of concern that became the hallmark of his life in Meeting for Worship.

In Friends worship we meet the resurrected Christ face to face. He promised his followers, "...lo, I am with you always, even unto the end of the world" (Matt. 28:20). He did tell us, "Behold, I stand at the door, and knock: if anyone hears my voice, and opens the door, I will come in to him, and sup with him, and he with me" (Rev. 3:20). George Fox was not proclaiming any new doctrine. He was simply calling the Church to rediscover some of the basic truths it had nearly forgotten or that had become lost in the tangle of dogma over the centuries. All of the first generation of Friends met the living Christ firsthand. The account of sweet-spirited William Dewsberry, the reconciler of the early Quaker Movement, is typical of the hundreds who left written records. He testified, "I lay waiting for the coming of Christ Jesus, who in the appointed time of the Father, appeared to my soul, as the lightings from the east and west, and my dead soul heard his voice, and by his voice was made to live...."[6]

The early Friends discovered that the experience of Pentecost is to be repeated in each generation. They proclaimed throughout England, Scotland, Wales, and Ireland, then wherever in the world an English sailing ship would carry them that "Christ is indeed here today to teach His people Himself." What a dynamic this gives to worship! It means that each Meeting for Worship is an adventure in communion with the Christ who lives. We can do without the bread and wine (or grape juice) because we have Jesus Himself. The account in the Gospel of John makes it so very clear. They said, "Our ancestors had manna to eat in the desert...." Jesus answered, "I tell you this: the truth is, not that Moses gave you bread from heaven, but my Father gives you the real bread from heaven. The bread that God gives comes down from heaven and brings life to the World." They said to him, "Sir, give us this bread now and always." Jesus said to them, "I am the bread of life. Whoever comes to me shall never be hungry and whoever believes in me shall never be thirsty" (John 6:30–36). Friends worship is communion with Jesus, who tells us that He is the bread of life. Such communion is the heart of the Quaker Movement.

Our spiritual forebears gathered for worship and trembled in their keen awareness of the Divine Presence—trembled to the point that we got our alternative name, "Quakers." Not many of us quake any more. We may be missing something vital. Richard Davies, the apostle of Welsh Quakerism, describes one of those early Meetings for Worship:

> When the first day of the week came, we went to a meeting
> at W. Panne's at the Wild Cop, where we had a silent
> meeting, and though it was silent from words, yet the word
> of the Lord was among us. It was a hammer and a fire; it

was sharper than any two-edged sword. It pierced through
our inward parts, it melted and brought us into tears, that
there was scarcely a dry eye among us; the Lord's power
overshadowed our meeting, and I could have said that God
alone was master of that assembly.[7]

Can we make such a claim about many of our Meetings for Worship
today?

The first generation of Friends realized that they were encountering
both the historic and the living Christ in their Meetings for Worship. It
was in later generations that we divided Christ. Elias Hicks stressed the
inward , while Jonathan Evans and the Philadelphia Elders emphasized
the historic. Old John Wilbur pleaded for the inward, while the eloquent
Joseph John Gurney proclaimed the historic. The great separations
would never have occurred if Friends had continued to hold up the
totality of Christ as George Fox and the Valiant Sixty had done.
Surprisingly, James Nayler makes the clearest witness of any of the
early Friends to the fact that Christ cannot be divided. This account is
taken from the time in 1653 when he was brought before the justices at
Appleby:

Question: Was Christ man, or no?

James: Yes, he was, and he took upon him the seed of
Abraham, and was real flesh and bone; but it is a mystery
not known to the carnal man; for he is begotten of the
immortal seed, and those who know him know him to be
spiritual; for it was the word that became flesh and dwelt
among us; and if he had not been spiritual he had not
wrought my redemption.

Justice Pearson: Is Christ in thee as man?

James: Christ filleth all places and is not divided; separate
God and man, and he is no more Christ.[8]

It is not surprising then that Christ who sent out the disciples in His
name should continue to send out others in His name. In the midst of
worship we meet Him, and He lays upon us the burden of the world's
suffering and sends us forth to do something specific about it.

CONCERNS SHOULD BE TESTED

Concerns are leadings that grow in intensity to the point that they become inward imperatives. Concerns do need to be tested if we are to avoid the errors that can result from rampant individualism and narcissism. We should keep in mind that early Friends' leaders spent about as much time writing against the anarchy of the Ranters as they did levelling broadsides against the established Church which seemed to have truth settled once-and-for-all and under lock and key. (Basically, Ranters were a group where each one did his or her own thing under the supposed leading of the Spirit, and it led to some bizarre aberrations.) Friends have several ways to test leadings within our traditions.

The first thing that one can do in regard to a leading is to pray about it. Offer it to God and ask for clearness. Be willing to act on it or to drop it. If the desire to pursue it or to carry it out grows steadily stronger, then it should be taken seriously.

Second, a leading or growing concern should be checked against Scripture. Friends believe that the ultimate source of authority is the Spirit that gave forth the Scriptures rather than the written word of God. They are convinced that they complement and answer one another and never contradict each other. At one point the great Quaker theologian Robert Barclay wrote "...whatsoever any do, pretending to the Spirit, which is contrary to the scriptures, [should] be accounted and reckoned a delusion."[9]

It is an understatement to say that George Fox knew the Bible well. A Dutch historian once remarked that if somehow all of the Bibles in the world had come to be destroyed, the Scriptures could have been reproduced out of the mouth of George Fox. As much as two thirds of some of Fox's recorded sermons are simply Scripture texts strung together. Occasionally I hear a Friend longingly say something like, "How I wish that we could recover the vitality that Quakers had during the time of George Fox." If Fox was so thoroughly rooted and grounded in the Scriptures, can we hope to recover vitality in our day without their being a significant part of our spiritual journey?

So, follow the practice of checking concerns against the message of the Scriptures. If they are in harmony, one can go forward with assurance.

I am indebted to Michael J. Sheeran and his insightful book, *Beyond Majority Rule,* for calling attention to the third checkpoint for leadings and concerns. He observes that for Friends, "The earliest major test of one's leading seems to have been whether one finds the Cross in what he is drawn to."[10] In 1652, Richard Farnsworth, a travelling companion of George Fox and a powerful minister in his own right, wrote that "you will be brought into a discerning to savour truth from error, both in yourselves, and in one another, if you will follow the cross which will 'cross and crucify that which would consult with human wisdom....' "[11]

Shortly afterward Farnsworth urged Margaret Fell, freshly come into the Quaker flock, to "keep in the cross, and purity will grow;—the safest way is the cross: take up the cross daily; mind to be guided by that which crosseth your own wills, and it will bring every idle word, thought and deed to judgment in you; and so the old...will be crucified."[12] When we recall the libertine behavior of the Ranters, it is easy to see why Friends insisted on this test. Friends were quick to point out that the Ranters "fled the cross."[13]

Sheeran also notes that in a right leading or concern amongst Friends one sees evidence of the fruits of the Holy Spirit.[14] Paul catalogues the fruits of the Spirit as "love, joy, peace, patience, kindness, goodness, faithfulness, gentleness [and] self-control..." (Gal. 5:22–23). Does your concern bring with it a deep sense of inward peace—not peace with the injustices of the world—but a sense of assurance that you are in harmony with the guiding forces of the universe? If so, you can probably go forward with confidence. But there are still two more tests.

Fifth, concerns should be checked with one's community of faith. There are no such things as Lone Ranger Christians or Friends. God has given us the gift of the beloved community, of being a part of a company of pilgrims on a shared journey. The Quaker theologian Robert Barclay spoke of the power of God at work in the fellowship of a Friends Meeting in a very moving way. He said:

> The seeing of the faces one of another, when both are
> inwardly gathered unto the life, giveth occasion for the life
> secretly to rise, and pass from vessel to vessel. And as
> many candles lighted, and put in one place, do greatly
> augment the light, and make it more to shine forth, so
> when many are gathered together into the same life, there is
> more of the glory of God, and his power appears, to the
> refreshment of each individual, for that he partakes not only
> of the light and life raised in himself, but in all the rest.[15]

The individual led by Christ has a significant amount of light. The committed group, dwelling together in Christ, has even greater light.

So, when leadings for concerns come to us, they should be shared with the larger body of the Meeting, with Ministry and Counsel, with a Clearness Committee. In prayer and waiting upon the Lord the larger group can either confirm the leading or urge one to seek further, or perhaps even suggest that one may be mistaken in his or her discernment.

Friends are certain that the Spirit is consistent. Hugh Barbour of Earlham College observes that the Light will not "contradict itself, either in history or among the members of the Spirit-led group."[16] The Spirit leads into unity, and when all the members of the worshipping group concur that a particular course of action or undertaking is the will of God, one would be mistaken to continue to question or to hesitate for long.

Such has been the way of Friends. John Woolman's social conscience seems to have been sharper than those of his neighboring Friends, but he never failed to clear a contemplated journey in ministry with them. The process can be seen vividly in the migration of Friends from the Carolinas to the "New West" states of Ohio, Indiana, Illinois, Iowa, and Michigan. When an individual or family felt a leading to leave the environment of slavery and settle in the new land, the concern was taken to the Monthly Meeting. If and when permission to migrate was granted, not just one family, but twelve or twenty, or sometimes the entire Meeting, would make the trek through the wilderness. Once they arrived in the new land they would carve out of the forest a community like the one they had left behind in the Carolinas with a Meetinghouse at its center. Often they would give the new community the same name as their former home. At their best, Friends have always highly valued and implicitly trusted the Spirit-led community. The community with which the concern is tested can be a support base for carrying out the concern.

A sixth test has come as Friends have sought to pursue leadings or concerns "as way opens." Perhaps no one has written of it more precisely than the fiery minister from Philadelphia, Hannah Whitall Smith. She states:

> If a 'leading' is of God, the way will always open for it. Our
> Lord assures us of this when He says in John 10:4, "And
> when he putteth forth his own sheep, he goeth before them,
> and the sheep follow him; for they know his voice." Notice
> here the expressions "goeth before" and "follow." He goes
> before to open a way, and we are to follow in the way thus

> opened. It is never a sign of a Divine leading when the
> Christian insists on opening his own way, and riding
> roughshod over all opposing things.[17]

So it was when the eleven Quaker missionaries in London felt the concern to take the Friends message across the Atlantic and the master mariner, Robert Fowler, built the good ship *Woodhouse*. So it was also when Penn set forth some of his theories of government in the Charter of Jersey and then received payment of the debt that King Charles II owed his father in the form of land between the southern boundaries of New York and the northern border of Maryland.

We run ahead of our Guide and risk a calamitous outcome when we endeavor to force action on a concern by bowling over everything that stands in the way. Friends proceed "as way opens."

CONCERNS FOCUS OUR LIVES

The pursuit of Spirit-led concerns can lead to an amazing simplification of our lives. For most of us there are too many heart-rending appeals, too many noble causes. Trying to respond to a large number, we become overburdened and weary until we reach the point of "social concerns burnout." We begin to question whether our little efforts scattered in so many different directions can really make any difference anyway. We begin to ask, "What's the use?" How many do we know who have taken this route and ended up cynical and sitting on the sidelines while the great cosmic battle between the forces of light and darkness rages on?

Remember we have already noted that a sense of inward peace about a particular project or course of action is a sure sign that it has the approval of the Spirit. Francis Wickes, a Jungian therapist, tells of a troubled patient whose life was crammed full of activity who had a recurring dream. In the dream, she dies and goes to Heaven. The gate-keeper inquires her name, and the only identification that she can give is that she was the woman who was the head of fifty-seven committees. She did not know the peace of the Holy Spirit.

Speaking of the Spirit-led concern, Thomas Kelly, the beloved professor at Haverford College in the 1930s, says, "...it is a particularization of my responsibility...in a world too vast and a lifetime too short for me to carry all responsibilities."[18] He goes on to point out that "...the loving Presence does not burden us equally with all things, but considerately puts upon each of us just a few central tasks, as emphatic responsibilities. For each of us these special undertakings are our share in the joyous burdens of love."[19]

While recognizing "the multitude of good things that need doing," Kelly assures us, "Toward them all we feel kindly, but we are dismissed from active service in most of them. And we have an easy mind in the presence of desperately real needs which are not our direct responsibility. We cannot die on every cross, nor are we expected to."[20] Paying close attention to the Inward Guide and responding positively to only those undertakings and appeals for service that have our name written on them leads to a life that is remarkably focused and effective in advancing the Kingdom.

CREATURELY ACTIVITY OR SPIRITUALLY MOTIVATED CONCERNS?

Do our social involvements spring from an inward imperative, or are we merely picking up on things that are given popular emphasis by our society and culture (or the political counter-culture)? The recent series of mass concerts featuring show business personalities to raise funds for some very pressing needs such as world hunger or farm aid is a good example of the way in which our society gets aroused about a particular cause, makes a dramatic gesture towards it, and then basically forgets it. Such emotional outbursts are no more permanent than a bubble in the summer sun. A spiritually based concern is for the long haul. It calls one to sustained involvement over a significant amount of time.

Today it is very easy for a community of faith to fall victim to American counter-culture religion and fads. Both are politically motivated rather than rooted in the Spirit of God. Instead of changing the world, the faith community is taken over by the world mindset.

In many of the main-line churches of the 1960s and early 1970s there was a saying, "Let the world set the agenda." The aim was for the Church to be dramatically relevant as it ministered to the world's most deeply felt needs. The problem was that in many instances the Church became so adept in the ways of the world that one could no longer tell the Church from the world. The Church utilized the world's strategies and measured its success by the world's values. The Church gave up on transforming the world and adapted to it. The salt lost its savor. The leaven no longer caused the loaf to rise. There has been a substantial amount of creaturely activity in faith communities in recent years.

In Jesus' prayer for his disciples and followers he made it very clear that their frame of reference did not come from the world. He prayed,

"...they are not of the world, even as I am not of the world. I do not pray that thou shouldst take them out of the world, but that thou shouldst keep them from the evil one. As thou didst send me into the world, so have I sent them into the world" (John 17:14, 15 and 18). The Church (or Religious Society of Friends) is in the world, but not of it. Hence comes the image of the Church (or Religious Society of Friends) as a colony of Heaven. Friends are citizens of a "city...whose builder and maker is God" (Heb. 11:10). Here we are "strangers and exiles" (Heb. 11:13). The trouble is that we have focused our attention to such an extent on the secular city, the city of mortar and stone, of flashing neon lights and freeways so numerously lined with cars that they back up for long, long distances at the exits—that we miss the city that God has prepared (Heb. 11:16).

Thomas Kelly sensed this trend decades ago when he warned us:

> We Quakers have become earthy. We are more at home with humans than we are with God. We have men of burning social passion, but not so many that burn for God, who long for God, who go down deep into the Waters of His life, who call to us, "O taste and see that the Lord is good." Social reformers we have now, men who are great in their contribution to social thinking, to war, to peace, to economic justice. ...But this epoch in history is weak in great prophets of the inner life, great voices who cry in the wilderness, "Prepare ye the way of the Lord within your hearts." ...skill in communion with Him [God], agile obedience to the Inward Glory, is less common today.[21]

We Friends have sold our spiritual birthright for a bowl of secular potage. We have fallen victim to a superficial and shallow age. We must reclaim our heritage as a Kingdom People. We must once again obtain our marching orders from an eternal source.

We must recall afresh that our local Meetings are "colonies of Heaven." As colonies we must be faithful to our charter. We have a commission from the homeland and Heaven's Ruler that is sealed with the Holy Spirit. We are to exhibit to the world a Kingdom mindset, Kingdom values, and a Kingdom lifestyle. Being in the world and not of it, we are the authentic counterculture of a better way, the only way that holds true hope and the promise of life for humankind. We are to demonstrate the Kingdom's reality to a world that generally sees little but rampant self-interest, greed, corruption, and the pursuit of pleasure.

As we act on Spirit-led concerns, we are the heralds of a dawning Kingdom day.

Those who pursue creaturely activities are generally driven persons. Driven persons are usually driven by a sense of guilt, intense insecurity, peer pressure, or the gnawing hunger for constant attention from others' applause, or to see one's name out front or at the head.[22]

Those who pursue Spirit-led concerns are "called persons." A concern comes to us as a call. Jesus calls persons. By the Sea of Galilee He called James, John, and Peter to leave their fishing nets and follow. He called Matthew to leave his tax collector's table, and Simon the Zealot to a better way than political intrigue. Several of the original disciples were not very promising, but they were called by Jesus. What an impact they made!

He called George Fox and Margaret Fell and Marmaduke Stephenson and Mary Dyer and John Woolman and Stephen Grellet and Elizabeth Fry and Hannah Whitall Smith and Thomas Kelly. In each generation of our life as a people of God, He has called Friends to vital and empowered ministry. He calls us today.

The called person is a person under orders. The called person has crossed the threshold to faith and made an irrevocable commitment. "Deep calls to deep" and the waves and billows of God's love sweep over us (Ps. 42:7). The called person's commitment is made to the person of the Living Christ, not to an ideology or to a program, but to Christ, the one who can satisfy the restless longings of our hearts.

The called person has a clear sense of identity. She or he can exclaim with Thomas Merton: "Who am I? My deepest realization of who I am is that I am one loved by Christ."[23] What more about identity need be said?

The called person knows the "power of a purpose." Austrian writer Viktor Frankl contends that "the striving to find a meaning in one's life is a primary motivational force."[24] The called person has that basic meaning. Aware of the gifts that God has given and sensitive to the needs of family, neighborhood, community, and humankind, purpose becomes clearer and clearer for one who is called. The called person can affirm with the apostle Paul, "...this one thing I do..." (Phil. 3:13).

Called persons abide in the living Christ even as the branch abides in the vine (John 15:4–8). Their relationship with the Christ who lives is nurtured through times set apart for meditation and communion, through regular participation in corporate worship, through conscientious stewardship practices, and possibly through journal keeping or fasting. The called person realizes and acts upon the fact that her or his relationship to the living Christ is the most important thing in life.

Jesus calls us today. As we hear, we are given Spirit-led concerns. We can respond affirmatively and live as called persons. When Friends have rightly understood their vocation, they have been a "Company of Called Persons."

CALLED TO WHOLENESS

The pursuit of Spirit-led concerns draws individual Friends, local Meetings and larger bodies of Friends toward wholeness. The vision of Christian Truth that inspired the first generation of Friends was so complete, total, overwhelming, and compelling that from 1652 to around 1700 Friends were the fastest growing movement in the western world. It would not be immodest to say that during that period of time Friends were the most vital and living part of Christ's Church on earth. Rarely is such vigor, power, and passionate commitment seen in the two-thousand-year-old story of the Church. The wholeness of the Friends witness is what appealed to so many seekers.

From 1827 until well into the 1900s the Friends story in North America has been a story of schism and fragmentation. Each splinter group has witnessed to a portion of the Truth that George Fox and the Valiant Sixty declared so forcefully—but partial Truth is Truth diluted in power. Somehow the ingredients of the original Friends under-standing of Christ's Truth which the various branches of the North American Family of Friends have divided amongst themselves must be reblended in the right proportion if another "Quaker explosion" is to be ignited.

The first generation of Friends were truly "full Gospel Christians." They had a passionate love for God, a breadth of vision for the Christian enterprise, and pentecostal fervor to carry out their mission that make us seem pale today by comparison. Faithful obedience in regard to Spirit-led concerns could enable us to recover that wholeness. The Spirit leads into wholeness.

We have seen this in some of the stalwart Friends of each generation. Laura Haviland was a flaming evangelist who probably did more for edu-cation of freed Blacks than any woman in America. Benjamin Trueblood was an architect of the "new Quakerism" of the frontier and Secretary of the American Peace Association in Boston. Clarence Pickett was an effective Friends pastor in Oskaloosa, Iowa, and guided the American Friends Service Committee to the Nobel Peace Prize in 1947 for its exemplary work in reconciliation in Europe following World War II.

For far too long we have had the false and artificial distinctions of "social concerns Friends" and "missionary-minded Friends" or "prophetic Friends" and "evangelical Friends." One of the greatest words that Jesus ever used was "and." In using it He made it impossible for us to ever truly follow His lead and settle for a partial witness. We are called to be socially concerned and missionary-minded Friends. We are called to be both prophetic and evangelical Friends. Anything less is unfaithful. We are called to be "Children of the Light" in both personal and social morality. Jesus will not let us settle for two or three "hobby horses" or to be "Susie One-Note" or "Johnny One-Note" in our witness.

The call to follow the path of Spirit-led concerns is a call to wholeness, and it is perhaps the greatest challenge facing this generation of Friends. We can no longer be comfortable to stay in our own little room in the Quaker house nor to endeavor to redesign the entire house to fit our personal tastes. There is a higher percentage of spiritual seekers today than there has been at any time in human history since the days of George Fox. A holistic Friends Movement could gain their attention and speak to their condition in an authentic and special way. A Friends Movement restored to wholeness, with a vital spirituality and cutting-edge social witness, could come as a refreshing rain to a land scorched by secularism and parched because the many clouds of false spirituality did not fulfill their promise. It could herald the beginning of a lush new springtime of the Spirit in North America.

NOTES

1. Douglas V. Steere, *Dimensions of Prayer* (New York: Women's Division of Christian Service Board, the Methodist Church, 1962), p. 106.

2. William Penn, "Preface," in the *Journal of George Fox*, Ed. John L. Nickalls (London: The Society of Friends, 1975), p. xliv.

3. Steere, *Dimensions of Prayer*, p. 97.

4. John Woolman, *Journal*, Thomas S. Kepler (New York: The World Publishing Company, 1954), p. 10.

5. Ibid.

6. *Christian Faith and Practice in the Experience of the Society of Friends*, (London: London Yearly Meeting, 1960), 30.

7. Richard Davis, *Journal*, 1877 edition, p. 30.

8. *Saul's Errand to Damascus* (1653), p. 31.

9. Robert Barclay, *An Apology for the True Christian Divinity*

20

(Philadelphia: Friends Bookstore, 1908), p. 89.

10. Michael J. Sheeran, *Beyond Majority Rule: Voteless Decisions in the Religious Society of Friends* (Philadelphia: Philadelphia Yearly Meeting, 1983), p. 24.

11. Quoted by Sheeran, Ibid.

12. Ibid., pp. 24–25.

13. Hugh Barbour, *The Quakers in Puritan England* (Richmond, IN: Friends United Press, 1985), pp. 110–120.

14. Sheeran, *Beyond Majority Rule,* p. 27.

15. Robert Barclay, *Apology,* pp. 364–365.

16. Hugh Barbour, *Quakers in Puritan England,* p. 120.

17. Hannah Whitall Smith, *The Christian's Secret of a Happy Life* (Old Tappan, New Jersey: Fleming H. Revell Company, 1970), pp. 98–99.

18. Thomas Kelly, *A Testament of Devotion* (New York and London: Harper and Brothers Publishers, 1941), pp. 108–109.

19. Ibid., p. 109.

20. Ibid.

21. Thomas Kelly, *The Eternal Promise* (Richmond, IN: Friends United Press, 1977), p. 116.

22. Gordon MacDonald, *Ordering Your Private World* (Nashville, TN: Oliver Nelson, 1984), pp. 48–51.

23. Quoted by Alan Jones, *Exploring Spiritual Direction: An Essay on Christian Friendship* (Minneapolis, MN: The Seabury Press, 1982), p. 113.

24. Viktor Frankl, *Man's Search for Meaning* (New York: Washington Square Press, 1959), p. 154.

SOME QUESTIONS FOR DISCUSSION

1. Define concern.
2. What is essential for a local Meeting to be a seedbed of concern?
3. How have you come by your concerns?
4. How have you tested them?
5. Is there a comfortable and hospitable place in your Meeting for the testing of concerns? How could you create one?
6. How can we "have an easy mind in the presence of desperately real needs"?
7. Do you feel that in some ways Friends and your Meeting have fallen victim to a superficial and shallow age? If so, how?
8. Are you a driven person or a called person?

9. What does it mean to say that Friends are a company of "called persons"?
10. Define your conception of wholeness for Friends.

ABOUT THE AUTHOR:

Growing up in Newton Square in eastern Pennsylvania, Jack Kirk is a graduate of Earlham College (A.B.) in Richmond, Indiana, and Christian Theological Seminary (M.Div.) in Indianapolis, Indiana. He has served as a pastor of Friends congregations in Indianapolis, Greensboro, North Carolina, and Wichita, Kansas. For four years the Director of the Quaker Hill Conference Center in Richmond, from 1978 to 1987, he served as one of the two chief executive officers of Friends United Meeting in his work as Field Secretary for the denomination and as Editor of *Quaker Life* magazine. He is currently pastor of Friends Community Church in Bakersfield, California. He and his wife, Janet Agan Kirk of Plainfield, Indiana, are the parents of two children, Jennie and Chad.

Chapter 2

Ordinary or Extraordinary Friends: Our Concerns about Ourselves

Leonard S. Kenworthy

Leo Tolstoy was once asked by an American visitor if he had any suggestions for him as he returned to his homeland. To that question the great philosopher and writer replied, "Yes, young man. You sweat too much blood for the world; sweat some for yourself instead."

Nearly all of this book is devoted to concerns about improving the world—and the importance of that aspect of life should not be minimized. Nevertheless, it may not be amiss to devote one chapter to the concern "to sweat some blood for ourselves."

Soul-searching and social change surely should be concerns of all of us—and should be considered complementary rather than contradictory. But alongside, or even ahead, of our confrontation with the world should be our confrontation with ourselves. Perhaps our prayer should be, "The kingdom come, beginning with me."

REALIZING AND RELEASING OUR POTENTIAL

At the heart of the Quaker message is the belief in that of God in every individual. That belief carries with it tremendous implications and makes of our lives an effort to discover and to carry out the full meaning of the verb "to become." If we do this we can say with the great Danish philosopher Sören Kierkegaard, "By the unspeakable grace of God, I have become myself"—meaning, of course, his best self.

The Psalmist believed in the vast potentialities in people, declaring that we are created "a little lower than God" (Ps. 8:5). Paul spoke of us as "children of God, and if children, then heirs of God and joint heirs of Christ" (Rom. 8:16–17).

22

In their attempts to recapture and reproduce the authenticity and vitality of first-century Christianity, early Friends stressed their belief in the extraordinary possibilities in ordinary people. They maintained that something of the Divine is implanted in each of us at birth and remains there always, waiting to be released and developed. Struck by the wonder of that revelation, they struggled for words to express it adequately, calling it variously the Inward Light, the Inner Light of Christ, the Seed. Having been liberated to be their best selves, they were driven forth to help others be liberated, too, and to try to transform the world of their day.

Those early Friends were incorrigible idealists and, yet, incredible realists. Throughout Quaker history there have been an amazing number of such truly liberated Friends. Have you known such individuals? Do you believe that there are such potentialities in you, too?

LIVING OUR LIVES FROM THE CENTER

We are not likely to achieve our full potential, lead purposeful, joyous lives, or contribute to the betterment of the world unless we cultivate the Center. If we do that, our lives will be enriched and the lives of those around us enhanced. Then the seemingly impossible will become the possible, for as Jesus said to His disciples, "With men this is impossible, but with God all things are possible" (Matt. 19:26).

In an incomparable passage Thomas Kelly wrote of such a life, saying:

> Life from the Center is a life of unhurried peace and power. It is simple. It is serene. It is amazing. It is triumphant. It is radiant. It takes no time but it occupies all our time. And it makes our life programs new and overcoming. We need not get frantic. He is at the helm. And when our little day is done, we lie down quietly in peace, for all is well.

Does that seem idealistic, impossible? Perhaps so. But most of us, possibly all of us, have known people who have lived such God-centered lives.

I knew several such persons when I was working in Nazi Germany in 1940–1941 for the American Friends Service Committee, helping persons of Jewish background to leave that hate-drenched land. In private conversations and in small, intimate Quaker groups, some of them shared with me the sources of spiritual sustenance which enabled them to live triumphantly in spite of the trials and tribulations of those times. They found strength and spiritual nurture through music, art, closeness to nature, friends and fellow seekers in small worship groups and Meetings, the Bible and a wide range of the world's finest literature, and most of all, prayer.

All of those sources of spiritual strength are available to each of us. Which are most helpful to you? Which could you use more to come closer to the Center?

FASHIONING AND REFASHIONING OUR PHILOSOPHY OF LIFE

How many times and in how many different situations do we wonder about the reasons for our residence on Planet Earth, and how best we can pay our rent for the tiny portion of it which we occupy for such a short time?

Fortunately, God has provided us with the equipment for such philosophizing. As Douglas Steere pointed out in his Pendle Hill pamphlet on *Contemplation and Leisure:*

> Curiously enough, each of us has a philosopher, a contemplator, if you like, within us. It is a gift that is not optional;...[it] is built-in equipment.

In our task of constructing and reconstructing our philosophy of life, many of us find help in the statements of others on the meaning and purpose of life. In the little computers in our minds we carry around the wisdom they have recorded, reflect on it, and try to act upon it. Above all is the succinct, glorious, and challenging statement of Jesus that the aim of life is:

> Thou shalt love the Lord thy God with all thy heart, with all thy soul, and with all thy mind...and thy neighbor as thyself (KJV Matt. 22:37-39).

There are also many other meaningful affirmations of life's goals and purposes. The following are a selection from my collection:

> Caring is the Christian thing. Caring is what matters most.
> —Baron von Huegel

The greatest aim of life is to spend it for something that will outlast it. —William James

To turn all we possess into the channel of universal love becomes the business of our lives. —John Woolman

The really big business in this world...is the business of being a coordinator, a transmitter, of the love of God, the love of God revealed in a person like us. —Rufus M. Jones

It would take many pages to develop all the aspects of a broad, inclusive philosophy of life, but there are a few questions we can ask . What does our philosophy of life say about evil? Do we recognize its existence and its power, as George Fox did in his famous passage about the ocean of darkness? Does our philosophy include the ocean of light which he saw flowing over the ocean of darkness, or, in another image, the shafts of light that pierce the darkness? Does it include the realization that we may not overcome some evil in our time, but as the great Jewish philosopher Hillel the Elder said, "It is not incumbent on you to complete the task but neither is it possible for you to desist from it altogether."

What does our philosophy of life say about the centrality of the Quaker belief in that of God in everyone? Does it transform our attitudes toward war, toward race relations, toward prisoners, toward the mentally disturbed, and toward other aspects of life?

And what does our philosophy of life say about simplicity? Have we examined carefully the baggage we are carrying and stripped it to the minimum, without omitting the beautiful possessions we need to enrich our life journey?

DEVELOPING OURSELVES AS UNIQUE INDIVIDUALS

All of us are under tremendous pressures to conform to what is considered normal for our group or culture. Yet the true aim of life is certainly to be oneself—"an original, being no man s copy," as William Penn described George Fox.

As Paul pointed out in his First Epistle to the Corinthians (12:4):

There are different kinds of spiritual gifts, but the same Spirit which gives them. There are different ways of serving, but the same Lord is served. There are different abilities to perform services, but the same God gives

> ability to everyone for their particular service, the Spirit's
> presence is shown in some way in each person for the good
> of all (The Good News Bible).

The question is not so much our innate ability, but how well we use the gifts with which we are endowed.

Sometimes as I sit in a concert hall and watch and listen to a symphony orchestra, I think of how my friends and the members of our Meeting resemble those musicians. Some are violins, cellos, or bass viols. Others are piccolos, flutes, or oboes. Still others are clarinets, saxophones, and bassoons. And there are harps, tubas, bass drums, and tambourines. Each of them is different, yet each contributes to the melodious music of the full orchestra.

Which instrument do you think you resemble? Are you an expert on it—or becoming one? Are you sensitive to the baton of the Great Conductor? Are you "unique, no man's copy"?

SETTING REALISTIC GOALS

How many demands there are on each of us. How crowded, cluttered, and chaotic our lives can become. Consequently, we all need to sort out our goals and priorities to the extent that can be done.

Some of those goals need to be for our entire life span, others will be for the year ahead, and some for shorter periods, including our plans for each day. In that regard it might be well for us to remember Rendell Harris' prayer, "Give us this day our daily discovery." Such plans often can be made in our personal times of devotion and in our Meetings for Worship, with the expectation that our aspirations will be consonant with those of the Divine for us. And certainly, some of our short-term goals should be attainable so that we can have the satisfaction of accomplishing them and the spur to set new, realizable goals.

LIVING IN THE LIGHT WHILE ON THE JOB

In our time Friends seem to be drawn increasingly to teaching, social work, and related fields. That is understandable. But we need to bear in mind the fact that one can live in the Light in most vocations. As Rufus Jones once wrote:

> God's work, the doing of His will, is extraordinarily
> inclusive—raising food on the land, ordering a nurturing

home, taking care of a child with loving insight, speaking simple truth, spreading love abroad in any spot of the world, praying and working for the Kingdom of God, being heroic in small ways, saying the right word when others do not dare, walking straight in the path of duty—these are some of the ways of doing God's will.

In a similar vein D. Elton Trueblood pointed out in his book *Your Other Vocation* that:

It is a gross error to suppose that the Christian cause goes forward solely or chiefly on weekends. What happens on the regular weekdays may be far more important so far as the Christian cause is concerned than what happens on Sundays.

It is not always easy, but the opportunities for doing good in the office, the factory, the hospital, the school, or in any other place, are legion. We can help set standards of industry, integrity, and good human relations. We can express appreciation and encouragement. We can help reconcile differences. We can console and counsel. And, upon occasion, we may feel called to chide—expressing confidence that someone can do better than he or she has done to date.

What opportunities have you found recently in your job for living in the Light? What opportunities have you by-passed?

IMPROVING OUR RELATIONS WITH OTHERS

In order to live life to the full and to spend it for something that will outlast it (as William James phrased the aim of life), some people pour themselves into movements, others into institutions, and still others into some kind of creativity—writing, composing, sculpting, or painting. But all of us can pour ourselves into people. As George Palmer said in his *Life of Alice Freeman Palmer:*

It is people that count. You want to put yourself into people. They touch other people; those, others still, and so you go on working forever.

So many of us stunt our growth in this respect by limiting ourselves to a small group of friends who are very similar to us. In speaking to groups of young people over the years, I have often asked them if they counted among their friends some older people, some younger people, some people of other religions, some people of other races, some people with different interests from theirs, and some people from other countries. Actually, that isn't a bad list for people of any age group. How would you reply to each of those categories? Is there one of them on which you might work profitably in the coming months?

Although some of us need to extend our circle of friends, some of us need to deepen our friendships with a few. Fortunate, indeed, are the people who have a few special friends with whom they have shared many of life's joys and sorrows and with whom one can be fearlessly and lovingly frank. Do you have such friends? Could you work profitably on this aspect of your life?

Of course there are scores of suggestions which might be made on this broad topic. Several will be made in Chapter Three of this book. Let us limit ourselves here to just two.

One is to remind ourselves of the importance of looking for the pluses in other people, accenting the positive. That does not mean ignoring the minuses; they will be all too apparent to most of us.

Second, nearly all of us need to learn to listen more, and more sensitively, in life. As Kara Cole wrote in a recent article in *The Evangelical Friend:*

> Listening is a lost art. And when I say learn to listen, I mean to our spouses, to our children, and to our fellow travelers in our communities of faith. But I also want us to learn to listen to God.

GETTING RID OF OUR "GROWN-UP RATTLES"

Many years ago the psychologist and popular writer Harry Overstreet wrote a book entitled *About Ourselves,* in which he urged adults to try to get rid of their "grown-up rattles" as quickly as possible. There are many such safety blankets which we use in much the same way as babies and young children cling to their teddy bears, dolls, and other toys. Among these are drinking, smoking, excessive sex, gambling, and overeating—the list could be lengthened.

Perhaps we should examine carefully and prayerfully some other obvious shortcomings or sins—our dogmatism, our procrastination, our easy discouragement, our overcommitment to causes and committees, our tendency to be overly pessimistic or unduly optimistic. Obviously, we cannot get rid of our "rattles" easily and quickly. To do so we may need the help of others (sometimes professionals) in order to discover why we need those possessions or habits.

Perhaps this is an aspect of our lives in which many of us need to work if we are to become fully-persuaded rather than almost- persuaded Quakers. What sayest thou?

ENJOYING OUR LIVES

As I have recalled some of the extraordinary Friends of the twentieth century, I have been struck by one of the characteristics they had in common—their sense of humor, their zest for living, and their joy. Rufus Jones will be remembered always for his stories and "down east" humor, Henry Cadbury for his dry wit, Heberto Sein of Mexico for his infectious smile, Tom Jones of the United States and Jack Hoyland of England for their hearty (and sometimes boisterous) laughter, and Margarethe Lachmund of Germany for her quiet radiance.

Thomas Kelly wrote, "Christians who don't know an inner pentecostal joy are living contradictions of Christianity." In another place he wrote more directly about Quakers, saying, "I'd rather be jolly St. Francis hymning his canticle to the sun than a dour old sombersides Quaker whose diet would appear to have been spiritual persimmons."

I always shall be grateful to A. Barratt Brown for his Pennsbury pamphlet, *Man of Joys*. In it he refers to the traditional picture of Jesus as the stern and solemn man, a man of sorrows, one acquainted with grief. But Barratt Brown points out that Jesus was also a man of joy and laughter, who revelled in nature, enjoyed the whimsicalities of human beings, and drew sustenance from His fellowship with His friends. I recall vividly my father's pleasure when he found a picture of Jesus playing tag with children.

Would that we could still the turbulent seas that occasionally rage in each of us and attain some of the placidity of the quiet pool. Perhaps as one way of achieving such serenity, we should revel more in the minor ecstasies of our lives. Of them Elizabeth Gray Vining has written in her usual inimitable style:

> Only a few people, and those few but infrequently, know ecstasy. ...With such grandeurs of experience I am not now concerned. I am thinking of what I have learned to call minor ecstasies—bits of star dust which are for all of us, however limited our opportunities. Everyone has these moments as they are recognized and cherished. Something

> seen, something heard, something felt, flashes upon one
> with a bright freshness, and the heart, tired and sick or sad
> or merely indifferent, stirs and lifts in answer. ...Exercising
> our faculty for minor ecstasies may actually increase the
> number of them we feel....

What were some of the minor ecstasies you have had recently? Did you really revel in them and feel enriched thereby?

Another aspect of our enjoyment of life is our ability to use our leisure time as re-creation. Thoreau said he loved a broad margin to his life; Whitman that he loafed and invited his soul. And what can we say? How wide are the margins of our lives? How replenishing is our leisure?

GROWING THROUGH GRIEF

In life we are all vulnerable. None of us escapes frustrations, disappointments, setbacks, and tragedies. Particularly painful are the losses of family members and close friends, sometimes in the early part of their promising lives.

Speaking to Friends in Southeastern Yearly Meeting, Elizabeth Watson once shared some of her tragedies and sufferings with those present. Then she commented:

> We are free to learn if we will. We can use the chronic
> disability, the unsought pain, the "thorn in the flesh," the
> incurable ailment, to heighten our awareness of beauty and
> our sensitivity to suffering in others. We can use it as a
> challenge to transcend our limitations. We can grow in
> depth through it as we seek to help God in the continuing
> process of creating a universe that is always breaking down.
> As Second Isaiah suggests, we can find beauty even among
> the ashes of our hopes and plans if we have the courage not
> to retreat from pain or be dominated by it.

Actually, some people turn adversity into an asset, becoming more compassionate because they have learned to live with pain and suffering. They triumph over tragedy. They grow through grief.

WIDENING OUR WORLD HORIZONS

A few readers of this chapter will complete their sojourn on Planet Earth before the year 2000. But most will live out their lives in the twenty-first century, many spending most of their years in that period of history. Much has been said in the past about the need for education about one's community. That is still true, but today our community encompasses the world; we live in a Global Village. People who once seemed far away are now living alongside us. People who were once distant inhabitants of our globe are now near neighbors.

As one who has written and spoken widely over a long period of years on the global dimensions of education, I hesitate to try to compress this topic into a few sentences. Nevertheless, it might be helpful to summarize here what I wrote recently in an oversimplified way in the *Brooklyn Meeting Newsletter* about "Catching Up With Our Changing World." Here are ten questions on which that essay was based:

1. Are you aware that we now have nearly five billion world neighbors and that the population may not stabilize until it reaches the eleven billion mark?

2. Are you aware of the tremendous rise in new nations and potential world powers?

3. Are you aware of the surge to the cities all over the world—with an estimated population of thirty million in Mexico City and of forty to fifty million in Calcutta by the year 2000?

4. Are you aware of the concept of cultures and of the eight or nine major cultural regions of the world?

5. Are you aware of the increasing international interdependence in our day?

6. Are you aware of the competing ideologies in the world today—politically, economically, socially, and religiously or philosophically?

7. Are you aware that the gap between the rich and the poor nations is broadening and of the desperate needs of the Third World?

8. Are you aware not only of the threats to our survival by nuclear holocaust, but also by pollution, making our Earth a plundered planet,—and by overpopulation?

9. Are you aware of the increasing number of regional organizations and their power and

        potential, as well as the many different aspects of the United Nations System?

10. Are you aware of the fun and beauty in our world, and enjoying aspects of it increasingly?

Together these ten questions might form a lifelong agenda for learning about our planet. From this list many readers might well select one question on which they would like to become experts in the foreseeable future. Which one would you choose?

CONCLUSION

Our stay on earth is short. Sometimes it is a difficult and even hazardous sojourn. But much of the time it is, or can be, exhilarating and rewarding. Our chief task is to love the Lord our God and our neighbors, as ourselves. Not self-love, but recognition of the potential in ourselves under God's guidance, making us not ordinary but extraordinary Friends.

SOME SUGGESTED READINGS

Brown, Lester R. *World Without Borders.* New York: Vintage, 1972.

Living with Oneself and Others. New England Yearly Meeting Committee on Ministry and Counsel, 1978. (Sold by the Quaker book stores.)

Maslow, Abraham H. *Toward a Psychology of Being.* New York: Van Nostrand-Reibhold, 1968.

Trueblood, D. Elton. *Your Other Vocation.* New York: Harper and Row.

SOME QUESTIONS FOR DISCUSSION

1. Have you ever written a brief statement of your philosophy of life? If so, have you updated it recently? If not, might that be a good idea?
2. Which of the philosophical statements on the aims of life on pages 24 and 25 appeals to you the most? Why? Do you have other statements to add to this list?
3. What opportunities do you find in daily life to witness to the Christian-Quaker way of life? What obstacles have you encountered in doing so? What have you tried to do about them?
4. Of the six types of Friends the author has urged young people to

cultivate, which do you find most interesting? Which would take the most effort?
5. What examples can you give of people who have grown through grief?
6. Which of the ten global themes mentioned by the author of this chapter would you like most to explore in depth?
7. What are your most satisfying sources of spiritual power?

ABOUT THE AUTHOR

Leonard S. Kenworthy is a graduate of Westtown School and Earlham College, with advanced degrees from Columbia University and Teachers College-Columbia. He has taught in Friends schools and was engaged for many years in teacher education at Brooklyn College of the City University of New York. He has worked abroad for the American Friends Service Committee and the United Nations Educational, Scientific, and Cultural Organization, as well as traveled in eighty-eight nations. He has written widely for children, teachers, Quakers, and other adults. His most recent books are Volumes I and II of *Living in the Light: Some Quaker Pioneers of the 20th Century.*

Chapter 3

The Quaker Prophetic Role: Repairers of Relationships

David Castle

> You shall be called the repairer of the breach; the restorer of paths to dwell in.
>
> Isaiah 58:12b

The warm weight of sunshine from a human being made my day. His coming broke the monotony of my loneliness and made me aware of the first principle of human relationships, namely, that none of us is anything except for the fact that there are other someones.

Our relatedness is the bulwark against disintegration and total collapse. R. D. Lain in his *Politics of the Family* says, "Until one can see the family [relationships] in oneself, one can see neither oneself nor any family [relationships] clearly." The one thing we have in common is the *fact* and the *quality* of our relationships. Some make us miserable and some make us happy.

The unfortunate, schizophrenic paradox of life is that we both covet and fear relationships. In our present democratic society we insist on more individuality and freedom to "do our own thing," while at the same time we are more dependent on one another than ever before. We are highly dependent on others for electrical power, highway safety, air travel, and nuclear protection, to mention a few. In our individuality we do not need each other as much as we did two generations back, but on the other hand we cannot survive unless we are in relationships.

The purpose of meaningful relationships at the personal level is to help one another to be more effective human beings. At the corporate level it is to create a social order in which people live in peace and develop a full expression of what they can be for the benefit of all. The

Ten Commandments were the guidelines of social order for the Israelites, just as the Beatitudes were for New Testament times and are today.

I believe there are gross problems in our time augering against relationship building, a kind of "arms length" syndrome. Here are three that come to mind:

First, dehumanizing biases keep people apart. Research shows that people do not fail on the job for lack of skill nearly as often as they fail in behaviors or relationships. An ambitious study by the Lutherans of their members (*A Story of Generations*) found that nominal church members have more prejudice than non-church members. War is possible when it is impersonal and combatants do not know the enemy as individuals, or their culture. The Vietnam tragedy was possible with little guilt because United States citizens did not know the names of a single Vietnamese philosopher, musician, theologian, or artist—and probably not even of a citizen. A father says to his young son, "Clean up your plate, Johnny. Think of the starving people of Southeast Asia." Johnny responds, "Name one, Dad."

Every situation or profession loses spirit when the personal emphasis gets sacrificed. The "It" becomes more important than the "Thou."

Second, truth loses when it belongs to the strongest. Power does not decide truth. Two teenage brothers had a fight. The oldest boy won the fight and was taken aside by his father for a talk. The boy reported having had a bad day and wanting to hit someone. He admitted being in the wrong. The older boy had won the fight and yet was obviously wrong. Power is a poor substitute for truth, a hard lesson in human relationships.

A competitive society has a power base stemming from a win-lose syndrome which puts a strain on depth in human relations because others are too often viewed as adversaries. Competition for jobs, for church members, for attention, for a livelihood, for a winning season, and for being "Number One" in international affairs tarnishes relationships. Some parts of this power play are healthy, and some parts of it degrade truth and relegate many to the role of victim and to fragmentation.

Third, when the Christian faith is a *theology* more than a *ministry*, it loses authenticity, realness, honesty, and responsibility. Much of our emphasis in church life is on Jesus' first commandment at the neglect of the second commandment (Luke 10:25–28). Thus we could wisely take our theological pulse to see if we are into an overdose of theology which needs to be balanced by a ministering approach, emphasizing relationships—persons to persons.

Much could be said about the strengths and weaknesses of various theological views and their effect on human relationships. Keep in mind this principle: each of us tends to choose a theology that is made authentic by our need. To understand the motive behind one's beliefs may be as useful as knowing what the beliefs are.

An example of the fusion of theology and ministry is a church in Philadelphia with all the problems of the inner city. One Sunday Pastor Tom Yoder's sermon was, "Bless This Mess," in which he said, "I feel proud that in this church we are in a mess; we seem to affirm messes...and the point of the whole Drama of Grace is that God works in messes...with people who know that they have problems and are working on them." A pamphlet entitled *Eight Good Reasons Not to Join This Church* includes, "(1)...if you're looking for a church comprised only of people like yourself, (2)...if all your faith questions are answered, and all answers are unquestionable, (3)...if you're sure that faith can be divorced from politics, economics, and social policy—then, this church is not for you."

THE QUAKER DAYSPRING

Friends are held in high esteem around the world because they build significant relationships. Service projects in situations of need are attractive because conflict gives way to love, self-centeredness to a reaching out to others, fear to assurance, aggression to caring, fences to frontiers. When that of God in me meets that of God in thee, Christian grace is experienced. People in every country hunger for these positives.

From the beginning Quakers have been "people persons." We call ourselves "Friends," a descriptive term of positive, intentional relationships. Historically our Churches have been called "Meetings." Worship was not a Worship Service but a "Meeting for Worship," and Church buildings "Meetinghouses." Note the relational character in these terms.

These Quaker terms suggest that meeting another at a deep level is the equivalent of meeting that of God in that person. Early Friends were often called "Friends of God." Indeed, all real life is meeting, and when the world of things becomes master more than servant, the spirit has departed.

William Penn stated the goals of our relational character as follows: every one is a temple, every family a church, every place a meeting-place, and every visit a meeting.

Because Friends held relationships in such high regard, they were forerunners of the contemporary group dynamics movement in several ways:

1. Our concept of shared or functional leadership was written into the practices of early Friends who made every member a participant and a minister, with full responsibility for bringing in the Kingdom of God. In this sense groups need leadership invested in the members more than in *a* leader.

2. In decision-making, Friends valued relationships so much that they would not take a vote in the group, but would wait for "the sense of the Meeting in which God healed brokenness and difference." In this there are no losers, no minority; and everyone wins.

Anthropologist Lionel Tiger believes the hunter in us is innate. The hunter is out to capture, to roam, to outmaneuver and conquer, to bring nature under its rule. The seeker thinks differently—wants to be in tune, appreciative, and open, seeking cooperation rather than conquest. In contemporary group dynamics, decision-making by consensus tends to make seekers rather than hunters out of group members.

3. The emphasis on peacemaking stems from the notion that conflict is the great divider. Early Quakers held to a positive peace more than a negative or transcendent personal peace (see Kenneth Boulding's *Stable Peace*). They did not view peace as an absence of conflict, but a resolving of differences in a way that used conflict to create new options for more truth and more humanization.

The biblical call for the "repairer of relationships" is in the first and second commandments which Jesus gave us, "You shall love God with all your heart...and your neighbor as yourself" (Matt. 22:34–40; Mark 12:28–34; Luke 10:25–28). We spend most of our energies on that first commandment and neglect the second. The Quaker movement today would have more of a ministry emphasis than a personal commitment emphasis if this second commandment gained more attention.

The relational quality was in whatever Jesus did. He went home for dinner with the despised Zaccheus (Luke 19:1–10). He told the disciples to "be as one," which appears four times within twelve verses in John (17:11–23).

The invitation for being in relationship reaches its zenith in the role of the servant, combined with the central dimension of love. Read how Isaiah (40–55) wrote of the servant as a messianic role-model over five hundred years before Christ's coming. Note especially the four servant songs in Isaiah (49:1–4; 50:1–11; 52:13–15; 53:10–12). Then read of Jesus and the servant and friend who loved one another (John

13:13–20, 34–35; 15:12–17).

Catch the flow in Paul's writing on spiritual gifts in First Corinthians, chapters 12–13. Chapter twelve, describing spiritual gifts, is followed by the greatest gift of all: love. In Chapter 14, verses 25–33, Paul centers on that great passage on togetherness. This fountain continues full when we read and reread the First Epistle of John.

SIX GUIDEPOSTS

My years in the pastorate—in the training for ministry workshops, working with college students, teenage delinquents, and families in conflict—have all meant defining my ministry as God's work in new "investments in relationships." What have I learned?

One's Attitude Is One's Aptitude in Human Relations. Attitudes tend to elicit themselves. Thankfulness tends to produce thankfulness, kindness begets kindness, anger elicits anger, and so on.

The word "Beatitude" from the Sermon on the Mount (Matthew 5) holds special meaning. To *Be* an *Attitude* is to be a blessing or to be happy.

We know that attitudes effect learning. The attitude a student has toward a teacher (or vice versa) will effect the learning of that student. Attitudes depend on the way we think. To develop positive attitudes, think rather than react. As a teacher, my first order of business is not to find out *what* a student thinks as much as *whether* he or she thinks. The key is to develop the mind without swelling the head! Creative thinking enlarges the possibilities and searches the alternatives.

Attitudes are conditioned by what we disclose and also by what we hold back. You cannot build an honest relationship until you deal with your secrets. With problem teenagers we work always on two psychological dimensions: denial and dependence. First, problem teens tend to cover up and not to be honest. Second, they want to be taken care of and loved so they can avoid being responsible. Any one of us who would take his or her spiritual and psychological pulse will get at secrets through a close look at the denial and dependency factors. Imagine how that would improve your attitudes.

Communication Is to Relationships What Blood Is to the Body. When the flow of blood stops, the body dies. So, when communication stops or is strained, love stops and resentments are born.

The importance of clear communication was noted when Western Union decided a few years ago, after the following incident, to print punctuation marks in words. A wealthy woman traveling in Paris saw a high-priced coat and wired her husband to get his approval to buy it. He wired back: "No. Price too high." Western Union left out the period, and thus was open to a lawsuit.

Communication is understanding. A definition of understanding came through one of our children who concluded that to understand means to stand under, which means to look up to, which is a good way to understand. Communicating helps relationships to be without pressure, by mutual agreement.

Where people have similar meanings and values, they communicate well. Communication is not in a message or in words as much as in people. Meanings are in people. Individuals associate, but persons communicate. To communicate meanings, do what Douglas Steere suggested: "Be totally present where you are."

Two things help communication, according to Joseph Luft (*Of Human Interaction*): self-disclosure and feedback. Self-disclosure, in which two or more people risk sharing personal information, helps define the level of relationships. The underdiscloser controls by not revealing self-information, and the overdiscloser, in revealing too much, fails to discriminate qualities in different relationships.

The second thing that helps communication is feedback. Feedback is the return to you of information about you that you would not otherwise know, had the conversant not offered it. Mirrors, cameras, and tape recorders give feedback, but the human response is the most powerful feedback method. Feedback is not criticism and lifts the level of relationship rather than destroying the person.

Growing-edge Living Increases the Possibility of Positive Relationships. On the signboard at the Friends Fellowship Home in Richmond, Indiana, is Will Reagan's observation: "People do not grow old; they get old by not growing."

A college professor asked freshmen arriving at his institution, "Are you a refugee or a seeker?" They knew what he meant after he explained that a refugee is trying to move away from something whereas a seeker is trying to move toward something. Growing-edge living is a movement toward something.

Badgered by a "proliferation of piffle," we escape into a cocoon world with a cocoon theology. Lacking purpose and direction, we give up creative thinking and adventure. Growing-edge persons know that we human beings are as pressure cookers, but they handle the pressure and move on to what is next in the life adventure. Likewise, they are realistic in knowing themselves as garbage cans where truth and love get smothered and discarded. Yet, the challenge remains.

Growing-edge relationships depend on whether you see your acquaintance as a bad person trying to manipulate you or as a needy person stumbling in an attempt to grow up.

The Purpose in Relationships Is to Lift the Level of Any Situation to the Level of the Holy. This is the Christian's calling.

> The two kinds of people on earth that I mean
> Are the people who lift and the people who lean.
> —Ella Wheeler Wilcox

There are the lifters and the leaners, the builders and the wreckers, the helpers and the spongers. "Learned helplessness" is a term discribing a sizeable group of people in our society.

Friend Robert Greenleaf's book *Servant Leadership* suggests that the best leadership comes from having been a servant. The same theme is surfacing in educational circles today under the heading of "service learning" (Brendtro and Ness, *Re-Educating Troubled Youth*).

In our work with problem teenagers, we are having great success emphasizing the "helping and caring" value. Teens start feeling better about themselves when they start helping someone else. This becomes possible when they stop blaming others for the way they are. The alternatives in any situation are that we are either helping or hurting. Helping and caring build the "hope factor" and can cost very little. Persons need to move outside themselves in order to complete themselves. To lift a situation to the level of the holy and to gain God's clarity, go into the quiet to get a picture or image in your mind of what the holy would look like in a given situation. Then create steps to help move toward that goal.

The heroic role of Christianity today is to lift our egoism to altruism. Begin with a sense that whatever is worthy of censure is deserving also of compassion and keep in mind the old Scotsman who suggested, "Be kind to everyone you meet, for everyone is having a hard time." In that frame of mind, move into situations of need as a prophet of God repairing relationships redemptively.

Relationships Are Tuned and Lubricated by Faith in God. Living in the Spirit is living the lubricated life. There is a flow and a rhythm. John and Charles Wesley sang their theology. Charles wrote over six thousand hymns and John put them together in over fifty volumes. They were to attune the laborers who sang them daily to the Spirit.

Jesus put positive values into situations and made events out of relationships. Quakers have been practical people who have kept their faith close to the common life. They have done this by making all life sacramental. Their communion has been the common meal. Grateful for food, yes—and for being around a table with others. That is a meeting with God.

There is a correlation between one's concept of God and the way one is in relationship to others. If God is seen as a judge, one is apt to be in a role of benevolent autocrat or in a legal orientation. If one sees God as having a sense of humor, one is more apt to have a sense of humor.

A friend spent much of his life praying and writing letters to people he did not particularly like. He did not require them to answer his letters. He was a seed-sower, tuning and lubricating his own life and the lives of others because of his faith in God. My friend says, "Where people see the real Jesus, they will tend to want Him."

Conflict Can Be As Much an Opportunity As a Crisis. Without conflict our person would remain rubricized. Ministry gets defined where there is conflict. The Quaker authors, David and Vera Mace, in *How to Have a Happy Marriage,* have titled a chapter "Never Waste a Good Conflict."

The way we think about conflict conditions the way we will act when faced with conflict. One's acceptance or fear of conflict contributes to one's action. It is a good thing to bruise your ego if it mends your heart.

The paradox is that we both appreciate and fear others. Many think in terms of destroying others in order to hold on to what they have. Charles Beard summarized history by saying that those whom the gods would destroy, they first make mad. These people like to define their enemies. The best antidote to conflict is to overcome dehumanizing biases. Where people are in relationship, conflict is an opportunity. Resentment is possible because we appreciate something. When you feel resentment, think about what you value or what is of worth that is missing. It is there we create anger. Focus on what you appreciate that makes possible the anger.

To avoid conflict, keep your relationship up-to-date and completed insofar as possible. If the past is unfinished, we will carry it with us.

In thinking about my life in human relations, one plus stands out. I think I have learned how to think creatively in situations of need. Creative thinking adds redemptive possibilities. We do not sharpen our minds by narrowing them or by making "close out" statements. To move conflict from a frustration to a motivation, think in terms of options or alternatives. This is an invitation to practice creative problem solving. To do this, brainstorm for options and go through the steps of problem solving.

FEWER MEETINGS AND MORE MEETING

The Meeting that gets serious about relationships will look at the large number of one-person households, not the fact that over a third of adults do not belong to any formal group, that over a fourth of our citizenry live marginal lives as victims; and be aware of the large number of one-parent families, most of whom got there through conflicts in relationships.

A Meeting could help by holding human relations training workshops, having continuing growth and therapy groups, maintaining a library on relating, having messages on redemptive "people building," learning to turn resentments into joy, lifting the level of each situation, and praying that you can "love your neighbor as yourself."

Many Meetings have built significant relationships through small groups where participants share their lives. These may take the form of prayer groups, study or discussion groups, Bible study groups, or personal growth groups. Successful groups need two things: some time of worship together to project them beyond self-centeredness, and someone in the group who can think psychologically, which tends to keep the group on a personal and practical level.

In human relationships, keep aware of Carl Whitaker's reminder to family therapists, "Maintain some sense of the absurd." What he is saying is that we need a sense of humor and the admission that we are more human than we usually want to admit.

Finally, the summation of human relationships is in this principle: *If we do not choose to love, we will learn love the hard way, which is out of necessity.* The Christian life at best moves toward the growing capacity to love. We go through all kinds of endeavors to experience love. We fight wars in the hope of finding a way of building relationships so we can live together. Perhaps the rule of law must prevail until we are ready for the rule of love.

> Some day, after we have mastered the winds, the waves, the
> tides, and gravity,
> We shall harness for God the energies of life.
> Then, for the second time in the history of the world,
> Man will have discovered fire.
>
> (Pierre Teilhard de Chardin)

There will come a time, I know, when people will take delight in one another, when each will be a star to the other, and when each will listen to his fellow as to music. Then free men will walk upon the earth, men great in their freedom. They will walk with open hearts, and the heart of each will be pure of envy and greed, and therefore all mankind will be without malice, and there will be nothing to divorce the heart from reason. Then life will be one great service to man! His figure will be raised to lofty heights—for to free men all heights are attainable. Then we shall live in truth and freedom and in beauty, and those will be accounted the best who will the more widely embrace the world with their hearts, and whose love of it will be the profoundest; those will be the best who will be the freest, for in them is the greatest beauty. Then will life be great, and the people will be great who live that life.

(Maxim Gorky in *Group Process*)

SOME SUGGESTED READINGS

Boulding, Kenneth. *Stable Peace*. Austin: University of Texas Press, 1978.

Brendtro, Larry K. and A.E. Ness. *Re-Educating Troubled Youth*. Hawthorne, NY: Aldine Publishing Company, 1983.

DuBois, Rachel D. and Mew Soong Li. *Reducing Social Tension and Conflict Through Group Conversation*. Piscataway, NJ: Association Press, 1971.

Greenleaf, Robert. *Servant Leadership*. Mahwah, NJ: Paulist Press, 1977.

Laing, R.D. *Politics of the Family and Other Essays*. New York: Vintage Books, 1972.

Luft, Joseph. *Of Human Interaction*. Bethesda, MD: National Press Books, 1980.

Mace, David and Vera. *How to Have a Happy Marriage*. Nashville, TN: Abingdon Press, 1977.

Satir, Virginia. *Peoplemaking*. Palo Alto, CA: Science and Behavior Books.

Stevens, John O. *Awareness, Exploring, Experimenting, Experiencing*. Moab, UT: Real People Press, 1977.

Strommen, Merton P., Milo L. Brekke, Ralph C. Underwager, and Arthur L. Johnson. *A Study of Generations*. Minneapolis, MN: Augsburg Publishing House, 1972. (Plus the study guides for this volume.)

44

1. How do you assess the "arms length" game and the problems suggested that auger against relationship building?
2. Describe the extremes of your own dilemma (paradox) of coveting more profound relationships on the one hand and fearing them on the other.
3. To what degree are you now using your potential? (Those in the Human Potential Movement say that most of us use about five percent of our potential.)
4. If Quakers were "contagious," what would others see in us as "repairers of relationships?"
5. A research project by Judy Brutz found that there is more violence in Quaker families than other families. Do we need some lessons on peacemaking to upgrade our testimony among our families? Discuss.
6. What are the specific implications of the idea that Quakers have a head start in ministry as investments in relationships?
7. Read fully from the suggested biblical passages referred to in this chapter. Then write your summary of Christian relationship-building.
8. Write and rewrite the six guideposts to describe your experience and to map your (or your Meeting's) next step in repairing relationships.
9. What could your Meeting do to help us to love out of choice rather than the more traumatic experience of learning to love out of necessity?

ABOUT THE AUTHOR

David Castle grew up in Western Yearly Meeting at Ridgefarm, Illinois. He really discovered the value of his Quaker heritage while studying under Roland Bainton at the Yale Divinity School, and during a Quaker Youth Pilgrimage in Europe. He and his wife, Elinor, have three children: Shari, Rick, and Gret. They have been involved in several alternative ministries, such as a teenage coffee house (The Speckled Ax), the establishment of a Human Relations Training Lab, pioneering in in-home therapy, and development of a Spiritual Checkup. The Castles now work at Quakerdale, New Providence, Iowa—a residential treatment center for teenagers in need of assistance, where David is psychologist and family therapist.

Chapter 4

Families as Centers of Peace and Love: Paradoxes and Contradictions

Elise Boulding

"Is your home a center of peace and love for all who enter therein?" reads one of the earlier forms of the query on family life. In setting out to collect some views on Quaker concerns about the family I have found a very different question in many minds. In fact, I have been taken aback by the vehemence and intensity of the concern about violence—not just in the world but in Quaker families.

As someone who joined marriage and Quakerism simultaneously a few months before U.S. entry into World War II, I have worked at the challenge of applying the Quaker peace testimony to everyday practice in the family for my entire adult life. My first pamphlet, *Friends Testimonies in the Home,*[1] was written when only two of our five children had been born. The circle of young parents in the Ann Arbor Meeting which was our support group through the births and rearing of our five children must have spent hundreds of hours over the years talking about how to practice both spiritual and physical nonviolence in the home and how to rear our children to be peacemakers in the larger world. Our conversations always assumed that the home was the starting point and training ground for the practice of nonviolence.

If anything, my feeling about the importance of the family as a training ground has intensified over the years as my understanding of what constitutes a family has broadened well beyond the traditional husband-wife-children concept. Furthermore, my Pendle Hill pamphlet, *The Family as a Way into the Future,*[2] expresses my conviction that intentional social change in the larger world is rooted in the family experience.

The Meeting never ran away from the fact of conflict. Conflict between spouses, between parents and children, difficulties of finding the right approach to handling anger nonviolently, were fully acknowledged. But conflict was always discussed in terms of *nonviolence*. The unasked question was, what about violence when it occurs? Yet today the big question, for those who are willing to discuss it, is not whether there is more or less violence in Quaker families, but whether there is more or less violence in Quaker than in other families.

How could I, and my generation generally in the Society of Friends, have missed this question? Certainly that violence did not begin yesterday. Willful blindness to unpleasant facts is not an adequate explanation, although there is some truth to the willful blindness theory.

Now I know the statistics on child abuse and wife abuse in society generally, and I am following recent studies on abuse in Quaker families as well. But it is taking a strong effort of the will to assimilate that information in the same way that I have assimilated information about violence in Vietnam, Northern Ireland, Lebanon, India, and Central America. And yet those are also violences I have never seen. Why do I resist the one and not the other? Perhaps because it does not match my map of the world. Many of us are operating with outdated maps in our minds, and it is time we took some lessons in social geography.

At another, and deeper level, I wonder if we in the Society of Friends do not have a particular kind of spiritual problem. As is often pointed out, every major religion uses the family as a metaphor for our relationships with one another and the creator in the created order. What is less often pointed out is that the family is used in two senses. In one, God is the stern patriarch who punishes his children with suffering and sometimes death when they disobey. In the other, God is our Loving Mother and Father, tender and nurturing. That nurture has been made flesh in the Holy Family for Christians and stands as the template for nonviolence in the Western World. The Bible gives us both families, and both are imprinted in our hearts in ways that defy rational analysis.

There is no question of our strong, conscious, intellectual, and spiritual commitment as Friends to the nurturing model. But I suggest that the continued coexistence of both models at a deep level of our awareness creates opportunities for self-deception for Quakers. We slip back and forth between these two models without realizing it. Hence both the violent and nonviolent behaviors can be unconsciously rationalized. This self-deception is further aided for some by the very real experience of having dealt with bitter conflict through prayer, having found spiritual resources that give strength to cope with conflict without resort to violence. What often remains, however, is a residue of hidden emotional turbulence along with a fierce commitment to behavioral nonviolence. The self-deception lies in the unacknowledged residue of anger. It can show in violently nonviolent silence—a perversion of Quaker silence if there ever was one! The more anger is repressed, the more emotional investment there is in maintaining the appearance of nonviolence. Thus, undealt with, the patriarchal God lives on.

For those who cannot maintain their own standard, but succumb to violence or are its victims, the need to maintain the appearance of the nurturing model must be even stronger. The fact that most Quakers belong to a protected middle-class sector of society further aids the self-deception. We have created a fictive social reality of family life to match our Quaker teachings, and it is taking a new generation to challenge that fictive reality.

Self-deception may be too harsh a term, but I use it out of deep respect for those who are struggling to awaken Quakers to the fact that violence is not only in the outside world but in our own Society as well. They are finding Friends very resistant to that message.

This essay began with a statement of this most difficult problem because I am convinced that our continued spiritual growth as a Society, and the effectiveness of our work in the world in this Nuclear Era, depend on a deeper understanding of the workings of violence in the heart. New mechanisms, new strategies, new social arrangements can do little by themselves to ensure a continuing human society on the planet if we do not learn how to rechannel those human energies which repeatedly drive us to hurt one another. The lion will never lie down with the lamb on a "let's pretend" basis, and too much of what we do as Quakers is "let's pretend."

In what follows I will examine further several aspects of the role of Quaker families in the hope of laying the basis of a realistic Peace Praxis in today's Quaker families.

SOME CONTRADICTIONS IN QUAKER FAMILY LIFE

Never underestimate the strong and continuing affirmation by Friends generally of the family as a source of strength and joy to each member and as the vital source of Meeting energy. Friends often speak of how much the intergenerational aspects of Quaker life, in family and in

Meeting, means to them. Many Quaker events are for all ages, which means that children are not left at home with baby-sitters. Consequently, Quaker families do more things together than many other families—such as the shared silence in Meetings for Worship, shared recreation, and shared social action. Quarterly Meeting, Yearly Meeting, and other special occasions can be family gatherings, too.

Yet some Friends are concerned that we do too much special programming for children at these intergenerational events. One wonders how much programming is out of concern for children and how much of it is out of a desire to keep children out of the way.

Parents comment, also, on the abundance of resources which Quaker teachings provide for family living, particularly the concern for answering that of God in everyone. That creates a gentle, divine pressure to seek the best in one another in family interaction. The sense of the family as a place where one is accepted and loved for oneself, a place from which to go out to the world and to come back to, is not unique to Friends. But the family is more important to groups which are trying to live a way of life different from that of the larger society. So it literally becomes a sanctuary.

Side by side with these affirmations of family life come complaints that the family becomes a source of stress in trying to practice Quaker testimonies outside the home. Every age since the founding of Quakerism has seen its forms of social turbulence as the Pandora's Box of industrialization has released one evil after another on the modern world. Twentieth-century strayings—the threat of nuclear war, environmental degradation, and growing social and economic inequalities—have, however, been particularly heavy. The demands for social action in the light of Quaker testimonies are very great, and many find that family needs are a hindrance or a distraction from attending to pressing social needs. Others feel there is a pressure for social witness that devalues the family, and they feel guilty when spending time on family togetherness.

Lack of time to meet both family and community needs is a great problem. Parents often feel that this means that they do not deal adequately with the pressures of materialism, do not attend enough to the individuality of each child, do not have enough listening dialogue in the home, and do not spend enough time teaching and practicing nonviolence.

Single-parent families feel these pressures in an extreme way, as do families where husband and wife are already in conflict over differing priorities. Even back in the 1940s family therapists commented on how much more guilt Quaker parents seemed to suffer over how they were carrying out their family responsibilities than other parents. This would seem to be even more true today.

SOME FURTHER SOURCES OF CONCERN

Quaker Conformity. While Quakers like to think of themselves as nonconformists, there is a special kind of Quaker conformity hinted at in the previous paragraph. There is an imaginary ideal Quaker somewhere, living out all the testimonies at every moment of every day. Such a Quaker is a collective myth which Friends use to put pressure on each other to conform to expectations which cannot be realistically met by human beings as we are presently constituted. Adults feel this pressure, and they often put these pressures on their children. According to Fortunato Castillo,[3]

> A conscientious pacifist couple with high standards may dutifully rear their children without being aware of the silent cruelty of their perfectionist drives. Instead of verbalizing feelings of anger, a silent, cold disapproval is felt by the growing children, compounded by their awareness of their smallness vis-à-vis the grown-up, powerful parents. The aggressive drives of the children become greater by the inability to find expression.

Some adults who were raised as Quakers have bitter memories of being forced to share when there was no inward assent to the sharing. Hence, succumbing to Quaker conformity without developing the capacity for discernment and autonomous choice builds up the hidden residue of anger.

In fact it can be argued that we have been too successful in creating appearances. David and Vera Mace, who first developed marriage enrichment retreats as a Quaker project and then moved to non-Quaker settings in which to work, on the assumption that Quakers did not need it—are now turning back to look at the Society of Friends in a state of shock. They have found that Friends need such programs as much or more than than anyone else![4]

The Society of Friends can be hard on those who do not conform. I am thinking particularly of the storms caused by Quakers who witness to personhood by declaring themselves lesbian or gay and choose publicly to affirm new types of family relationships or new types of roles for men and women. That witness is usually based on strong inward leadings and involves a kind of affirmation of equality, nonviolence, and community for which many Quakers in traditional gender-identified roles are not prepared. Are they perhaps new twentieth-century combatants in what George Fox called "the Lamb's War?"

The Absence of Quaker Disciplines. The opposite problem to that of Quaker conformity is the absence of knowledge and experience in Quaker ways, traditions, and disciplines. Those who are concerned about Quaker over-conformity usually come from Meetings where there has been an active passing on of Quaker ways from generation to generation. There are many Meetings in which this does not take place, whether because of a predominance of newly convinced Friends or because of the lack of energy and interest on the part of experienced Quakers in the work of religious education. The result may be a spiritual vacuum which leaves families floundering in the secular culture. One major concern today in many Meetings is that too many convinced Friends have not really gone through the process of "convincement."

That is a very serious problem, indeed, for in terms of family life it sets up a vicious cycle. Because they are not learning Quaker ways, these families live out their secular culture in the midst of the Meeting, unintentionally weakening by dilution the Quaker practices in families that do follow them. This further taxes the Meeting's capacity to serve as teacher for new members.

What are Quaker family practices? They are varied, and each family that takes its Quakerism seriously develops its own variant of Quaker culture. The uses of silence are important, including all kinds of special occasions—from meals to family celebrations, and in the attempt to create a listening dialogue at times of conflict and disagreement. Quaker values also make themselves evident in the choice of books, in other literature and media, and in recreational patterns. It will be found in a very basic way, too, at the level of household expenditures. The responsibility of a Meeting to introduce its new families to the meaning of the Quaker culture, then, goes beyond its responsibility to new members; it is also a responsibility to keep strengthening and supporting the families already in membership.

Role Pressures from the Larger Society. The pressures toward secular values come from both within and without. From within, the strains are associated with not being able to assimilate new members with little knowledge of Quaker disciplines. From without, Quakers feel the same role pressures that non-Quakers feel because the boundaries between the Quaker and the secular culture are increasingly permeable.

There was a time when Quaker communities were more separated from the larger community. Today, for most of us, there are far more secular than Quaker influences in our daily lives. One effect of this situation is that the testimony on equality between men and women, long considered a major feature of Quakerism, is eroded daily through non-Quaker sex role socialization experiences from early childhood to old age. Some, like Demie Kurz, see the problem of the erosion of the testimonies on equality and peace in Quaker families as part of the larger problem of increasing cultural violence—again emphasizing the permeability and vulnerability of Quaker culture in the larger culture.[5] She suggests that women are less affected than men by the new models of violence because sex role stereotypes still call for nonviolence on the part of women.

Should we infer from this line of thought that the leadership which Quaker women have given to the peace movement in recent years is simply a function of differential gender socialization, with little additional impact from Quaker rearing? We cannot answer that question because we know so little about the development of pacifism in individuals over the life span. Judy Brutz, who has done the pioneering studies of violence in Quaker families, has turned to a very positive approach in an otherwise very painful problem.[6] Instead of focusing simply on why violence occurs, she is asking how people ever become nonviolent. With that focus, it becomes possible to see the subtler influences of Quaker ways in shaping perceptions and behaviors over a wide range of situations during a lifetime.

Thinking in Life Span Terms. In doing oral histories of Friends of all ages, Brutz is finding that the understanding of the peace testimony and the ways of defining nonviolence and pacifism change over the life span. From thinking in terms of specific behaviors, the pacifist approach broadens to include all areas of life, with increasing sensitivity to the many dimensions of violence in human experience. Most important, Brutz finds a gradual discovery over the lifetime of the interconnection between spiritual development and pacifism.

This corresponds with my own research and personal impressions gained in trying to identify what the growing-up process is for peacemakers.[7] It is important, for example, to know that individuals may enter into public peace witness for the first time in middle age, but usually there are early childhood events that triggered the process of growth. The combination of receiving love and acceptance in early childhood, the experiences of separation and solitude that encourage reflection in puberty and adolescence, and early responsibility for self and others seems to produce peacemakers. Always we come back to what is happening in the most intimate setting of our lives—the household, in its many manifestations. It is the space in which much of what we are is formed and re-formed over the life span.

If we call those who live in our household our immediate family, then we can say that the family is the practice space or testing ground for all our Quaker testimonies—such as equality in personhood, nurturing, and decision making between women and men. If we do not work at such approaches to life, what basis is there for abstaining from violence when things do not go our way?

It is the developmental character of pacifism, the fact that the peacemaker in us ripens slowly through a process of lifelong learning, discipline, and prayer, that links the peace testimony so powerfully to the family. Everywhere else we are dealt with as segments of ourselves; in the family we are willy-nilly whole. Though we may try, no part can be completely hidden. The family may help or hinder, but it is definitely a part of the process.

DOES THE FAMILY HAVE A FUTURE?

Asking this question has been a favorite parlor game inside and outside the Society of Friends for at least the past four decades. Once again the permeability of the boundary between Quaker and non-Quaker becomes evident as women from both sides of the boundary stream into the labor force. Consequently, the question on both sides of that boundary is—who is going to look after the children? The concept of shared parenting and neighborhood child care as a community responsibility, which can strengthen rather than weaken family life, is still slow in developing. Nowhere is the Quaker testimony on equality more pertinent than in the case of shared parenting, for it is a weak concept of the family that depends on a traditional gender-based division of labor to keep it going.

Divorce and remarriage rates have apparently stabilized after a period of rising marriage dissolutions. An important concern for the future is how to help divorced and recombined families stay as support networks for one another after recombinations have occurred. The Meeting community, with its clearness committees and ministry and counsel structures, will need to shift some of its attention away from the more dramatic struggles of marital dissolution toward the disciplines of long-term involvement and support over considerable distances for members of recombined families.

Economic hardship is frequently the aftermath of dissolutions, much more for women than for men. With the prospect of a continuing decline in the availability of well-paying jobs, many families will experience a decline in their standard of living. The structure of the labor force is changing, and the salaries of the 1980s will be available chiefly to a professional and technological elite. What, then, will it be like living in a society in which children cannot afford homes as large and comfortable as those their parents had?

This is the time to remember that there have been longstanding complaints from Friends about the inroads of materialism and the consumer culture on family life. Is there, consequently, an opportunity to rethink within local Meetings what the testimony on simplicity means?

Another looming problem area is the greatly lengthened life span. Children these days not only have living grandparents; they often have living great-grandparents. Treasured when there were few of them, grandparents are now being seen as a future burden to the economy as the children, whose own economic expectations have already been lowered, face the burdens of a staggering social security budget to support their long-lived elders. In fact, articles are already being written about the war the young will be waging on the old.[8]

What does the Society of Friends have to say to the larger community about this? At least Friends are beginning to answer that question by such measures as the appointment of committees on aging and the construction of retirement homes and communities. But will this be only a physical care approach? What about the social insight and spiritual wisdom which our elders have stored up over the decades? How will these treasures be drawn upon? If the rest of society is preparing for war on the elderly, how do we prepare for their role as peacemakers—and our own?

Hence, once we start thinking in life span terms, all important social questions come to roost in the family.

THE RECOVERY OF THE QUAKER FAMILY

Is there a way forward for the family, in spite of the many problems that beset it? Can Quaker homes become centers of peace and love—colonies of heaven? Colonialism has a bad name in our time, yet the kind of colony that is a center of peace and love for all who enter it is an outward-turning colony, an inclusive, sharing community seeking ever new bonds with the larger human family. What are the signs of hope for this kind of family?

First and foremost, there are many such families already in our midst. We should celebrate them and learn from them.

Second, we should appreciate the extent to which the current focus on family problems, including family violence, is in fact a process of correcting our mental maps and redrawing the social contours to reflect the reality of the bumpiness of family living in this difficult age. No more whitewashing!

Third, we have in our recent Quaker history the experience of incorporating refugee families into our Meetings, going back to the 1930s when Meetings often "adopted" refugee families from Europe. That experience is taking on new dimensions as Meetings today are not only adopting refugee families from Central America, but increasingly offering sanctuary, either literal or symbolic. The courage and love which such families bring in our midst, as well as the problems, remind us how basic that human grouping is and how closely it is related to the issues of a just world order, just national policies, responsible community behavior, and the vitality of the local Friends Meeting.

Fourth, another type of claiming of space for a just world order in opposition to governmental policy is the declaration of the Meetinghouse and the homes of Meeting members as nuclear free zones, or zones of peace. While this is a symbolic act, it also creates the opportunity for living in those zones of peace as if the Peaceable Kingdom had already arrived.

Many more signs of the new seriousness with which family life is approached could be given. Instead, I will close with one that is powerful because it knits together people whose individual family ties may have been shaken through death, divorce, moving or reaching the empty nest stage. I refer to the extended family projects many Meetings have undertaken. In them family-type groups are formed with anywhere from eight to twenty participants. Meeting regularly, they share at many levels—from worship to recreation to deep discussions of personal and social issues. A special additional characteristic is that they include individuals of all ages and foster closer bonds among members than ordinary Meeting activity can sustain.

ROOM FOR GROWTH

To balance the problems and promises in this discussion of family life, I will close with some suggestions made by Friends for strengthening the new trend of dealing realistically with family problems.

1. Ministry and Oversight, or Ministry and Counsel, is the body within the local Friends Meeting charged with the responsibility for the spiritual health of its members. Frequently this body is unprepared for dealing with some of the more severe family problems which exist within the Meeting, particularly problems of child and wife abuse. Sending members of these bodies to workshops dealing with those issues is one way of strengthening the ministry to families in the Meeting. Making sure that the composition of Ministry and Oversight reflects the range of spiritual and social wisdom in the Meeting is another.

2. In order to make the best use of two often excluded perspectives in dealing with family and Meeting concerns, Meetings might well appoint intergenerational teams, including adolescents and the elderly. Such teams could serve as task forces, bringing recommendations on various concerns before the Meeting, carrying on family visitation, and sometimes serving as mediators in conflict situations. Drawing on both ends of the age spectrum could add measurably to the vitality of the Meeting as well as strengthen the individuals involved.

3. Family to family visiting can be encouraged, perhaps even including sign-up sheets so that families not otherwise included can be involved. The revival of the traditional practice of visitation, individually or in pairs, on Meeting members and attenders, for worship-sharing and discussion, might also be considered.

4. The joint planning of Meeting Forums by the Junior and Senior High School First-Day School classes and the Adult Religious Education Committee, to deal with the application of Quaker testimonies in the home and larger community, would enable the adults of a Meeting to see their children in a new light—and vice versa.

5. The development of an oral history project by teenagers and adults is another promising project, focusing particularly on the experiences of elderly Friends as Quakers. Putting such histories on tape (and in some cases in written form) can help families at various stages of life to appreciate the challenges and changes that lie ahead for them in their expanding life span.

Once a Meeting starts to think of projects that can bring the family aspect of its corporate life into clearer focus, there will be no lack of ideas, especially when children are encouraged to participate in that process.

CONCLUDING REFLECTIONS

A few years ago I began living in what I call the two-hundred-year present. That means that my present begins each day with the date of birth of those who are celebrating their hundredth birthday and extends to the coming hundredth birthday of the babies born on this day. I can do this because my life is intertwined in so many ways with the lives of those born and to be born within that extended present moment, through all the human beings I have known and will know, inside and outside the family. Thus, those two hundred years are very much a part of the time in which I live and move.

Sensing the immediacy of that time span makes the wisdom of those lives, the knowledge and experience accumulated and yet to come, more vividly accessible to me and makes my sense of connectedness to the future as well as the past very strong. I believe such an approach gives us a new hold on the problems that beset us when we realize that much of what we are struggling with now in the 1980s was also struggled with in the 1880s and will probably be with human beings in the 2080s.

By living in this extended present a widened wisdom, love, and joy become available to build on. And the ignorance, hatred, and envy remain usefully visible to learn from.

It is my hope and prayer for the Society of Friends that we can collectively live that two-hundred-year present. May every Friend be able to draw on the rich resource of human experience for building the next generation's world in that setting which can nurture the best of what makes us human—our families.

RELATED READINGS

1. Elise Boulding, *Friends Testimonies in the Home* (Friends General Conference, 1953, Reprinted in 1959 and in 1964).

2. Elise Boulding, *The Family as a Way into the Future,* (Pendle Hill Pamphlet 222).

3. Fortunato Castillo, "Aggression and Hostility in Quaker Families," Rufus Jones Lecture, 1974. (Available in mimeographed form from Friends General Conference.)

4. David and Vera Mace, "Violence in Quaker Families," *Friends Journal* (October 1, 1984).

5. Demie Kurz, "Violence and Inequality in the Family," *Friends Journal* (October 1, 1984).

6. Judy Brutz, "How Precious Is Our Testimony?" *Friends Journal* (October 1, 1984). Also "Religious Commitment, Peace Activism and Marital Violence in Quaker Families" (with Craig Allen) to appear in a forthcoming issue of the *Journal of Marriage and the Family;* "Parable and Transforming Power Among Friends" (an address to Ohio Valley and Illinois Yearly Meetings in 1985), and "Conflict Resolution in Quaker Families" (with C.B. Ingoldsby) in the *Journal of Marriage and the Family* (February, 1984).

7. Elise Boulding, "Who Are These Women: Report on Research on the New York Women's Peace Movement," in *Behavioral Science and Human Survival,* ed. M. Schwebel, (Palo Alto, CA: Science and Behavior Books, 1965); "The Child and Nonviolent Change," in *Strategies Against Violence,* ed. Israel Charny (Boulder, CO: Westview Press, 1978).

8. Philip Longman, "Age Wars: The Coming Battle Between Young and Old," *The Futurist* (January-February, 1986).

SOME QUESTIONS FOR DISCUSSION

1. How do you react to the author's comments on "the unasked question" about violence in Quaker homes? Why?
2. To what extent do the Friends you know incorporate some of the characteristics of God as a patriarch as suggested in this essay?
3. What "support groups" are there in your Meeting and/or in your community for dealing with the problems of violence, including wife or husband abuse? How successful are they?
4. What advantages are there in traditional Quaker approaches and disciplines? What disadvantages?
5. Which of the suggestions made regarding actions by local Quaker Meetings could be implemented in your group now? Which might be implemented in the foreseeable future?
6. How do you react to the author's suggestion of trying to live in a "two-hundred-year present?"

ABOUT THE AUTHOR

Elise Boulding, now retired and living in Boulder, Colorado, has taught at Dartmouth College and the University of Colorado. She is a member of Intermountain Yearly Meeting, the wife of Kenneth Boulding, the mother of five, and the grandmother of thirteen. In addition to several Pendle Hill pamphlets, she has written numerous

58

articles on conflict and peace, development, family life, and women and the future. Among her books is *The Underside of History: A View of Women Through Time*. She is currently working with several United Nations bodies and national and international peace commissions.

Chapter 5

Finding the Taproot of Simplicity: The Movement between Inner Knowledge and Outer Action

Frances Irene Taber

It may surprise some of us to hear that the first generation of Friends did not have a testimony for simplicity. They came upon a faith which cut to the root of the way they saw life, radically reorienting it. They saw that all they did must flow directly from what they experienced as true, and that if it did not, both the knowing and the doing became false. In order to keep the knowledge clear and the doing true, they stripped away anything which seemed to get in the way. They called those things superfluities, and it is this radical process of stripping for clear-seeing which we now term simplicity.

Because of this interrelationship with core experience, simplicity is not a topic which we can very usefully talk about in an isolated sense. It is not something which Friends set out to achieve for its own sake, but is rather the by-product of a single-hearted intention to follow God all the way, wherever we may be led. Attempts to talk about simplicity in itself, without recognizing its vital root, usually end by going in circles around the impossible question of deciding just what is simple.

The taproot of simplicity is to be found at that point in the life of a Friend when the realization comes that his or her inner and outer lives are connected, that for the inward life to continue to grow, there must be a response from the outward life. It is at that point where awareness dawns that spiritual knowledge itself comes from an open relationship between one's inner and outer lives, and from a free movement between the two.

EARLY FRIENDS FIND THE TAPROOT OF SIMPLICITY

Among seventeenth-century Friends, Mary Penington was very much aware of this movement between one's inner and outer lives. The second time she met Quakers, she heard the Scripture quoted, "He that will know my doctrine, must do my commands." She thought at once, "If I would know whether that was truth they had spoken or not, I must do what I know to be the Lord's will." That is a striking statement of the experimental nature of the way of early Friends. The same truth that Mary Penington understood comes in twentieth-century language in Henri Nouwen's words, quoted by Parker Palmer: "You don't think your way into a new kind of living; you live your way into a new kind of thinking." Sven Ryberg, a Swedish Quaker, suggests the same understanding in his phrase, "the new situation, necessary to remake a man."

In their effort to ground themselves by living their way into a new relationship to life and to God, many early Friends found that they had to strip away superfluities in their lives. They also discovered that when they did that, they were given new joy and power.

For Mary Penington, whose social circle was fashionable, uppercrust London, the struggle to bring her outer life into accordance with her new-found understanding of truth was intense, even though she had been a frustrated seeker of inner peace all her life. It became clear that for her the inner peace which had been so elusive would be connected with some outward changes, and she could not bear the thought of them. Her statement about her struggle is characteristic of much of seventeenth-century Quaker experience:

> I never had peace or quiet from a sore exercise for many months, till I was, by the stroke of judgment, brought off from all those things,...and I was given up to be a fool and a reproach, and to take up the cross to my honor and reputation in the world. The contemplation of those things cost me many tears, doleful nights and days; not now disputing against the doctrine preached by the Friends, but exercised against taking up the cross to the language, fashions, customs, titles, honor and esteem in the world.

Once the leap had been made and she was "brought off from all those things," Mary found herself at last content. She wrote, "But Oh! the joy that filled my soul in the first Meeting ever held in our house at Chalfont."

First-generation Quakers found not only joy, but power, resulting from their efforts to make their outward lives congruent with their deepest interior sense of reality, or truth, as they often called it. Stephen Crisp describes the sense of empowerment he felt when he finally made the leap to bring his life into accord with his inward convictions:

> And the cross of Christ was laid upon me, and I bore it. And as I came willingly to take it up, I found it to be to me that thing which I had sought from my childhood, even the power of God; for by it I was crucified to the world and it to me, which nothing else could ever do: but oh, how glad was my soul when I found the way to slay my soul's enemies.

To understand what Crisp means, we need to know that before becoming a Quaker he had tried the whole range of dissenting sects in Puritan England without finding satisfaction. None of them could show him how to have "power over corruptions," or in other words, strength against the big and petty temptations of life. Finally, among the Quakers he found what he was looking for. He calls it the Cross, which "was laid upon me, and I bore it." He means that when he made the decision to actually live in his own life what he knew was right, he felt a release from powerlessness and received the empowerment which he had vainly sought. He had discovered "that thing which I had sought from my childhood, even the power of God."

Not all Friends of the seventeenth century record the same kind of struggle about customs and fashions. Those not of London society had less of lace and "ribbons" to take off. A review of journals from that period gives the impression that the specifics which exercised each Friend had to do with his or her temperament and spiritual needs as well as station in life—which is exactly what we would expect. For instance, Margaret Fell makes no mention of issues of superfluities in her brief story of her convincement by George Fox.

However, John Gratton's entrance into Friends Meetings was so swift that he was already speaking in a Meeting for the third time when he realized that:

> The People looked earnestly upon me, at which I marvelled, but perceived it was at a laced Band which I had upon my Collar; at this I was smitten and sorry, for until now I had not minded it since my Convincement; besides, Friends in those Days shewed no Appearance of Pride in their Apparel, neither was I pleased with myself; for I saw that the Holy Spirit did not allow of any Superfluity, either

> in Apparel or any thing else, from a Sense of which I took
> it off, and wore it not more.

Gratton's record shows unity with the testimony against superfluities, but suggests that at that date (1671) no one was enforcing uniformity. It even hints that the greater uniformity of a later period actually involved a greater pride in appearance.

Whatever their personal journeys, all of those Friends would have been in unity with John Banks when he wrote:

> Now the way of my Prosperity in the Truth and Work of
> God, I always found was by being Faithful unto the Lord,
> in what he in the light manifested; though but in little and
> small Things, which Unfaithfulness in, is the Loss and
> Hurt of many in their Growth and Prosperity in the Truth.

"LIVE UP TO THE LIGHT THOU HAST, AND MORE WILL BE GRANTED THEE."

It is important when thinking about the experiences of early Friends to remember that this movement between the inner life and the outward one which resulted in the testimony of simplicity was a pivotal one in their faith. And it is no mistake that it is called a testimony. It testifies, or witnesses, to a perceived inner truth. It might even be called the outward and visible sign of an inward and spiritual grace—the phrase used to define a sacrament. Caroline Fox, a nineteenth-century British Quaker, recognized the importance of these life-statements of Friends when she wrote in a letter:

> The "inner life" amongst our worthies is, I think, as, or
> more, legible in their outward existence as in their most
> earnest writings—they...conceive themselves...as simply
> taking our Lord's declarations...translating *them*—however
> imperfectly—into Life.

Caroline Fox also recognized the relationship of this translation into life to the continuance of that inner life in this quotation from her writings, which Susan Stark has turned into song:

> The first gleam of light, "the first cold light of morning,"
> which gave promise of day with its noontide glories,
> dawned on me one day at Meeting, which I had been
> meditating on my state in great depression. I seemed to hear

> the words articulated in my spirit, "Live up to the light
> thou hast, and more will be granted thee."

It is no accident that John Woolman is the Friend most often quoted
on the subject of the congruence between the inner and the outer life,
and the resulting simplification of the outer. Surely in no other journal
is the path between the two walked so often. Woolman was also far-
seeing in terms of the social implications of a simplified life. Fox had
spoken of unity with the creation in personal terms; Woolman's vision
saw that that personal unity also had implications for the welfare of his
fellow humans and for the animals in their care. It would be only one
step more to a concern for the entire ecology.

Woolman's characteristic phrase on the subject is "the right use of
things," and his continuing care was "to apply all the gifts of Divine
Providence to the purpose for which they were intended." He was firmly
convinced that as God "is the perfection of power, of wisdom , and of
goodness, so I believe he hath provided that so much labor shall be
necessary for men's support in this world as would, being rightly
divided, be a suitable employment of their time." His correlative was
always that "Every degree of luxury of what kind soever, and every
demand for money inconsistent with Divine order, hath some
connection with unnecessary labor," and that we cannot pursue such
luxury "without having connection with some degree of oppression."
The link of oppression to war was only too evident, and he
recommended: "May we look upon our treasures, the furniture of our
houses, and our garments, and try whether the seeds of war have
nourishment in these our possessions." In the late twentieth century we
might properly add our food to John Woolman's list.

Woolman's view of divine order clearly allowed for the enjoyment of
what we can in good conscience possess. He observed that "Treasures,
though small, attained on a true principle of virtue, are sweet; and while
we walk in the light of the Lord there is true comfort and satisfaction in
the possession." At the same time, the connection between what we do
with our outer lives and the progress of our inner being was continually
before his mind. At one point he wrote:

> Sometimes when...I have been drawn into retired places and
> have besought the Lord with tears that he would take me
> wholly under his direction, and show me the way in which
> I ought to walk, it hath revived with strength of conviction
> that if I would be his faithful servant I must in all things
> attend to his wisdom, and be teachable, and cease from all

customs contrary thereto, however used among religious people.

The same "tenderness," or sensitivity, to truth which led Thomas Ellwood to take the rows of useless buttons off his coat and John Woolman to see a connection between that sort of luxury and the causes of war is still able to sensitize our consciences to the implications of our lifestyle, both to our spiritual growth and to the cause of justice.

The unostentatious life of one Friend I have known spanned and can symbolize the movement from a traditional to the mid-twentieth-century interpretation of simplicity. Born before 1890 in an area of Conservative Quakerism, his desire to live the truth as he understood it led him to adopt a collarless suit-coat worn without a tie when he was about twenty years old. By the early 1940s, he felt it to be more consistent with his understanding of simplicity not to have a dress suit, and for the last forty years of his life he wore a fresh, clean outfit of work clothing for Meeting and other dress occasions. Other parts of his life showed the same Woolman-like sensitivity. He and his wife sold their wedding silver in order to have funds to help meet the needs of others less blessed than they felt themselves to be. As long as they lived they kept informed about many areas of human need, and, with an income bordering on or below government definitions of poverty, they managed to live in frugal comfort and to give generously to help others.

Such experiences of Friends make it clear that simplicity, when it has been a live practice, has not been incidental to Quaker faith, nor an isolated feature which can be admired for its elegance or rejected for its inconvenience. It has rather been a core or pivotal testimony, a way of honing or making oneself available to God's work in one's life, a necessary corollary to other testimonies. These qualities will become even more apparent in exploring other twentieth-century witnesses to simplicity as a part of the vital workings of a Quaker's experiment with faith.

SOME TWENTIETH-CENTURY WITNESSES TO SIMPLICITY

Seven Ryberg's story as described in his pamphlet, *Return to Simple Living*, is a strong witness. In it he reviewed the spiritual seeking, both unconscious and deliberate, which led to his joining Friends in Sweden and deciding to leave his work in the film industry to become a farmer, an occupation about which he knew nothing. Of that decision he wrote:

> But the main impetus, by far, was a dim, in fact a most dim and unidentified feeling, growing more and more awkward, that we had to do something before "religion" had run out of us completely. When "it had no root, it withered away." (Matt. 13:6).

Sven and his wife Eivor took up farming in the search for a life root to nourish their "religion" and found unexpectedly that the taproot out of which sprang a growing faith was also the root of simplicity. He feels that simplicity cannot live without this root, saying:

> After more than twenty years of experience as a farmer (by choice) and of simple living (by compulsion), I can hardly believe that any serious decision "to live simply" will last for long or work out positively if it is not part and parcel of an inner context.

The Rybergs found that for them a simple life was a necessary component of their intention to dig deeper. Sven describes the result of "our transformation through action," saying about it, "Most precious of all, in our souls the Divine Seed has, by the Grace of God, begun to germinate," an outgrowth of their commitment to live and work within the limitations of a way of life to which they felt called. He suggests the process involved in this growth by saying, "The bread of life within has to be harvested, baked, broken and shared by deeds, not read about in a recipe."

The radically experimental nature of the Rybergs' "transformation through actions" and its consequent kinship with the experiences of seventeenth-century Friends, are apparent as he speaks out of his life in these words:

> In the New English Bible, in the 12th chapter of Paul's letter to the Romans, the second verse is rendered: "Adapt yourselves no longer to the pattern of this present world, but let your minds be remade and your whole nature thus transformed. Then you will be able to discern the will of God and to know what is good...." My reading of that bit relates the text to our actual situation. The essence of simple living is to know what is good. Therefore adapt yourself not to the wicked values of the current system. They only breed destruction and pollution in all directions. Disobey, revolt, but not in a pretending or theoretical way, [as] it will never put you in a new situation, necessary to

remake a mind. To transform our whole nature goes even further and requires to be in the test-tube body and soul,—in other words, a discipleship. Living without any sort of security, true discipleship is shaking our very foundations. When we have gone down into the silent crypt of our soul and discovered our true relations, we may discern the will of God.

Another radical challenge to consider what we may be missing if we are not serious about simplicity comes out of twentieth-century American Quakerism through the lives and writings of Wilmer and Mildred Young. Like the Rybergs, the Youngs left professional life (teaching at Westtown School) for farming. They lived and worked with local farms in rural Mississippi and South Carolina for nineteen years. Their convictions about the relationship of simplicity (or functional poverty, to use Mildred Young's unambiguous term) to our other testimonies as Friends was forged in that and other contexts of working with the poor. Out of that life experience and the understandings which it brought to them, Mildred Young wrote several Pendle Hill pamphlets.

She is unequivocal in blaming our inflated standard of living for our ineffectiveness in other testimonies—conspicuously peace and the related issue of justice. She said in A Standard of Living:

> I shall impugn our admired standard of living elevated to an ideal, as a main cause of the distress and violence of our world. I shall announce the choice of poverty a reasonable corollary to our refusal to participate overtly in that violence, almost a condition to our constructive approach to that distress. I shall have to say that, to me, it no longer seems possible to reconcile pacifism with physical ease, or with the effort to get and to hold property.

In her essay "Another Will Gird You," Mildred Young describes the purification which she feels the Society of Friends must undergo if we are to be effective witnesses to our testimony on peace with justice:

> If Friends are to be able to contribute their insight and leadership to the effort to find a substitute for war—if they are to make their ancient testimony existential—we shall individually need such purification of life as Friends made when they set their slaves free. Corporately, we have never known, since Friends were first out of the early persecutions, such a purification as we shall need now.

She feels that there is among us a worldliness which is "throttling our witness and giving a hollow ring of pretension to what we say" and identifies that worldliness as "characterized by our uncritical and insensitive attitude toward our insatiable material wants." Mildred senses that our effort to speak to a testimony for peace without wrestling personally with related economic issues is creating a split in our Quaker personality, and states in *What Doth the Lord Require of Thee?* that, "It is in this split, this need to maintain ourselves in a sharply felt contradiction, that I find the root of most of the causes of our spiritual decline." Aware of the two-way nature of the movement between testimony and spiritual life, she points out that "The testimonies grow out of the relatedness, but on the other side, they are also the means by which we clear the path *to* the relatedness."

DIALECTIC

A CONTEMPORARY MOVEMENT TOWARD VOLUNTARY SIMPLICITY

There is a current in contemporary American life, larger than the Quaker stream, which is moving toward simplicity. This current is described in a recent book, *Voluntary Simplicity,* by Duane Elgin, who states that it is also present at the grass roots in almost every western industrial nation and has been growing through the decade of the 1970s. He says that "one of the principal qualities of voluntary simplicity is that of an unfolding balance between the inner and outer prospects of our lives." One might call it the process of achieving a congruence between the real, as we most deeply perceive it within, and the reality which we express in our daily lives.

A reading of that book leaves the distinct impression that the kind of voluntary simplicity he advocates is nothing less nor more than the Quaker testimony under another name. The impetus to it, the basis in spiritual reality or inner experience, the type and patterns of its working out in everyday life, are certainly congruent with Quaker experience. One has the feeling one is watching a non-Quaker pick up a theme which our spiritual foreparents worked with, taking the ball from our flagging hands and running with it into the future.

Nine distinctive characteristics which I have found in the Quaker testimony on simplicity are all shared by the contemporary voluntary simplicity which Elgin describes.

1. These two traditions of simplicity hold in common an unfolding, developmental, or process quality. One does not come full-blown into the practice of simplicity or lay hold of it suddenly. Elgin says that:

> Overall, the journey into this way of life seems to be a
> relatively slow, evolutionary process—one that unfolds
> gradually over a period of months and years....One
> conclusion that I draw...is that if change is too abrupt, it
> may not have the staying power to last.

2. The traditional Quaker and this contemporary experience also have
in common a balance between attention to the outer and to the inner
life, and of continual movement between the two. I have already emphasized this aspect in Quaker experience. In talking about the same
quality, Elgin says that " 'voluntary simplicity' refers to a way of experiencing the integration and balance of the inner and outer aspects of life."

3. Quaker and contemporary voluntary simplicity both involve the
development of an immediate awareness of world reality. This is
contributed to by internal and also by external experience. Elgin finds
that:

> ...it is the very deepening of insight through the inner
> quest that reveals the entire world as an intimately
> interconnected system. The interior journey is indispensable
> in revealing that we inhabit an ecological reality.

At the same time he observes that "when people deliberately choose to
live closer to the level of material sufficiency, they are brought closer
to the reality of material existence for a majority of persons on this
planet." As life simplifies itself, we awake from what he aptly calls
"the hypnosis of a culture of affluence."

4. Both in traditional Quaker and in non-Quaker contemporary
experience, there is an awareness of personal empowerment as a result
of taking action. This was significant in Stephen Crisp's seventeenth-
century experience mentioned earlier. These persons whose experiences
Elgin surveyed also spoke in a variety of ways about feeling enabled,
and more positive about the effectiveness of their lives.

5. Both in Elgin's concept of voluntary simplicity and in Quaker
experience, the level of consumption suggested as appropriate is one
which takes into account the needs of humanity as a whole; which
adequately meets the physical and other needs of persons; and which
does not prescribe a uniform standard of material wealth and possessions
for everyone.

6. Both contemporary voluntary simplicity and Quaker convictions
about it say something about one's means of livelihood. Elgin reports
that persons practicing voluntary simplicity prefer work which provides

a "contributory livelihood," that is, work which gives "opportunity to support others by producing goods and services that support a workable world." Woolman's concern was that the manner in which he earned his living and acquired his possessions be entirely consistent with "that use of things which is agreeable to universal righteousness."

7. Classic Quaker simplicity has, in common with present-day voluntary simplicity, a connection with directness and honesty in personal communication. Elgin finds that contemporary persons practicing voluntary simplicity are led not only to a concern for plain honesty and for "letting go of idle gossip and wasteful speech" and for "respecting the value of silence," which have Quaker echoes, but also for "greater eye contact with others," and for "greater openness to nonsexual, physical contact."

8. Another common characteristic of these two streams of simplicity is that both tend to lead to a spiritually-based activism. Elgin finds such activism to be an almost universal characteristic among the persons he surveyed, saying that "an ecologically oriented, nonviolent activism seems to characterize" their political orientation.

9. In both of these streams of experience, the development of congruence between one's inner and outer life involving a practice of simplicity has led to joy and to a sense of contentment with life. One contemporary practitioner of voluntary simplicity wrote that the "Dissatisfactions of V.S. are minute, not because they don't exist, but because they are part of the process—not obstacles but humps on a road that I choose to follow." Another declared that "Satisfactions are the fulfillment of the heart; dissatisfactions are the rumblings of the mind." Mary Penington, you will recall, after her struggle about joining the life of Friends, reported a long-sought and long-remembered joy.

It is clear that Quakers are involved in the contemporary movement toward voluntary simplicity which Duane Elgin describes. It also seems clear that few of us are in the forefront of it, and that it is a challenge to our faithfulness to our own vision. It is also a challenge to that vision in another way. Elgin sees in the movement towards voluntary simplicity our strongest hope for the revitalization of civilization. He asserts that "the emergence of voluntary simplicity as a widespread way of life seems crucial to the birth of some form of peaceful global civilization." He sees in this movement the hope, at last, for making the ethic of love normative on a world scale as well as in personal relations. Elgin's bold statements are both humbling and exciting to a Quaker struggling with the specifics and the implications of the testimony on simplicity.

OUR PERSONAL ENCOUNTER WITH SIMPLICITY

It does not seem necessary to go into detail about ways in which a concern for simplicity can affect our lives. For most of us the question is not what those ways are. The struggle is rather how we can personally move one step at a time into such a reality. That is an intensely personal journey, and also an immensely hopeful one, both personally and for our planet.

As we approach that journey, we must remember that it goes on by a constant movement between our inner and outer lives, and that it may not be possible to tell in which place it begins.

Thomas Kelly in his essay on the simplification of life, in *A Testament of Devotion,* does not talk about food as testimony or about our attitude towards cultural elaborations. Rather, he speaks insistently of the inner core of devotion in our lives and of how the effects of that seep out through the texture of our days, rather like water from a hidden spring. In his words, "The life with God is the center of life and all else is remodelled and integrated by it. It gives the singleness of eye." He is aware that the greatest complexity many of us now face is one of schedule and feels that a solution to that lives in a clear understanding of the Quaker idea of *concern*. He writes:

> I wish I might emphasize how a life becomes simplified when dominated by faithfulness to a few concerns. Too many of us have too many irons in the fire. ...Quaker simplicity needs to be expressed not merely in dress and architecture and the height of tombstones but also in the structure of a relatively simplified and co-ordinated life-program of social responsibilities. And I am persuaded that *concerns* introduce that simplification, and along with it that intensification which we need in opposition to the hurried, superficial tendencies of our age.

Through the beautiful confessions of an unnamed Friend, Mildred Young also recognized that there exists a spiritual center, in which all the hard choices involved in the journey toward simplicity are clarified and made easy. She recalls in *"Another Will Gird You"* that:

> During a recent discussion, one Friend said very humbly that some time ago he had found himself brought into that perpetual sense of the presence of God which *is* simplicity. In this Presence, he knew what work or travel he had to

undertake, and what to lay down or leave for others; and when called on to do work beyond his strength, he found the strength to do it.

We live in a difficult era for simplicity. It is difficult because we live in such a very pluralistic society, and, therefore, there are a great many choices to make. If our lives are to have any sense of simplicity at all, we have to live in constant awareness of our primary goals and very consciously make our choices in the light of them. As we approach closer to simplicity, however, it can become our window into reality, our clarifier of murky places, the opener of our blind eyes. Simplicity can become our discipline, our preparer, our stone for sharpening the tool of the self. Simplicity can itself be the tool without which our other testimonies will falter and fail.

SOME SUGGESTED READINGS

Elgin, Duane. *Voluntary Simplicity*. New York: Morrow, 1981.
Foster, Richard. *Freedom of Simplicity*. San Francisco: Harper and Row, 1981.
Prevallet, Elaine. *Reflections on Simplicity*. Pendle Hill pamphlet 244.
Ryberg, Sven. *Return to Simple Living*. Friends World Committee: European and Near East Section, 1973.
Smith-Durland, Eugenia. *Voluntary Simplicity Study-Action Guide*. Portland, OR: Alternatives, 1978.
Young, Mildred. *Another Will Gird You; Inured by Hope;* and *A Standard of Living*. Pendle Hill pamphlets 109, 90, and 12, respectively.

SOME QUESTIONS FOR DISCUSSION

1. Has there been a situation in my own life experience in which I struggled to put into practice what I believed and found that after doing so my spiritual understanding and insight was set free to grow?

2. Does my understanding and use of the Quaker idea of concern simplify or complicate the direction of my energies? How?

3. Is there an area in my life about which I feel a sense of uneasiness? What might this sense of uneasiness be telling me about a conflict between my values and the way I live, or about a work I am called to? What is hindering me from responding?

4. How could we, as members of the Meeting, support each other in our efforts toward simplicity? Could we share the use of possessions? the care of children or of elderly parents? How could we take responsibility for each other in emergencies? What circumstances, such as where we live, might need to be changed to facilitate such mutual support?
5. What difficulties sometimes arise for children when their parents decide to change their previous practices in favor of a more simplified life style?

ABOUT THE AUTHOR

Frances Irene Taber grew up in Iowa and Ohio Conservative Yearly Meetings. She was educated at Olney Friends School, William Penn and Earlham Colleges, graduated from Brown University, and had a student year at Pendle Hill. As a young Friend, she spent a summer traveling among Friends in Germany. She and her husband, William Taber, co-directed the Friends China Camp in New England Yearly Meeting. She spent twenty-one years at Olney Friends School as a faculty wife and in various positions, including seven years as manager of the kitchen. Now on the cooking staff at Pendle Hill, she also helped initiate a personal retreat program there. She has taught Quakerism for the Quaker Studies Program of Philadelphia Yearly Meeting and in the fall of 1985 at Pendle Hill. The Tabers have two grown daughters.

1. DOES THIS DISCUSSION OF SIMPLICITY FEEL MORE LIKE A BURDEN THEN A JOYFUL LIBERATION FOR YOU? WHY?

2. WHAT WOULD HELP YOU IN FEELING MORE JOY + LIBERATION THROUGH SIMPLICITY?

Chapter 6

Creating Centers of Contagion: Quaker Education in the United States

Eugene S. Mills

In lines that were addressed to his namesake Quaker colony in California, an aging John Greenleaf Whittier wrote:

> Fear [not] the sceptic's puny hand
> While near the school the church will stand.
> Nor fear the blinded bigot's rule
> While near the church shall stand the school.

Whittier's association of church and school reflected a strongly held view of the importance of education. The American history of the Religious Society of Friends is marked by the establishment and perpetuation of schools, academies, and colleges. Indeed, Quakers in the United States are probably best known for their efforts in human service and in education.

A RELIGIOUSLY GUARDED EDUCATION

From the beginning of the Society of Friends more than three centuries ago, there have been concerns to provide young Friends with "a religiously guarded education." A pious and fervent George Fox stressed the importance of education in his ministry. Hence the early years of Quakerism saw the development of schools and the clear call for co-education. In the context of contemporary concerns for co-educational opportunities and equality of access, that early approach to education seems remarkably prophetic.

The small scale and intimacy of Friends communities and the concern

73

to provide children with a "religiously guarded education" often led to the establishment in the American colonies of schools alongside Friends Meetinghouses. The archives of American Quakerism reveal many long-abandoned schools and academies, particularly in the east and midwest. Throughout the eighteenth and nineteenth centuries the Meetinghouse, school, library, and cemetery were tangible evidence of small, but vital, religious communities that tried to live within the faith.

As Elbert Russell noted in his excellent book, *The History of Quakerism:*

> On the frontier the schoolhouse appeared promptly beside the Meeting House and an effort was made to have a monthly meeting school in every community. ...In the states of Ohio, Indiana, Iowa, Kansas, North Carolina, and Tennessee the monthly meeting schools laid the foundation of the public school system or materially influenced its character.

Russell states that over fifty academies were founded between 1860 and 1900 and cites statistics of Indiana Yearly Meeting in 1865 revealing a total of 8,685 children enrolled between the ages of five and twenty. His comment that Friends schools laid the foundation for the public school system was true in a special way in Philadelphia where a number of Friends schools became public schools as this more general approach to education developed.

Clearly, Friends took seriously the need for a "religiously guarded education" and committed their energies and resources to the creation of the schools and academies that would make this possible. But, the growth of population, industrialization, and a burgeoning public school system made difficult the preservation of those special communities. More than a century later, those factors and others continue to pose difficulties for Quaker schools and colleges.

COMMUNITY, HARMONY, EQUALITY, AND SIMPLICITY

In his book on *Quaker Education: In Theory and Practice,* Howard Brinton noted the following educational policies that were derived from social testimonies concerning community, harmony, equality, and simplicity:

COMMUNITY
1. Development of a sense of belonging to the Quaker community
2. A religiously guarded education
3. Dedicated and concerned teachers

HARMONY
4. Non-violent discipline and methods
5. Appeal to the inward sense of rightness

EQUALITY
6. Equal education of both sexes
7. Equality in education of races and classes

SIMPLICITY
8. Moderation in dress, speech, and deportment
9. Scholastic integrity
10. Emphasis on practical subjects in the curriculum

While Friends succeeded only in part in making their schools the instruments for achieving these worthy goals, the continued vitality of the Society was due in no small degree to the propagation of values in those learning centers. Throughout the history of Quakerism both prominent and unremarkable lives were devoted to fulfilling the quiet and yet fervent ideals of the Society. Impressive testimony to the linkage between Quaker education and Quaker contributions is to be found in Leonard Kenworthy's book, *Living in The Light: Some Quaker Pioneers of the 20th Century* (Volume I—In the U.S.A.). Creating the educational conditions for community, harmony, equality, and simplicity remains an important task for contemporary Quakerism.

A DELICATE BALANCE

From the beginning, Quaker schools and academies have had to ask themselves just how Quakerism is to be brought into the lives of students and faculty. In the early years it was generally assumed that teachers would be Friends, fully involved with the faith of the Society. But, never monolithic, the Society was a diverse and changing religious community. In time, even Methodist and Episcopalian (and non-believing) teachers of competence were to be found in Quaker classrooms!

Further, there was always a concern that the materials of study be appropriate to the values and beliefs of Friends. While there were early efforts to produce texts and classroom materials for the special needs of Friends schools and academies, this was a necessarily limited practice, and more often than not, the Bible and a miscellaneous collection of

Friends publications and periodicals became supplementary to standard materials. As Elbert Russell observed in his *History of Quakerism,* nineteenth-century Friends schools included the teaching of the Bible and instruction in Quaker principles, but while "...the system proved fairly effective as a means of transmitting the Quaker ideal of life...[it] fell short of teaching men and women to do original thinking and in developing freely chosen virtue."

Across the years, Friends schools and academies have had to face the related problems of enrollment and financial resources. While they differ substantially, institutional histories share a focus upon questions of curriculum, faculty, students and money—though not necessarily in that order! Because of the limited number of Quaker students, the spread of public education, and the financial problems that seemed unremitting, Friends gradually and reluctantly discontinued many of their earlier schools and academies.

There were a number of sturdy survivors and some have achieved distinction (e.g., George School, Westtown, Friends Select, Sidwell, Moses Brown). It is revealing that three of our Friends schools still operating were founded in the seventeenth century (Penn Charter, Friends Select, and Abington Friends), twelve were founded in the eighteenth century and sixteen in the nineteenth century. There were 15,901 students in Friends schools in 1984–85. Furthermore, a number of elementary schools have continued as quality institutions across two centuries (e.g., Frankford Friends School, 1768; Plymouth Meeting Friends School, 1780; Haddonfield Friends School, 1786; Westfield Friends School, 1788; and Buckingham Friends School, 1794).

In its current roster of Friends schools, the Friends Council on Education lists seventy institutions in the United States and Canada. This list includes a number of new Friends schools and pre-schools that have been established in recent years. The founding of educational institutions is not a closed chapter in our Quaker history. The life of the Society of Friends continues to give birth to new educational experiments.

Wherever it has happened, the survival and more recent establishment of Friends schools and academies have been achieved by way of a delicate balance of those factors and practices that, according to Kay Edstene, Headmistress of Brooklyn Friends School, permit the institutions "...not only to teach the educational basics but also to preserve the qualities of the Life of the Spirit." It has been a balancing, as well, of the needs for a critical mass of students, for financial support, and for institutional identity in a society that is heavily committed to public and non-sectarian education. Operation and institutional growth and development have required the admission of substantial numbers, even a heavy majority, of non-Friends students and faculty members. Creating the conditions for a Quaker education will continue to require a delicate balance of competing demands.

THE INNER LIGHT AND HIGHER LEARNING

> Friends had to learn by sad experience
> that the "Inner Light" is not an easy
> substitute for the encyclopedia...
>
> —Elbert Russell

As one might infer from Elbert Russell's comment, Friends were led to establish schools and academies and, subsequently, collegiate institutions. While most of our colleges have had their ups and downs across the past century, and a few, such as Nebraska Central College, have discontinued operations, the remaining Quaker colleges have been influential in American higher education far beyond what might have been expected when considering their number and size.

The sixteen Friends institutions of higher education listed by the Friends Association for Higher Education have today a combined enrollment of approximately 12,250. They are a highly varied group of institutions, as the following sketch illustrates:

Date of Founding	Haverford College was founded in 1833 and Friends World College in 1965.
Enrollment	Whittier College enrolls 1,650 students and the Friends Bible College approximately 103.
Purpose	Most are four-year liberal arts colleges, but Pendle Hill is an adult Quaker Center for study and contemplation, and Friends World College is a non-traditional, decentralized college in which students "treat the entire world as their university" and focus their studies on urgent human problems. The Earlham School of Religion is the only accredited Quaker seminary in the United States.

| Relation to the Society of Friends | The institutions vary from those that are under the direct ownership and authority of Yearly Meetings to those that are independent and have largely historical relations with the Society. |

In addition to the sixteen Quaker institutions referred to above, one or more Friends were substantially involved in creating Cornell, Johns Hopkins, Duke, Brown and Lincoln Universities. Certainly, Quakers have considered higher education to be an important instrument for human service and for furthering the life of the Society of Friends.

As has been the case with schools and academies, the colleges have had to face problems of resources, programs, availability of qualified Quaker teachers and students, and the general question of relationship with the Society of Friends. Each of the institutions continues to work in its own way toward an appropriate expression of what it means to be a Quaker institution of higher learning.

FRIENDS IN PUBLIC EDUCATION

Although Quakers established their own schools very early in the history of the Religious Society of Friends, there also were many members of the Society who served nobly, and sometimes conspicuously, in the public school movement. As the public schools spread across the land, they became teachers in those schools, members of boards of education, and active participants in local parent-teacher organizations. Today, hundreds of Quakers are involved in public education at all levels.

By providing leadership in their own communities and schools, Friends have helped to improve the quality of education for all citizens. Drawing upon their beliefs, they have searched for ways to introduce Quaker values and concerns into non-sectarian education and into public life. Peace, service, social justice, and governance concerns have found expression in the selection of teachers, the choice of speakers, and the establishment of curricula. Often, lives of quiet principle have had an uncommon and beneficial effect upon the educational process.

There are many fine Quakers who have played important roles in non-Quaker educational institutions, foundations, or agencies. To cite but a few examples: Clark Kerr, formerly president of the University of California and later chairman of the Carnegie Commission on Higher Education and the Carnegie Council for Policy Studies in Higher

Education; Ernest Boyer, formerly chancellor of the State University of New York, United States Commissioner of Education and now president of the Carnegie Foundation for the Advancement of Teaching; Landrum Bolling, formerly president of Earlham College, president of Lilly Endowment, and then chairman of the Council on Foundations; Paul Braisted, formerly president of the Edward Hazen Foundations; Elizabeth Gray Vining, author and tutor to the Crown Prince of Japan; Kenneth Boulding, economics educator and professor at the University of Michigan and the University of Colorado; Elise Marie Boulding, sociologist and educator, University of Colorado and Dartmouth College; and Leonard S. Kenworthy, author, editor, professor at Brooklyn College of the City University of New York and member of United Nations and international education commissions and committees.

SUPPORT AND A LINK WITH TRADITION

Following a number of preliminary discussions, in June 1980, a conference of Friends educators and Friends Meeting leaders was held on the campus of Wilmington College to launch the Friends Association for Higher Education (FAHE). The creation of the association had been inspired by an observation by Helen Hole in her book, *Things Civil and Useful*, that "perhaps the time has come to form a broad national committee which can provide support and a link with tradition in the Quaker educational world." Since that time, the association has met annually on Quaker campuses. The organization is similar to the Friends Council on Education which for many years has worked on behalf of Quaker elementary and secondary schools.

The Friends Association for Higher Education resulted from a widely recognized need to bring together those who have Quaker concerns about education, both within Quaker-related colleges and on non-Quaker campuses. The association's creation and its early years are to be credited especially to the devoted leadership of two Quaker educators, Charles Browning of Whittier College and T. Canby Jones of Wilmington College.

The purposes of the FAHE are both important and ambitious:

1. To strengthen the Quaker mission in higher education which, in the words of George Fox, means "to bring all persons to the Teacher within themselves."
2. To reawaken members' appreciation of Friends Judeo-Christian heritage and to nurture the individual and corporate search for Truth.

3. To assist Friends colleges in their efforts to deepen their Quaker character.
4. To establish a supportive relationship among all Friends engaged in higher education on both Quaker and non-Quaker campuses.
5. To help foster a caring relationship between Yearly Meetings and the Friends educational institutions related to them.
6. To nurture a caring relationship among Friends organizations and Meetings at all levels and all persons concerned for higher education.

FAHE has provided a point of focus for Quaker educators, and it has helped to establish a professional Quaker personnel network. Through its meetings and the publication of a directory it also has shared information about job openings in Friends colleges.

CENTERS OF CONTAGION

> Here, then, are our seven Quaker words which together provide us with a Quaker philosophy of education. We have a Quaker philosophy of civilization, a theory about the way the world can be changed. It will be changed by people planted in all walks of life, each of whom becomes a center of contagion. The central purpose of Quaker education is the production of such contagious people, people marked by veracity, discipline, simplicity, individuality, community, concern and peace.

With these important words, D. Elton Trueblood summarized his address to a Friends conference on education, held at Earlham College in November 1946. Viewing each Quaker school and college as "a holy experiment," Elton stated that "...our responsibility is not to educate all but to demonstrate to all...." It is significant that he did not focus upon prescribed curricula or formal institutional arrangements; rather, he stressed the characteristics of individuals and the dynamic and functional concerns of people who, in familiar Friendly terminology, "live in the light." Quaker education is to be concerned with the development of individuals who are "planted in all walks of life" and who become "centers of contagion."

As we have seen, the long and noble history of Quaker higher education in America reveals a variety of institutions, each relatively small. The combined enrollment of over 12,000 students is but a tiny fraction of the total national collegiate enrollment; moreover, there may be no more than 1,250 Quaker students in these colleges. There is certainly a larger number enrolled in non-Quaker colleges. It is understandable that a participant in the first annual conference of FAHE would comment, "There just aren't enough of us to go around!" It is apparent that the existing Quaker colleges are going to continue to serve a largely non-Quaker population.

Would it be desirable to have a larger Quaker enrollment? The answer to this question would seem to be a qualified "yes." There is the need for a critical mass, to use an inelegant term, but the special characteristics of Quaker institutions are well suited to a mission that benefits a varied student population. While this is the case, there is a need to encourage qualified Quaker students to consider the value of enrollment in one of our Quaker institutions. If the number of Quaker students, teachers, and board members should dwindle to a negligible level, then the Quaker character of each institution will cease being a vital educational influence and will become, instead, a historical footnote to the story of American higher education.

What we do well, in our best moments, is to create the conditions for academic learning and personal growth along the lines that were sketched by Elton Trueblood. We create no great body of doctrine and we do not indoctrinate. We are institutionally rather informal, and characteristically we are democratic in going about our business. Veracity, discipline, simplicity, individuality, community, concern and peace—these characteristics might well guide our often faltering efforts to develop thoughtful and responsible men and women. Academic rigor in a special learning environment can mark people for life, thereby making them "centers of contagion."

"WE ARE ALL TEACHERS FOR GOOD OR EVIL"

Opal Thornburg's fine history of Earlham College provides this quotation from a student's journal which was written after the Civil War. The evangelical fervor of the time may have produced a rather large oversimplification, but it does speak eloquently of the personal sense of responsibility that has been at the heart of Quaker education in the wider world. Much of our educational effort has taken place outside of the school, academy and college.

In Leonard Kenworthy's book *Quakerism, A Study Guide on the Religious Society of Friends,* there is a helpful sketch of the educational efforts of Friends outside of formal educational institutions. The Quaker concern to teach and to witness to a needy and often confused world has been evident in prisons, mental hospitals, work camps, United Nations organizations, and foreign missions. Kenworthy cites Eric Johnson's comment that perhaps the American Friends Service Committee has been our "largest Quaker school." Friends seem to have labored under a special sense of responsibility to minister to a world in need and to be "teachers for good."

SUMMARY COMMENTS

1. The spiritually direct, highly personal, non-dogmatic, socially responsible characteristics of Quakerism provide a special context for the conduct of vital educational institutions.
2. The search for consensus and the effort to resolve conflicts peacefully are basic concerns in the governance of Quaker educational activities.
3. An insistence upon scholastic integrity and a continuing search for education that has both personal meaning and social relevance have given Quaker education at its best an openness to innovation and experimentation. This is often expressed in non-traditional and even non-institutional educational initiatives.
4. Educational efforts that have been launched or inspired by Quakers vary greatly in program, scope, style, and prominence, and they share the problems and pressures that are experienced by all private educational ventures. Many Quaker educators have expressed their values and concerns through service in public education.
5. The vitality and permanence of Quaker education are dependent upon the continuation of a viable Religious Society of Friends. It is probable that, ultimately, the Society will not survive as a religious movement without the survival of vital Quaker educational organizations and initiatives.

SOME SUGGESTED READINGS

Brinton, Howard H. *Quaker Education: In Theory and Practice.* Pendle Hill Pamphlet 9, 1945.

Heath, Douglas. *The Peculiar Mission of a Friends School.* Pendle Hill Pamphlet #225, 1979.

Hole, Helen G. *Things Civil and Useful: A Personal View of Quaker Education.* Richmond, IN: Friends United Press, 1978.

Kenworthy, Leonard S. *Living in the Light: Some Quaker Pioneers of the 20th Century* (Volume I—In the U.S.A.). Friends General

Conference and Quaker Publications, 1984.

Quaker Education Considered. Report of Friends Conference on Education. Earlham College, November 21–22, 1946. (On file in Earlham, Whittier and other Quaker libraries.)

Russell, Elbert. *The History of Quakerism.* New York: The Macmillan Co., 1942.

SOME QUESTIONS FOR DISCUSSION

1. Is it still important for Friends to provide young people with a "religiously guarded education"? If so, how can this be done in our contemporary society?
2. What characteristics of Quaker belief are especially important in the teaching and learning process?
3. Is a "critical mass" of Quaker students and teachers needed in order to make a school or college a Quaker institution?
4. How does one go about making a Quaker school or college the kind of place that develops students who are to become "centers of contagion"?
5. Can the Religious Society of Friends survive as a vital movement without healthy and independent Quaker schools and colleges?
6. In what ways have members of your Friends Meeting or Friends Church been able to introduce some Quaker concerns into public educational institutions? What else might you do?

ABOUT THE AUTHOR

Eugene S. Mills, a lifelong member of the West Newton, Indiana Friends Meeting, is a graduate of Earlham College with advanced degrees from the Claremont Graduate School. He has taught psychology at Whittier College, the University of Victoria, and the University of New Hampshire. He is the author of numerous psychological publications, including a major biography of one of the founders of American psychological science. Following a number of administrative positions, he served as the president of the University of New Hampshire from 1974 to 1979, when he became president of Whittier College.

Chapter 7

Some Quaker Perspectives on Sexuality

Peggy Brick

With respect to sexuality, we live in the best of worlds and the worst of worlds. A sexual revolution, the feminist movement, and the gay liberation movement have challenged a myriad of destructive assumptions and myths about sex. Simultaneously, a new science—sexology—offers a rich new body of knowledge about the physiology, sociology, and history of human sexuality. More liberated than before from prejudice and ignorance, we can seek to understand the meaning of sexuality in the light of our fundamental Quaker values.

That is an awesome responsibility—to create for ourselves and our children a new way of being in the world as males and females, of affirming our body feelings and capacity for sensuousness, and of nurturing our drive toward intimacy and communion. The possibility of that enterprise is what is best. What is worst is that we struggle to achieve such wholesome sexuality while living in a society where sexual exploitation is pervasive in relationships, in the media, and in many other facets of public life. Fortunately, during the last twenty years a number of Friends have joined the search for Quaker perspectives on sex, and their insights can give seekers direction.

I recall the beginning of my own journey when, in 1965, I sat under the maple tree in our backyard in Baltimore, our children playing nearby, and read the pamphlet *Toward a Quaker View of Sex*. That short publication jarred all my convenient and conventional assumptions about sexual morality—assumptions that were really amoral because they had never been examined any more than most people examine their assumptions about patriotism and war. The British Friends who wrote that pamphlet as a response to young homosexual Friends were one of the first religious groups to examine sexuality in contemporary society. Their statement in the preface to that booklet challenged me then, and can guide us now. It said:

> Christianity is not a book of rules, the application of which has to be worked out in a pattern. It springs from living relationships with each other and with God and its fulfillment is in relationship. Its implications can therefore be reached only through an understanding which is personal and intimate: without compassion there can be no understanding at all. The compassion of Jesus was his point of entry into each human situation. We must accept and begin from the truth about each human being in his own predicament, here and now in the modern world.

Indeed, the questions Friends currently ask regarding sexuality illustrate the inadequacy of any traditional rules in guiding their search. The following questions are a sample of those collected at three recent workshops: What are the characteristics of a sexual relationship that is spiritual? Does a lot of energy toward sexuality hinder spiritual growth? What kinds of expressions of sexual energy are "acceptable" for unpartnered people? Can love link sexuality and spirituality? Is there spiritual significance to being celibate? What happens to unexpressed sexuality? How do you retain your sense of self in a relationship? What effect does age have on sexuality? Is non-monogamy ethical; does it go against something fundamental? How can a single parent offer a role model that communicates sexuality to children in a living, healthy way?

The questions are endless: individuals face decisions about cohabitation; couples confront the failure of their marriages; families struggle with the disclosure of sexual abuse; young people realize that they are gay or lesbian; older Friends cope with the death of a spouse. What is a Quaker view of sexuality that will affirm it as a fundamental part of every person's humanness: all the experiences, learnings, knowledge, dreams, fantasies, experiences, and relationships that have to do with our being male or female?

There seems to be little in Quaker history that will help Friends today. Even the slightest deviation from the established puritanical norms of the early days was a cause of concern and very often of being "read out of Meeting." The records of Friends Meetings indicates that Quakers were disowned frequently for "fornication with a fiancee," fornication, adultery, and incest. Much more common was disownment for marrying someone outside the Friends community.

However, several Quakers in recent years have studied human sexuality intensely and have shared their thinking in books, pamphlets, and reports of various conferences. We turn, then, to some of those reflections.

THE CHRISTIAN RESPONSE TO THE SEXUAL REVOLUTION

In *The Christian Response to the Sexual Revolution*, written in 1970, David Mace, a well-known Friend, defines the sexual revolution as "a radical change in our *thinking* about sex,"—a change that proceeds from " a negative attitude to a positive attitude toward it." He predicts that the new attitudes, based on the scientific study of sex, the collapse of taboos, the emancipation of women, the advances in medical knowledge, and a new era of individual freedom, will, in time, gain almost universal acceptance.

David Mace believes that the sexual revolution launched a quest for the true meaning of sexuality. Christians, coming from "a tradition that encouraged dogmatism and authoritarian assertiveness," are confronted with the need to think about the standards of sexual behavior they ought to proclaim and practice. He charges that the "Christian view of sex is a shambles—a hodgepodge of superstition and prejudice that answers to no set of coherent principles," and he proposes that Christians adopt a standard of sexual morality based on the ethical teachings of Jesus: the Golden Rule and the commandment to love our neighbors as ourselves.

The "New Morality," says Mace, like the teaching of Jesus, stresses inward motives rather than outward acts, the well-being of people over respect for institutions, and requires followers to live not under the law but under grace. Thus, he urges giving up "a deeply ingrained pathological conceptualization of our sexual nature" and "freeing ourselves for the urgent task...of bringing religion and sex back together."

THE WORKING PARTY ON HUMAN SEXUALITY

Confronted by the impact of the sexual revolution on some of its members in the assignment of rooms at its annual Gathering, Friends General Conference (FGC) sought clearness on a number of difficult issues. To explore those questions a Working Party on Human Sexuality was organized by the Religious Education Committee of the FGC, and they met one Saturday a month for more than four years.

Then, in 1977, that Working Party held a weekend conference on

"The Meeting's Response to Issues of Sexuality and Marriage," with workshops tackling such topics as "Clearness for Marriage," "Marriage Enrichment," "Roles of Parents and Meetings in Sex Education," "Communication between Adults and Youth about Sexuality," "Homosexuality and Bisexuality," "Living Without a Partner," "Living Together and Not Married," "Sexuality in the Later Years," "Spirituality and Sexuality," "Intimacies Outside the Primary Relationship," and "Marital Distress and Divorce." Although the Working Party never achieved the written document it had hoped to produce, it did publish an *Annotated Bibliography and Resource Materials for Discussion Leaders.*

HUMAN SEXUALITY AND THE QUAKER CONSCIENCE

In 1973 the Religious Education Committee of Friends General Conference had recognized that "a searching look at our attitudes toward sexuality is going on within Quakerism today," and they decided to ask Mary Calderone to give the Rufus Jones Lecture on Human Sexuality and the Quaker Conscience. To them she was the obvious choice to open a dialogue on that sensitive topic, as she was a physician, a Quaker, a grandmother, and a pioneer in sexual relations, concerned with "liberating human sexuality from the unhealthy atmosphere of suspicion, guilt, and fear that [has] surrounded it."

In that searching and provocative lecture, Mary Calderone identified three major components in the sexualization process of human beings: the establishment of core gender identity, the learning of appropriate gender behavior, and the development of the capacity for genital sensation. Since these are learned behaviors, in contrast to reproductive capacity, they are extremely vulnerable to environmental lacks and emotional deprivation—a crucial fact in considering sexual morality.

She maintained that sexuality and society are often in conflict over issues concerning heterosexuality and homosexuality, male and female relationships, and forms of erotic behavior because "while we accept the right of the individual to free choice and decision as a basic principle in a free society, many of us tend to reject this as a right when it comes to certain kinds of sexual behavior or certain kinds of individuals." She maintained further that many such issues could be resolved by "a broad distribution of sound sexual information and by protection of the rights of others in their use of it."

Raising the question about the Quaker conscience, she asserted that "The great challenge of being a Friend has always been for me that only one of us may hear—each one for his or her own self—God speaking to

us. No other human being can overhear our message nor our response
to them...." Thus, she said, each person must wrestle with the many
meanings of sex in life. On that theme she commented in this way:

> For reproduction? Obviously. For lusty pleasure? Unques-
> tionably. For deep, mutual passion? Hopefully. For tender-
> ness and caring, for fun and laughter, for companionship,
> for communication? A thousand times yes. To bring us
> closer to God? If an affirmative relationship can do this, sex
> may or may not be a part of it...if sex enhances such a
> relationship, lends a radiance, a special meaning to it, how
> fortunate for both people—and who among those not so
> fortunate will have the temerity to judge another's state of
> being? Such judgments as were made by Jesus were always
> in the side of generosity and love.

WHAT IS SEXUAL MORALITY?

Seven years later, Eric Johnson, a well-known Quaker educator long
associated with the Germantown Friends School, told the Friends
General Conference Gathering that in order to discover what sexual
morality is, we first need to unlearn ideas that confuse our
understanding of sex. In that category he included the following: that
sex and genitals are equal (sex organs do not fall in love with each
other); that sex is bad; that sex is *the* best thing (there are lots of other
wonderful things, too); that sex has to be either an orgy or a sacrament
(actually it is somewhere in between); that you can have sex without
consequences; and that you can prove yourself by sex ("if you want to
prove yourself by having a lot of sex, you're in competition against
hamsters, mice, rabbits, guinea pigs...").

He also stated that we must unlearn that sex is natural (in fact, we
learn how we are going to express our sexuality). We must also unlearn
the idea, common among teenagers, that it is okay to have sex if you
are carried away by passion and things get out of control, but if you go
out and prepare for sex by getting birth control, it is a bad thing (it is
not okay if you are carried away unless you are carried away in a
responsible, loving environment).

Eric Johnson proposed six values on which we can base our sexual
behavior: information, responsibility, control, consideration, the
ultimate worth of every individual person, and communication.

WHAT IS MARRIAGE—BEYOND LIVING TOGETHER?

In 1979 a conference at Pendle Hill, the adult Quaker study center near

Philadelphia, addressed the issue of unmarried cohabitation as an emerging life style in the culture generally, and among some Friends. Led by David and Vera Mace, co-presidents of the Association of Couples for Marriage Enrichment; Eleanor Macklin, a professor of Human Ecology; and Dorothy Steere, a much respected Quaker leader; the group assembled there identified the topic as particularly important to three Quaker groups: young people, especially college students; people in mid-life who are separated, divorced or widowed; and senior citizens.

At the final session participants reported how they as Quakers had reacted to what they had learned. Their responses, although not unanimous, were sufficiently representative to be recorded and indicated that Friends were "moving toward a new openness" and "could not dismiss cohabitation as a wicked practice." Overall, they "felt constrained to ask whether our major duty as Friends is to recognize and nourish that of God which is in every individual or to preserve the sanctity of a particular social institution."

The participants indicated that while they recognized the importance of "divine assistance" in the achievement of successful marriages, yet "in the light of the Quaker concept that all life is sacramental, it seemed [that] a relationship between a man and a woman which demonstrated the 'inward spiritual grace,' but lacked the 'outward and visible sign' might be at least as sacramental as one which had 'the outward and visible sign' but lacked the 'inward spiritual grace.' "

The conference concluded with the following *Suggestions and Recommendations:*

1. A full, open discussion of this subject should take place in many Meetings to overcome the "conspiracy of silence" that exists concerning these sensitive questions and which can breed evasion and misunderstanding unworthy of our Quaker heritage of honesty and openness to the truth.

2. Friends should examine their attitudes to members of Meetings who become involved in marital difficulties; who experience separation and divorce; who seek in unregistered marriages to find answers to their personal and interpersonal needs; or whose children go through such experiences. We need to reaffirm in these new life situations our traditional Quaker principle of extending caring and loving service to those who suffer rejection and condemnation from other sections of our society.

3. In this new human situation we may be called to a new application

of our peace testimony: the issue of cohabitation places some parents and their children, some Meetings and their members, in a state of tension—if we reject them as being outside the scope of "divine assistance," we fail ourselves to act as agents of that assistance.

4. We need to reexamine our practices of guiding young couples through their first year of living together and of providing all couples in our midst with easy access to couple enrichment.

5. To guide their own attitudes, Friends can ask the following questions:

   a. Do I see marriage as different from cohabitation; if it is different, how? Do I see some unique value in legal marriage; and if so, what is it?

   b. Would I ever feel comfortable cohabiting outside of legal marriage; and, if so, under what circumstances?

   c. How do I now react to (think about, feel about, behave toward) persons who are living together outside legal marriage? How do I wish to react?

   d. What can I do to help my Meeting deal constructively with the issue of marriage and cohabitation?

   e. If as Quakers we believe that "divine assistance" is an important element in a relationship, how do we define this? allow ourselves to be open to it? communicate the concept to others?

FRIENDS FOR LESBIAN AND GAY CONCERNS

Ever since 1971 a group of Quakers, known as Friends for Lesbian and Gay Concerns (FLGC), have labored to avoid a "conspiracy of silence" concerning homosexuality in the Religious Society of Friends. FLGC seeks "to encourage fellowship, friendship, support, and self-affirmation among gay men and lesbians; and to promote a dialogue within the Society at all levels, with a view toward achieving a deeper mutual understanding and affirmation." In their pursuit of those goals, members have promoted some of the deepest and most soul-searching discussions about the meaning of sexuality that have occurred in Friends Meetings.

In fairly recent years Australia, Baltimore, Illinois, Intermountain, New York, Pacific, Philadelphia, and Southern Appalachian Yearly Meetings have minuted their support of homosexual persons. A 1973 Baltimore Yearly Meeting Minute reads:

We urge Friends to put new energy into the struggle to end oppression, often unconscious, that is imposed on people because of their sex or their sexual orientation. Men and women must be freed of the rigid roles society teaches them.

The myths about bisexuality and homosexuality, myths that perpetuate deep rooted discrimination, need to be dispelled through educational efforts, perhaps undertaken by the monthly meetings. Equally important are the efforts each individual must make to develop positive attitudes toward his or her sexuality and the sexuality of others, and to build mutually affirming relationships. In accordance with Friends testimony of the right and responsibility to follow the Inner Light, we hope we will come to respect the decisions of others about their own sexuality.

It would be misleading, however, to indicate that all Friends are united in such conclusions. With deep sincerity and conviction, other groups of Friends have spoken out against homosexuality. Among them have been Southwest Yearly Meeting, Evangelical Friends Church—Eastern Region, and Iowa, Indiana and Mid-America Yearly Meetings. A 1982 Indiana Yearly Meeting minute states:

We believe homosexual practices to be contrary to the intent and will of God for humankind. We believe the Holy Spirit and Scriptures witness to this (Lev. 18:22, Lev. 20:13, Romans 1:21-32, I Cor. 6:9-10, I Tim. 1:9-10). We further believe that, whatever our condition of sinfulness and forgiveness, redemption and wholeness are freely available through our Lord Jesus Christ (I Cor. 6:11, Eph. 1:7). Adopted with the disagreement of a few Friends as noted.

LOVE AND SEX IN PLAIN LANGUAGE

Meanwhile, Eric Johnson was pursuing his tireless efforts to make accurate and responsible sex education available to children and youth. His three books on that topic: *Love and Sex in Plain Language; Sex: Telling It Straight;* and *Love and Sex and Growing Up,* still give Quaker parents—and thousands of others—a way to open honest communication about sex. Responding to a student's request that he tell "everything," his writing acknowledges the healthy curiosity of children about sex, as well as the discomfort that many adults still have in talking to them about it.

In 1981 Eric Johnson joined Mary Calderone in writing *The Family Book About Sexuality,* affirming the family as the best setting for learning to develop and use one's sexuality responsibly and for learning to give and receive love. In the preface they declared: "Quakers believe that all human beings have a right to all the information that can help them to arrive at rational and responsible decisions about the conduct of their lives" and that "as Quakers, our moral values depend on our belief in the infinite worth of each human being and on our belief that as human beings we are obliged to deal with others as we would like others to deal with us—trustingly, caringly, and responsibly." Then, in 1982, Mary Calderone co-authored another volume giving more specific recommendations for *Talking with Your Child About Sex.* These books are an invaluable resource for Quaker parents who want to successfully fill their inevitable role as the primary sex educators of their children.

Although some parents and teachers are committed to helping children understand sexuality within a Quaker context, most Friends Meetings have done little, if anything, on sexuality education. Meanwhile, some other religious groups have developed excellent programs that help young people understand sex information as related to their religious beliefs. For example, the Unitarian-Universalist Association used sex educators to help them create a comprehensive curriculum and teacher-education program, known as *About Your Sexuality.* Parents take the course in advance of their puberty-aged children so that they can supplement the lessons with informal discussions at home. Recently the Unitarians added a carefully designed component for sexual abuse prevention.

Friends Meetings that are concerned about the confusing and exploitive sexual messages that children are subjected to in American society should consider emulating such programs and taking a much more active role in the sexuality education of their young people.

SEXUALITY: A PART OF WHOLENESS

At a 1982 conference sponsored by the Family Relations Committee of Philadelphia Yearly Meeting, Elizabeth Watson contended that the reason sexuality is such a problem for the human race is that "we have taken sexuality out of the context of wholeness" with each of us "working at being all we were meant to be...living life to the circumference."

She analyzed the way the historical orthodox Christian church perpetuates myths that destroy such wholeness: 1) *Dualism*, "that divides things into opposites: body and soul, God and man, life and death..." and "lays out our lives in terms of 'thou shalt not!' rather than in terms of affirmation and seeking...;" 2) *Patriarchy*, that limits our view of the human race to the male half so that women are the possessions of men and the female body is an object, a view that considers masculine ways of thinking, making decisions, and making moral judgments as the only human way; 3) *Sex is evil.* Sex, permissible only for procreation and only within marriage, is best denied for more spiritual matters.

Elizabeth Watson imagined how different life would be when sexuality is experienced as a part of wholeness: 1) Love will be a relationship of equals; 2) Sexuality will be a normal, beautiful part of life; 3) Children will explore and enjoy their bodies and will grow up armed with knowledge of what is involved in intercourse and parenthood; 4) Sexuality will be seen as a continuum that includes homosexuality, bisexuality, and heterosexuality—and probably masturbation. Individuals at different places at different times in their lives will not pass judgment on those at other places; 5) Most people will probably still prefer to make long-term commitments, though there have always been people who cannot live within this framework; 6) In both long-term and less formal relationships people will be honest with each other; 7) Celibacy will be a viable option; and 8) Women will be freed of the double standard.

Finally, Elizabeth Watson suggested what individuals who accept this vision of sexuality can do to make it a reality. 1) Grow into wholeness. When lives are interesting and rewarding, sex is more likely to assume its rightful place. 2) Resist exploitation, recognizing that the domination of others and submission to others are both evil and preclude peace between individuals and nations. 3) Love ourselves so we can love others—being in touch with our needs, listening to our bodies, leaving our "sexuality up to God, holding it in the Light, seeking answers to [our] problems." 4) Cultivate non-judgmental attitudes, for "so long as people are not harming others, their life styles and sexual practices...are not our business." 5) Create time and space for our children's honest questions. 6) Resolve conflicts creatively, using outside help when appropriate, but willing to release a partner who needs a different space in which to grow. 7) Live our relationships as a "holy experiment," for the kingdom of God is within us. And 8) Hallow our sexuality, saying "yes" and "no" with assurance—out of the centeredness of our lives.

Not all Friends will accept Elizabeth Watson's call to wholeness, to "let sexuality and spirituality walk hand in hand," but the process she suggests is a challenge to individuals and Meetings alike. Surely Quakers of varying backgrounds need to continue to seek an understanding of sexuality today in a Quaker perspective.

Participants in one workshop on sexuality sponsored by Friends General Conference attempted to do just that by developing a list of *Queries on Sexuality* for Friends. That list was revised by members of a workshop at New England Yearly Meeting and by individual Friends. It is presented here as an invitation to other Quakers to engage in active dialogue about sexuality, and perhaps to develop their own set of queries.

QUERIES FOR FRIENDS ON SEXUALITY

1. How does your life reveal that sexuality is a gift of the spirit, to be celebrated as an embodiment of that spirit in each of us?
2. In what ways do you recognize that sexuality is a vital and basic part of our humanness, present at birth and continuing throughout the life span?
3. How do you recognize that as we mature, our values and the values of those with whom we have intimate relationships may change, necessitating continued mutual seeking in order to respect the needs of each individual involved?
4. How do you recognize that a long-term relationship committed to the nurturance of both partners may provide unique support for the development of both personalities?
5. In what ways have you examined your sexual values? How are you open to new information and insight into these values?
6. How are you open to a growing understanding of varying sexual preferences, orientations, and life styles?
7. Are you aware that masturbation is a normal and healthy sexual outlet?
8. How are you open to understanding different values on the issue of abortion?
9. How do you avoid sexual exploitation of other people, particularly those under eighteen; those with significantly less experience; those especially vulnerable mentally, emotionally, physically, or socially; and those who are in some way dependent on you?
10. In making decisions regarding your sexual activities, how do you consider all the consequences for yourself, your partner, your

family, and your community?

11. How do you accept yourself as a sexual being, rejoicing in your own body?
12. In what ways do you seek equality and mutuality in your intimate relationships?
13. How are you sensitive to the feelings of others when expressing sexual intimacy in public?
14. How do you support and encourage good sexuality education in home, school, and Meeting?
15. What are the sexual values you model? What do your children believe your sexual values are? Do they perceive you as a sexual person? How do you make sexual information available to your children? Do you dialogue with them to facilitate their healthy and responsible development? Have you discussed the fact that values concerning appropriate sexual behavior may be different for different age groups?
16. How have you encouraged family planning and the provision of birth control information to those who want and need it?
17. How is your response to that of God in yourself and in others the foundation of your relationship?

SOME SUGGESTED READINGS

Barnett, Walter, *Homosexuality and the Bible*. Pendle Hill Pamphlet 226.

Calderone, Mary S. and Eric W. Johnson. *The Family Book About Sexuality*. San Francisco: Harper and Row, 1981.

Calderone, Mary S. and James W. Ramey. *Talking with Your Child About Sex*. New York: Random House, 1982.

Friends for Lesbian and Gay Concerns Newsletter. Box 222, Sumneytown, Pennsylvania 18084.

Nelson, James. *Embodiment: An Approach to Sexuality and Christian Theology*. Minneapolis, MN: Augsburg Publishing House, 1979.

ABOUT THE AUTHOR

Peggy Brick, the Director of Education for Planned Parenthood in Bergen County, New Jersey, trains New Jersey teachers for the implementation of the state's new Family Life Education Mandate. For fifteen years she taught Human Sexuality in a public high school. She has written numerous articles about sex education and recently co-authored *Positive Images: A New Approach to Contraceptive Education*. A member of the Baltimore Yearly Meeting, she has led workshops on sexuality for Friends General Conference, Pendle Hill, and New England Yearly Meeting.

Chapter 8

Beyond Equal Rights: The Quaker Concern for the Rights of Women

Margaret Hope Bacon

In Indonesia, young girls are recruited to work in multinational industries under unsafe conditions and at low wages because they are considered "docile." When they cease being docile, they are dismissed. In famine stricken Africa, where more than half of the refugees are women, relief programs are tailored for men, with consequent increased suffering and death for women and children, who make up ninety percent of the refugee population. In the United States, the majority of women who work at wages of fifty-nine cents to the dollar paid to men are expected to carry the double burden of work and housework without help and are vulnerable to domestic violence, rape, and a poverty-stricken old age. Two out of every three poor adults in this country are women.

Despite some apparent, spectacular gains for a small segment of middle class women, the worldwide statistics still show women around the globe suffering from oppression based solely on their gender. Like its twin, racism, sexism uses a multitude of rationalizations and subterfuges to cover the naked truth of exploitation. Historically, men have exercised their power to subordinate women, in order to reserve for themselves the largest share of the pie.

QUAKER ROOTS

One of the distinguishing features of the Religious Society of Friends since its birth in seventeenth-century England has been its insistence on the spiritual equality of women. George Fox argued with the clergy to defend the right of women to preach and prophesy, and he later defended

97

women's capacity to conduct Business Meetings against schismatics within the Society. Margaret Fell wrote the first treatise since the Reformation defending women's right to the ministry. Both quoted from St. Paul's Epistle to the Galatians, "There is no room for Jew or Greek, there is no room for slave or freeman, there is no room for male and female; you are all one in Christ Jesus."

The equality granted women within the Society was one of the reasons for the persecution of Friends by the male-oriented Puritans of New England. When William Penn founded Pennsylvania as a haven for Friends, he defended the separate women's Meetings for Business. Speaking of the ideal relationships between men and women, he said that "in souls there is no sex."

Many of the first traveling Quaker ministers, particularly in the American colonies, were women. Their capacity to endure separation from their families and the hardships of travel, and to play a vital role in the planting of the Seed, taught Friends of both sexes something about the previously buried talents of women and made a lasting impression on the larger society. Many of the early Friends schools were designed for both girls and boys; and as a result, Quaker women were consistently better educated than the women of other denominations. When women began to enter the professions in the nineteenth century, Quaker women consequently led in many fields. In the developing reform movements, such as the reform of women's prisons, Quaker women were often the pioneers.

The early Quaker concept of equality went far beyond a question of rights and was, instead, based on a spiritual premise. Having been brought again through Christ into a state of grace, men and women together participated in a Peaceable Kingdom where no one dominated another and all power-based, hierarchical relationships were dissolved in a pure democracy of the Spirit. This was the condition in which Friends felt they lived, which they believed would take away the occasion for all war. The equality of women was as fundamental a testimony as the peace testimony and preceded the peace testimony in the evolution of Quaker belief.

But Quakerism developed, and has survived for well over three hundred years, in a society where sexism is pervasive, as unseen as the sea in which fish swim. Inevitably, the Society of Friends began with some of the unconscious sexism of the larger society as part of its world view and has continued to absorb new sexist views as they have developed. In particular, as Friends prospered and became part of the business establishment, they were vulnerable to the attitudes of their non-Quaker business counterparts about the special sphere of women. That is why the Hicksites, who remained rural, more fully preserved the ancient testimony of gender equality. In consequence of these trends, it has taken Friends many years to see the implications of their testimony on women outside the walls of the Meetinghouse. Just as Friends came slowly, over a period of almost one hundred years, to realize that their faith in that of God in everyone precluded the holding of slaves, so it took Quakers two hundred years to begin to advocate equal rights for women in the larger society. And, as in the case of slavery, a few courageous spirits within the Society first raised the issue and entered into the struggle despite a lack of support, or even faced active disapproval, from their home Meetings.

In the field of women's history, the Quaker contribution to the struggle for women's rights in the nineteenth century is acknowledged as a major factor. Angelina and Sarah Grimke, Abby Kelley Foster, Lucretia Mott, Sarah Pugh, and Susan B. Anthony—all pioneers of women's rights, were Quakers. Their original commitment to the abolition of slavery led them to see that all rights were "tied up in one bundle," as Abby Kelley Foster put it, and that they must advocate equality for women in order to play a responsible share in ending slavery.

Both the abolition and the women's rights movements, however, meant mixing with "the world's people," and Friends in the early part of the nineteenth century were deep in a period of withdrawal. As a consequence, most of the women active in either of those causes received a cold response from the very Society which had inspired their devotion to equality. Many gave up Quakerism because of this lack of support. Only a handful stuck it out, and only Lucretia Mott kept up a valiant, lifelong battle to convince her beloved Society that the struggle for equality had its roots in the original Quaker vision.

In the latter half of the nineteenth century, commitment to women's rights became more general as Quakers began to move out of their period of withdrawal from the world and as Friends in the Midwest, as well as in the East, became active in such causes as temperance and the reform of women's prisons. An allegiance developing between the temperance and the suffrage issues brought many of these women into work for political rights for women, although only the Hicksites advocated suffrage as a religious body. Alice Paul, a Hicksite Friend from Moorestown, New Jersey, led a dramatic, nonviolent campaign for the vote during World War I and later arranged for the introduction in Congress of the original Equal Rights Amendment. Feeling rebuffed by

Quakers for her militancy, she maintained only a token relationship with the Society for many years.

QUAKER WOMEN IN THE TWENTIETH CENTURY

At the time the battle for woman's suffrage was raging, many Quaker women were becoming involved in the development of two institutions that were to have a profound effect on the evolution of Quakerism in the next seventy years. Those were the Women's International League for Peace and Freedom (the WILPF), founded in 1915 and the American Friends Service Committee (the AFSC), organized in 1917. Once suffrage was won, the National American Woman Suffrage Association, which had been founded by Susan B. Anthony and had originally led the fight, became the League of Women Voters. Many Quaker women turned their energies to League activities, while others worked through the WILPF and the AFSC.

Quaker families continued to offer their daughters equal educational opportunities, and Quaker schools and colleges provided a high quality of education for girls as well as for boys. But only a handful remained active in Alice Paul's continuing fight for the Equal Rights Amendment and for worldwide commitment to equal rights under the League of Nations, and later, the United Nations.

Consequently, when the current women's movement developed in the late 1960s, it took Quaker women by surprise. Most of them felt that they had been treated as equals all their lives and that they had no need for the consciousness-raising which was an integral part of the reawakening of this movement. Many also shared the typical Quaker aversion to politics, and the new movement was soon active politically. Also, many were deeply involved in struggles for world peace and for racial equality, which seemed at the time more pressing than the concept of working for women's rights.

Gradually, however, this original perception began to change as younger Quaker women brought to the attention of Meetings and of Quaker institutions the fact that patterns of sexism adopted from the larger society were to be found within the structure of the Society of Friends. Top positions in Friends United Meeting, Friends General Conference, and AFSC continued to be occupied by men; women were predominate at the secretarial level. In Meetings, women frequently served on the hospitality or First Day school committees; men on the property and finance committees. There were more men than women in tenure-level positions in the Quaker educational institutions, and the women's salaries were lower.

Along with these discoveries came increased information on the toll of sexism worldwide. Friends of all persuasions conducted service projects or missions in developing countries. In them they saw women who were expected to raise food for the family through backbreaking agricultural work, haul the water, and still cook the food and make the clothes for large families. Statistics on women's health and mortality under such circumstances were alarming. Meanwhile, new programs in the U.S. being developed for women, often with a few individual Quakers in the lead, were bringing to light the buried fact of violence against women in homes, sexual harassment on the job, and the ever-present use of women as sexual objects in advertising, pornography, and rape. Statistics on women as victims of poverty were also becoming more compelling.

THE DEVELOPMENT OF A NEW QUAKER WOMEN'S MOVEMENT

Here and there, within Monthly Meetings, Quaker women began to meet to discuss some of these issues, starting in typical Quaker fashion with their impact on their own lives. Younger Quaker women spoke of their despair at the use of sexist language, which they considered an affront to their existence in the community of worshipers, in Meeting. Quaker wives and mothers of the Civilian Public Service generation began to acknowledge that they had accepted the post-World War II cultural swing toward reemphasizing the role of homemaker and had stayed home and raised families at the expense of not only their own education and career development, but of the closeness between father and children.

Many of those original groups continue to meet. Some women find worship with a group of other women very nourishing, though few see it as an alternative to regular First Day Meeting. For some women the local women's groups has been a way station before committing themselves to taking action on women's rights. Thus, a number of Quaker women, as individuals, are involved in community-based programs providing safe houses for abused women, counseling for rape victims, help to mothers in prison, health care for women, and protection of the civil rights of homosexuals.

How many such women's groups have been formed during the 1970s and 1980s is difficult to say. Some of those scattered women's groups began to coalesce in the early 1970s into Yearly-Meeting-wide groups on either a formal or informal basis. Women from these wider groups met in 1974 and 1975 in week-long seminars at Pendle Hill, the adult Quaker study center in Wallingford, Pennsylvania. Following the second of those meetings, a newsletter called *The Friendly Woman* was started with editing responsibilities moving among several Yearly Meetings. That task has served also as a tool in strengthening each organization.

Since 1974 women have maintained a women's center at the annual Gathering of the Friends General Conference where women can participate in worship and sharing. And each year there has been a work-study group devoted to some aspect of women's rights. Following the 1983 Gathering, a network was established among women who are in the ministry and wish to revitalize it. Their newsletter, called *The Friendly Nuisance,* is circulated among some forty women.

Interest in women's issues is high at Earlham School of Religion. Many women train for pastoral work there in programmed and unprogrammed meetings, often centering their attention on feminism and Quakerism. Pendle Hill has recently appointed educator and administrator Margery Walker as executive secretary.

Within the Friends United Meeting community, the selection of Kara Cole to be the Administrative Secretary of the Friends United Meeting from 1978 to 1987 has been a tangible sign of change. The United Society of Friends Women has also been interested in studying the roots of the Quaker emphasis on equality and has scheduled a number of Quaker feminist speakers at its annual sessions.

Among members of the Evangelical Friends Alliance, a Task Force on Women has been formed to study the ministry by Quaker women and to keep in touch through *The Priscilla Papers*, a newsletter. One member of that group has studied the decline of the ministry of women in Oregon Yearly Meeting; several are now studying at graduate schools of theology, preparing for careers in the Quaker ministry.

Within the American Friends Service Committee a group of younger women, primarily secretaries, began to meet in the late 1960s. Gradually they were joined by other, older women, in an informal group which pressed for changes on several issues, including child care in the national office. Following a meeting of AFSC women for the regional offices, a Nationwide Women's Program was formed with the twofold purpose of bringing a feminist perspective to bear on all current AFSC programs and assisting the regional offices in developing programs for women. An initial program in Cambridge, Massachusetts, centered on child care and abused women; in New York City on abused women and counseling for abusing men; and in San Francisco on women's health issues. Members of local Friends Meetings also supported those programs. More recently the Nationwide Women's Program has concentrated on contacts with Third World women's organizations in this country and in the developing nations, as well as with women active in the movement against nuclear weapons. Its publication, *Listen Real Loud*, has a national distribution both inside and outside the Society of Friends.

Through its Affirmative Action Program, the AFSC has increased the number of women in executive positions. That includes Asia Bennett, the executive secretary of that organization and the first woman to be appointed to that post. (In the 1920s Anna Griscom Elkinton served for a short time as Acting Executive Secretary.) Several of the Committee's major programs are now focused on women's issues. Those include an important Women in Development program in Mali and Guinea Bissau, helping women to increase their earning power; and Women in the Workforce, providing networking and information for women in Appalachia who are often heads of families in a region where jobs are scarce and the highest paying ones are reserved for men, and where violence against women has been an accepted part of the culture.

THE PROBLEM OF LANGUAGE

Probably the most difficult aspect of the current women's movement for Friends has been the struggle over the elimination of sexist language.

There are some indications that early Friends were conscious that use of the word "man" and its grammatical derivatives to indicate all people was a slight to women. In founding Pennsylvania, William Penn was careful to guarantee religious liberty to persons "whatever his or her conscientious persuasion," and the women of Philadelphia Yearly Meeting once suggested that "followers of Christ" be substituted for "brothers" in the *Discipline*. In 1830 New York Yearly Meeting (Hicksite) indicated that it was using "his," rather than "his or her," in the *Discipline* merely to save space. Nevertheless, this early sensitivity did not last into the twentieth century, and many Friends were shocked and even annoyed when the women's groups began to suggest a change to a more inclusive language.

The early resistance, experienced by other denominations as well, was perhaps natural. People do not like to change their habits, not because they are lazy, but because habits maintain a certain adjustment to one's world. In the case of language, the new ways always sound awkward at first and the change seems trivial—not worth the bother.

But there are deep-seated reasons why language must change to fit changing perceptions. For many years the use of the word "native" helped the colonists feel justified in their occupation of the lands of other people. The assumption was that the native was primitive and needed the help of the great white father. So, in the South the use of Nigra or nigger helped to insulate slave owners from the realization that the men and women who did the work on the plantations were also fully human. The generic use of male language has helped to reinforce the myth that the world was created for the use of males, and the white, Anglo-Saxon males of the Western world at that, and that women were simply an adjunct.

Early Friends understood the power of language, and their insistence on using thee and thou instead of you and yours (which infuriated their contemporaries as trivial) was based on an understanding of the need to get rid of hierarchical structures in society and to develop a Holy Community under the leading of the Spirit. Modern Friends have slowly come to understand the importance of using inclusive language, although there remain many pockets of resistance. Several Yearly Meetings are now in the process of revising their version of *Faith and Practice* in order to avoid sexist language. The AFSC, Friends General Conference, and other Quaker institutions have adopted inclusive language in their style books.

Even more troublesome has been the idea of trying to use descriptions of God other than as the all-powerful father. This should not be so, for early Friends used language about God which emphasized both maternal and paternal aspects of the Divinity. George Fox's *Journal* is full of images of the Holy Spirit as nurturing the eternal life in men and women. He speaks of the bread of life, of the living food of the living God, and of being gently led by the love of God. Many other early Friends used the language of nurture, likening the love of God to that of a mother who holds her nurslings to her breast. Friends spoke, too, of being tendered and melted together.

Some of the most beautiful expressions of Quaker belief speak of God in asexual terms. Thus James Nayler's much quoted dying words begin, "There is a Spirit which I feel...." A century later, John Woolman said, "There is a Principle placed in the human heart...."

Jesus was of course male, and few Quaker feminists wish to quarrel with the acceptance of this fact. Most see Jesus as embodying the best qualities of both the male and female; assertiveness and courage with love and tenderness. Quaker feminists believe that if both men and women are freed from the stereotypical sex roles which have been taught them by the sexism that runs through society, both men and women will be free to develop this androgyny of values. Lucretia Mott stated in the nineteenth century that if women were granted equality, the "elements which belong to men as such and to women as such would be beautifully and harmoniously blended" and one can hope there would be less war and injustice in the world.

Through the centuries, from Fox onward, Quaker men have worked to create equality within the Society of Friends. Quaker men supported the nineteenth-century women's rights movement as well as the suffrage struggle. Still, as Mott pointed out, men have a handicap. Enjoying the fruits of privilege, they are simply less apt to see injustice. (Exceptions, perhaps, result when men like Jesus or Fox are highly attuned spiritually.) It has therefore been the role of women to call attention to the need for change, just as the slave had to speak up against slavery.

FEMINISM AND NONVIOLENCE

While Quaker women have traditionally worked alongside Quaker men on many issues devoted to peace, or separately in such organizations as the WILPF, some Quaker women have been asking themselves if there is a specific connection between feminism and nonviolence. When not dominated by men or a masculine-oriented way of thinking, women's approach to peacemaking is less ideological and more empirical. It involves working with people in local situations on their own perceived needs rather than mounting national campaigns, often in response to and serving as a mirror-image of the campaigns of militarists.

Women interested in exploring what a feminist peace movement might be like have been meeting to share experiences and to plan campaigns. A number of Quaker women have participated in such all-women actions as Women's Pentagon Action and the encampments at the Greenham Common U.S. Military Base in Great Britain and at the Seneca U.S. Army Base in New York. Others have met with women in Europe interested in their interconnections. The use of silence and the seeking of consensus in decision-making have been contributions of Friends to those occasions. Also a number of Quaker authors have contributed chapters to a new book, *Reweaving the Web of Life*, exploring the relevance of feminism to nonviolence.

A VISION FOR THE FUTURE

The media presents the women's movement as a drive for equality. The young woman lawyer, doctor, stockbroker, or businesswoman who has participated successfully in the corporate world and is earning as high a salary as a man is the standard image. It might be called an "I'm all right, Jill," view. But most thoughtful feminists, and certainly those with a religious orientation, think instead of feminism as a path to a radically changed, more peaceful, more cooperative world. Getting rid of the notions that one group of people must control and have power over another group, that success is spelled by one's share of the world's goods, and that patriarchy and hierarchy are somehow written deep into the very universe, can free one to conceive of a wholly different world. When women have tried articulating their future vision, they find they are talking about the Peaceable Kingdom, the vision of the future which early Friends believed was a return to original Christianity.

That is why Quaker feminists believe their goal is beyond equality to a reawakening of the whole Society, male and female, to the need to purge itself of the sexism of the workaday world which has crowded into our lives and crowded out the capacity to envision a better world, or spiritual growth for oneself. A number of Quaker leaders have led sessions in imaging the future, imaging the world as one would wish it, and then stepping back to see what needs to change. Facing, uncovering, and eradicating deep-rooted sexism, with its ties to war and to the oppression of people of color, can be a way of ridding ourselves of outworn attitudes and preparing ourselves to move toward growth and change.

WHAT MEETINGS CAN DO

Friends have always worked best on issues when their actions were rooted in experience. Because Quakers tend to be white and middle class, it is difficult for them to understand the oppression of women unless they have some hands-on experience. Meeting participation and involvement in a local program designed to provide a shelter for abused women or homeless women, or a workroom for refugee women needing to gain employment skills, can do more to change attitudes and awaken sensitivities than a series of lectures on the subject. Some Meetings have been involved with visiting mothers in prison—another eye-opener.

An adult class discussion can also be devoted to the history of Quaker leadership in women's rights and the question of whether such leadership is being exercised today. A newly released film on the life of Lucretia Mott can be used to initiate and stimulate such a discussion.

If there is tension around the use of sexist language in the Meeting, it is usually wise to let it surface in the discussion hour or in the Meeting for Business. The revision of a brochure describing the history of the Meeting or of a handbook for overseers can be an occasion to thresh out strong feelings pro and con inclusive language.

Someone has said that the surfacing of the women's movement has been the most exciting surprise of the last half of the twentieth century. There is an enormous amount of energy wrapped up in this movement and a potential for social change as dynamic as—and some people believe more profound than—that perceived in the labor movement of the 1930s. Friends can find genuine satisfaction in the role the Society has played in the past in providing leadership in the women's rights movement. But rather than rest on our laurels, we need to see what the Lord requires of us today. We should enter into the search zestfully, knowing that the change and the transformation it will bring is a vital part of living in the Light.

SUGGESTED READINGS

Bacon, Margaret. *Mothers of Feminism: The Story of Quaker Women in America.* New York: Harper and Row, 1986.

Bacon, Margaret. *Valiant Friends: The Life of Lucretia Mott.* Walker, NY: Walker, 1980.

Boulding, Elise. *The Underside of History: A View of Women Through Time.* Boulder, CO: Westview Press, 1976. (An abbreviated edition is the Foreign Policy Association's Headline book *Women: The Fifth World.* New York: Foreign Policy Association, 1980.)

Watson, Elizabeth. *Daughters of Zion.* Richmond, IN: Friends United Press, 1981. (See also "Renaming the World," *Friends Quarterly* July, 1984. pp. 330–337.)

SOME QUESTIONS FOR DISCUSSION

1. Does your Monthly Meeting support and participate in community- based programs which speak to the specific needs of women?
2. Do you use inclusive language in worship and in the conduct of Meeting business?

3. Are members aware of the worldwide situation of women? Are you in touch with legislation affecting women through the FCNL and of programs for women in developing countries through the AFSC?

4. Have you scheduled a discussion hour or evening program on the history of Quaker women and their leadership in women's rights? Have you looked into the history of the women associated with your own Meeting in this regard?

ABOUT THE AUTHOR

Margaret Hope Bacon retired in 1984 after twenty-two years in the Information Services of the American Friends Service Committee. In private life she is an author whose short stories, poems, book reviews, and personal essays have appeared in many major magazines and newspapers. Since 1969 she has published six books of Quaker history and biography, three concerning Quaker women. She has received several awards, including the human rights award from the Philadelphia Commission on Human Relations and an honorary doctorate from Swarthmore College.

Chapter 9

Bringing the Family of Humanity into the Family of Friends

James A. Fletcher

What is the spiritual image of the Religious Society of Friends? I see a Meeting for Worship locked in silence, awaiting the Spirit of God—the nameless, faceless spirit who, we are told in Genesis, spoke from the burning bush "...I am that I am..." when asked by Moses to identify himself. That same spirit on whom Friends wait in silence is the logos of the Fourth Gospel and the eternal one, as the Muslims say, who has ninety-nine names "...not this...and not that...."

In the worship of God we have perfect freedom and peace. We cannot command God's spirit or shape it to our desires. It shapes us. Its power is unlimited. And from that unlimited nature of God have flowed our Quaker commitments for perfection, progressive revelation, and universal salvation.

LACK OF DIVERSITY AS A QUAKER PROBLEM

Yet, when one looks at the physical image of the Religious Society of Friends, the unlimited becomes the limited. In the world at large, Friends are mainly concentrated in the United States, Great Britain and related countries, and in East Africa. That reflects a historical pattern of migration and settlement and the more recent results of missionary activity. But it does not approximate the distribution of the world's population. Despite the multiethnic, multicultural makeup of the United States, the physical image of Friends is likewise limited. Rare indeed are the Black, Hispanic, Asian, and Native Americans in Quaker Meetings, even when Meetings are located in areas with large representations of those population groups.

Why is this a problem? It is one because the composition of our religious society can reflect how we view the human community and how we view the historic message of Friends. Who are "we" as Friends? Does the nameless, faceless spirit moving in us move only White, Anglo-Saxons to gather as Quakers?

Actually, the need for diversity in Friends Meetings is as broad as the full family of humanity. It embraces Blacks, Hispanics, Asians, and Native Americans, as well as other white ethnic groups who are not Anglo-Saxon. It also extends to those who are not middle or upper class and who do not have university degrees.

We must face the truth that the composition of many Quaker Meetings is now an anachronism in a world of change. Many people of goodwill have come to see the possibility, the actuality, and the potential benefits of racially integrated and multiethnic environments, as evidenced increasingly in the workplace, in schools, in neighborhoods, in governments, and even in world forums like the United Nations. In affirming and supporting this change, we recognize what is necessary for peace with justice. And we also recognize the great beauty in seeing God's creation coming together.

Unfortunately the lack of diversity in our membership can cloud our vision and blur our message to the world. We cherish our testimony of equality, but as the Scripture says, "...by your fruits so shall ye be known...." Furthermore, the scarcity of Third World Friends in Meetings often puts significant pressures on the few who do attend, causing them to ask sincerely, "Am I really welcome?"

This unfortunate lack of diversity in Quaker Meetings also helps to contribute to the sensitive relationships between some Friends and our own American Friends Service Committee (AFSC). Despite the fact that it has one of the most advanced affirmative action programs in our nation, sensitivity sometimes arises in it over the issue of "affirmative action for Friends." In fact some Friends are disturbed by what they perceive as a dilution in Quaker representation in the AFSC. If Quaker membership were more representative of the total population of the United States, Friends could provide more diverse membership in groups like the AFSC, and the experience of diversity itself could be less threatening to Quakers.

As a committed Friend who is also a Black American and the father of three children being raised within the Religious Society of Friends, I have a continuing concern about the lack of diversity in our group. We have been members of three Yearly Meetings and six Monthly Meetings in the East, Midwest, and West and have visited widely in

of diversity among Friends. At a recent meeting of the AFSC Corporation, the morning session was given over to a wonderful sharing on the need for encouraging diversity among Friends. But in the afternoon, a very practical matter arose concerning the AFSC Board By-Laws. At issue was the question as to whether regional AFSC clerks who are not Friends could be members of the AFSC Board. Such a change would officially recognize a situation that already exists, as there are regional clerks who are not Friends but who function fully as Board members.

The discussion went on and on, becoming very emotional and taking an ominous cast after one Friend voiced the fear that the approval of such a change would "open the floodgates." More than any other, that statement crystallizes what I see as an abiding Quaker concern that we continue as an exclusive cult. I felt appalled and ashamed for us then as Friends. Who was "flooding" whom? Why are we so fearful that the family of humanity will join the family of Friends? Somehow I have never noticed any overpopulation on the lonely, difficult social works in which we as Friends are engaged. Our membership is not growing rapidly. How we could use vigor, imagination, and sincere commitment from wherever it comes!

Because of the lack of diversity in our Friends Meetings, part of our Quaker vision is stillborn. Part of God's spirit is not heard or reflected in Meetings for Worship. I sense the image of a symphony which is incomplete because not all of the instruments are present. Friends suffer, and we all suffer because of this. As Mike Yarrow used to say, "cult Quakerism gets in the way of essential Quakerism."

EARLY FRIENDS AND THE IDEA OF DIVERSITY

At the core of the early Quaker message was a deep universalism. Early Friends like Fox, Barclay, Penn, and Penington dared envision the Quakerization of all England and an extension of the message to Friends throughout the world. In the words of Fox, they wanted to "walk cheerfully over the world, speaking to that of God in everyone."

We hear George Fox remarking on his visits to America about the workings of the Inner Light in Native Americans and their innate spiritual capacity. We hear Fox advising Friends to educate their slaves and to bring them to Meetings. Of course, the intent was to make Meetings open to all. But the word "slave" falls with a chill on our ears today, and it is not pleasant to realize that a number of early Friends owned slaves. It is even less pleasant for me to think that I might have been one of them, had I lived then, owned by a White Quaker of that day.

Nevertheless, many early Friends were inspired by the vision that Robert Barclay wrote about in his *Apology for the True Christian Divinity* and which he called "the universal and saving light." He wrote vividly on how the universal light was in individuals in China and India, as well as in those of the European Christian nations of that day. In one early incident in the life of that great Quaker apologist, we are told that when some Friends were objecting to having a Black speak in Meeting, Barclay rose in a powerful ministry on the meaning of Quaker universalism and said, "Let the Tawney speak," (Tawney being an expression then for Blacks in England).

In some respects that early Quaker movement failed. Exclusion replaced inclusion. Quakerism retreated from being a movement and became a sect.

In his account of *Democracy in America,* Alexis de Tocqueville wrote of the early United States as roughly one-third White, one-third Black, and one-third Native American. Those early demographics certainly held the seeds of future promise if those peoples would become unified.

Religiously almost one-third of the early White colonists were Quakers. Hence, it might have been possible for the seeds of that promise to sprout among Friends. However, that was a failed opportunity. A Society on the verge of contraction, concentrating on its inner preservation by exclusiveness, was unable to reach out to new people. The White, Western European bias and attachments to material possessions, including many Black slaves, prevented this development from occurring. In Quaker history one even reads of John Woolman's pleading unsuccessfully with his own Mount Holly, New Jersey Meeting to admit a Black person to membership. That application was denied despite the fact that that person had attended faithfully for many years, sitting on the back bench.

The story of Friends continues to record an endless series of missed opportunities. Even after Friends had freed themselves of slavery, there were racially segregated Meetings wherever people of color were allowed to attend. There also was a rise in a paternalistic, self-congratulatory spirit among White Friends who were proud of the work Quakers had done "for" Blacks and Native Americans. Blacks and Native Americans, however, were not represented among the membership of Friends, with the notable exception of a man like Paul Cuffe.

Most Friends today are unaware of how long segregation policies have persisted in Quaker Meetings, schools, retirement homes, and other institutions. As Friends have evolved into a generally well-educated and affluent White, middle and upper-middle class group, heavily professional and predominantly Anglo-Saxon in our ethnic background, we have become removed from many average Whites as well as from many Third World people.

SOME PERSONAL EXPERIENCES OF THE AUTHOR

There were no Quakers among the working class White ethnics and the Blacks I grew up with in Steubenville, Ohio. There were some Quakers in that area, but they were WASPS in the rural region outside the city. Most of the Whites in Steubenville were Roman Catholics from such "old countries" as Ireland, Italy, and Poland—with Czechoslovakia not far behind. There were also significant Jewish and Greek Orthodox groups. It seemed that all the churches had a racial and ethnic identity.

Our family church was African Methodist Episcopal (AME), founded in the late eighteenth century by the Black minister Richard Allen, who had been raised under the influence of Friends but who had turned as an adult to Episcopalianism rather than Quakerism. After he and some other Black worshippers were pulled off their knees and denied communion in a White church in Philadelphia, they formed the Free African Society in 1787, from which the AME church eventually evolved.

The Free African Society met in the Friends Free African School House in Philadelphia after 1791. Although a Black organization, its clerk and treasurer was a White Quaker, Joseph Clark, and its by-laws provided that position should always be held by a Friend. In his volume, *Richard Allen: Apostle of Freedom,* Charles Wesley asserted that that decision "shows the confidence and respect which the society had for the Quakers and the influence of Quakerism in the first Negro organization." He also wrote about their decision to open their proceedings with fifteen minutes of silence and meditation, commenting that "There is manifested in this action the influence of the spirit of the Quakers on this assembly."

That new organization evaluated carefully the form their society should take, considering the Quaker model but rejecting it as too little known among Blacks. Furthermore, Quakers were considered well-meaning, but basically White. Instead they chose to combine the Methodist and Episcopalian tradition with their African heritage, thus becoming the AME Church.

The prophetic black historian, W.E.B. DuBois, once wrote that "The problem of the twentieth century is the problem of the color line...." Bearing out his contention is the fact that our world today is in a state of revolution in the political, economic, and social relationships among its many peoples. And in the United States the true multiracial, multiethnic, and multicultural character which our country has always had is now asserting itself more forcefully and vigorously than ever before, demanding official recognition by all of us. It should be increasingly clear that we can no longer conceive of ourselves as a nation of real or acculturated White, Anglo-Saxon Protestants.

How do these winds of change affect Friends? There is more than a grain of truth in the old Quaker joke that Friends came to America to do good—and ended up doing well. The social and material privileges with which most Friends live give a welcome sense of comfort, but can also lead to smugness and help to blind us to the hurts and indignities suffered by those who lack such privileges. These privileges help reinforce the lack of diversity among Friends. They can also buttress the vested interests which some Quakers may wish to protect, even though this may conflict with the historic Friends testimonies and may separate us from the struggle and anguish of the disinherited of the earth.

SOME SIGNS OF HOPE AND SOME POSSIBLE COURSES OF ACTION

How do Friends "speak to this condition" of our Religious Society? I sense that there are mixed voices. Not all Quakers perceive that we have a problem of too little diversity. Some do, but they don't know what to do about it. Still others may either say the problem lies with those who are not represented in Friends Meetings, or else may want to celebrate and reinforce our right to hold ourselves apart.

But there are also many sprouts of hope. Although our numbers are small, there are more Third World people in our Meetings across the United States now than ten years ago. There is also an increasing awareness of the special circumstances of Friends in Africa, Latin America, Asia, and other places. There is greater participation of Quakers from those places in the gatherings of the worldwide society of Friends, often fostered by the AFSC and the Friends World Committee for Consultation.

As a result of the missionary efforts of Friends, there are now Quaker Meetings in several parts of Africa (including Madagascar), China (or

Taiwan), Cuba, India, Jamaica, Mexico, parts of the Middle East, and Alaska. Actually, the increase of Friends in East Africa in recent years has been phenomenal; few Quakers realize that the largest single concentration of Friends in the world is there and that the fastest-growing segments of the Religious Society of Friends are in Africa and in Latin America. Even in the midst of the escalating turmoil in the struggle against apartheid in South Africa, a Quaker Meetinghouse and Center is being constructed by Black Friends in Soweto, with funds largely donated by Friends in the worldwide Society.

By the turn of the century it is likely that half of the Quakers in the world will live in Africa and Latin America. Furthermore, a wider representation of non-Anglo-Saxon Europeans in the Religious Society of Friends has come about as a result of Quaker relief work after World Wars I and II. A number of German Jews and Jewish-Americans have become Friends.

Interesting developments in the United States have also furthered diversity in our Meetings here. For example, there are Cuban Friends in Miami, Florida; Jamaican Friends in New York City; and a large Meeting, composed largely of Vietnamese, in California. There has been an increased presence of Black American Friends, too, in the United States in recent decades, including such widely known Quakers as Hessye Castlen, Clarence Cunningham, Barrington Dunbar, Noel Palmer, Ira Reid, George Sawyer, Jean Toomer, and Dwight Spann-Wilson.

In the writings of the nineteenth-century Persian prophet and mystic, Bahaulla, the founder of the Bahai religion, appears the statement "ye are all the leaves of one branch and the fruit of one tree. The earth is but one country and [humankind] are its citizens." Those are words with which all Friends should agree. But words and thoughts are not enough. Our hearts and our hands must be fully enlisted in God's great work.

How can we work to achieve this goal? We must begin with a deep sense of humility rather than guilt, as we know there is hope. We should begin with ourselves and ask how we view ourselves and the message of the Religious Society of Friends. As we look at ourselves deeply and critically, and then at our Meetings, we need to ask with John Woolman "whether the seeds of war lie in these, our possessions...." Motivating a deeper view of the causes of war and conflict, we can ask whether the seeds of racial or ethnic and social exclusion lie in us. If we opt for a broader, more inclusive sense of community as an end to the fragmentation of humanity in our Meetings, we can be guided by the sense of power that will come when we know we are doing God's will. A sense of joy will come, too, as we overcome the final barriers to being whole again.

Likewise, we must recognize the scope of the problem. Centuries of Eurocentric expression have resulted in a language that abounds with views of blackness as dirty, wrong, and evil. To some, even the favorite Quaker expression of the oceans of death and darkness and those of light can convey a negative image. Hence, there is a crying need to change our language, our culture, and our approaches—moving beyond words, thoughts, and theories into the reality of wholeness, fullness, and unity in diversity. In our efforts we can gain much from the work of the women's movement to eliminate the male-centered language of the Scriptures and of our daily speech.

As we move from the broader view to specifics, we should be conscious that the primary goal is not only to understand the world, but to change it. One thing that Friends can do well, if they set their minds to it, is to be friendly. The power of friendship is a marvelous thing. Just as water is an almost universal solvent in the physical world, so friendship is in the social world.

Years ago our family moved to a new Meeting, about which we knew nothing. We were busy unpacking and getting settled in our new home when visitors arrived from that Meeting with loaves of freshly baked bread and an entire meal. That gesture broke the ice and was the beginning of a beautiful relationship with that group. Set in a small town, the feeling of closeness and community was fostered by many special events on different days, as well as on First Days.

Yes, friendship is an important first step. Relationships are formed as a result of people's pursuing common interests and enjoyments and coming to know each other in the process. That is good for individuals in their own right, but it is also an important form of outreach; many people come to know of Friends by the individual Quakers they know.

Many Quakers value education and learning. One good thing individuals and Meetings can do is to familiarize themselves more with the history, culture, and traditions of Blacks, Hispanics, Asian-Americans, and Native Americans, as well as other ethnic groups in our country. We can become more aware of and more involved in the needs and struggles of the poor and working people for economic justice.

Historically, Friends have sought a vision of group as well as individual testimonies and commitments through the use of queries. Here are some provocative queries developed at a recent world gathering of Friends in Kenya. Surely they should be read and responded to by Quaker Meetings everywhere:

Racial Concern Queries from the Kenya Conference

For Friends generally:

1. Are we aware of the way in which our social institutions contribute and continue to contribute to racialism?
2. Have Friends directly or indirectly supported commercial organizations thriving on racial exploitation?
3. Do Friends attempt to provide their children with enriching and positive interracial experiences?
4. Are Friends aware of the extent to which race and culture affect profits and privileges? Can Friends identify particular instances? Are Friends willing to share, materially and spiritually, with persons of other colors and/or races?
5. What efforts are made to welcome, and make easy, persons of cultures and color other than our own into Monthly Meetings of the Society of Friends and Friends committees?
6. Are Friends with responsibilities in teaching and media presentation careful of the canons of honest scholarship and research? Do we take care to examine such works for premises and assumptions that have roots in racialism?
7. Are Friends active in trying to help overcome the contemporary effects of past and present exploitation and deprivation of people who are racially different?

For Friends individually:

8. Am I sensitive to all aspects of racism, including discrimination and/or buried feelings of superiority/inferiority?
9. Have I tried to understand why the other person is, or feels, aggrieved? Do I *really* listen?
10. Am I being honest and forthright in my dialogue with persons of another color and/or race? Is it "that of God" in me which speaks to "that of God" in persons of other colors or race?
11. Am I willing to be open to the Light in matters of privilege and/or deprivation based on color or race?
12. Am I teaching my children that the love of God includes the equality of peoples and respect for cultural and racial differences?

These Kenya queries should enable us to reach very deeply toward the underpinnings of racism and the lack of diversity in our Meetings today. They focus our attention on the many subtle guises which systems of power and privilege can assume to divert us from the good way.

My hope and prayer is that the Religious Society of Friends will reach toward a new corporate testimony of expressing the oneness of humanity in our Meetings. In striving toward that goal we can be heartened by the affirmative action program of the American Friends Service Committee, the efforts of the Bahai group, and the work of other organizations. We can learn from their living witnesses of what can be done when there is a will and a way.

The path ahead is a rocky one, strewn with problems, false starts, and disappointments, as it always is when people try to relate to one another across what they believe are social distances. A little bit of humor and laughter can go far in helping to defuse tensions and spark the light of friendship. Good relationships need an absence of tension to germinate and grow. It is very difficult for anyone to get to know anyone else if the atmosphere seems threatening, defensive, or tense. We all share in a responsibility to help put others at ease, especially when the other is a stranger. In this instance, I am sure we would also be doing to others as we would have others do to us.

Through the years I have become increasingly convinced that the real barriers to our getting together as human beings are in our minds, our hearts, and our souls. They are reflected in our ways of thinking, and feeling, and acting. Other than that they have no physical reality. Even Blackness and Whiteness are basically masks—states of mind having to do with the history and current reality of the oppressed and the oppressors. As William Penn commented, "The humble, meek, merciful, just, pious, and devout souls are everywhere of one religion; and when death has taken off the mask, they will know one another, though the diverse liveries they wear here makes them strangers."

When I was a little boy of six, we lived for a while with my father's aunt, Emma, in Wheeling, West Virginia. At that time many places in that state, as well as elsewhere, were segregated by law and by custom. But there were many private spaces where the separate worlds of Blacks and Whites made contact. One of them, for me, was a little friend by the name of Billy, also six. Every day we played together.

One day my friend told me that he could not play with me any more because his parents had told him I was a "Nigra." He said I was dirty and needed to wash the color off my body. That really hurt because I did not know what he was talking about. My mother bathed me every day.

It also hurt me because I considered him my friend and liked to play with him.

I ran home and cried in the bathroom as I washed and scrubbed my hands to see if there was any change. Then Aunt Emma came by and asked me why I was crying. When I told her what had happened, she said, "Don't cry about it and don't let him call you that again. Just go back and call him a dirty little white trash."

At that point my mother appeared and overheard our conversation. Then she pulled me aside and said, "Jimmy, don't go back and call him that. Aunt Emma is older than you and me and should know better, but she doesn't. You really shouldn't say such things to people. Come with me and we'll talk about it."

So she took me into the garden where we always went in the cool of the evening and where she often read to me from an old, worn copy of the *Book of Knowledge*. This time she opened it to pages of beautiful flowers and different animals and told me how each of these fit together into a beautiful and varied plan like the instruments in an orchestra. She told me that people were like all the rest of God's creation and that their varied colors were like the different colors of flowers in our garden.

I remember experiencing a sense of incredible peace and beauty. I felt close to life and love, and the hurt and resentment I felt for what Billy had said were gone. All the colors of the garden flooded my senses, and I was conscious of life everywhere—chirping, creaking, and moving around.

Years later, as a grown man, my thoughts went back to that beautiful moment when I saw a Quaker wearing a T-shirt which said: "Our world is brought to you in living color." Indeed, our world is brought to us in living color: all the colors of the rainbow. We may be different in colors of skin, ethnicity, social experience or background; but we are all children of God in whom the same light shines.

Many times in Meetings for Worship I feel the same way I felt in that little Meeting my mother and I had many years ago. But in Meetings I do not yet see much variation in the colors and backgrounds of the Friends present. I long for the day when our Meetings will reflect the beauty and diversity of the family of humanity within our family of Friends.

THE CHALLENGE OF THE FUTURE FOR FRIENDS

I feel that the principal challenge God has placed before us as Quakers of this day and age is to see what love can do to build a worldwide family of Friends which transcends race, ethnicity, and social class, yet includes them. I envision a new unity with diversity. The light of such unity would shine as a living example of the Peaceable Kingdom foreseen by the prophets. It is this vision that sustains me through all the troubled times and keeps me working with our beloved old Society of Friends for a new Society that has never been, but can be, if we will it. If not now, then when? If not here, then where?

SOME SUGGESTED READINGS

Fletcher, James A. "Toward a Truly Multiracial Family of Friends," *Friends Journal*. Vol. 29, No. 9 (May 15, 1983).

Ives, Kenneth, ed. *Black Quakers: Brief Biographies.* Chicago: Progresiv Publishr, 1986.

Kenworthy, Leonard S. *Quakerism: A Study Guide to the Religious Society of Friends.* Dublin, IN: Prinit Press, 1981.

A Quaker Speaks for the Black Experience: The Life and Selected Writings of Barrington Dunbar. New York Yearly Meeting, 1979.

Taylor, Richard K. *Friends and the Racial Crisis.* Wallingford, PA: Pendle Hill Pamphlet 172, 1970.

SOME QUESTIONS FOR DISCUSSION

1. What friends do I have of different races, ethnic groups, or economic circumstances than my own?
2. How many Friends in my Meeting are of a different race, ethnic group, or economic circumstance than mine?
3. Is my Meeting representative of the diversity of God's family where I live? In my state? In the nation at large?
4. What experiences do my children or the children of my Meeting have with others of different races, ethnic groups, or economic circumstances?
5. What have I done to broaden the diversity of my circle of friends and Friends? What more could I do?
6. Am I and my Meeting familiar with the Queries on racism from the recent triennial of the Friends World Committee in Kenya? Do we read and respond to them?

ABOUT THE AUTHOR

James A. Fletcher is a member of the Ann Arbor, Michigan, Monthly Meeting of Friends and of Lake Erie Yearly Meeting. Currently he is a member of the Michigan Area and the Great Lakes Regional Committee of AFSC, the AFSC Corporation, and the FCNL General Committee. In 1980 he visited South Africa as a part of an AFSC delegation.

His past activities with Friends include membership on the national board of the AFSC and membership in the Quaker UN Committee, the Oakwood School Board, the Barrington Dunbar Fund for Black Development and clerk of the Committee for Black Concerns of New York Yearly Meeting. He co-edited the booklet on Barrington Dunbar.

James Fletcher is married to Karen Fletcher. They have three children: Howard, Jamie, and Lancelot. They are former members of Meetings in Arizona, Colorado, Connecticut, and New York.

Chapter 10

Alcohol and Drugs:
A Quaker Concern

James F. Neff, M.D.

During the past two centuries there have been a number of changes which have produced a stressful environment and unpredictability in our daily lives. Those conditions continue currently. In that period we have faced the industrial and scientific revolutions, overpopulation on a worldwide basis, and an increased ability to destroy each other.

Simultaneously, the remarkable creation of new knowledge has given human beings tools which, if used properly, can raise civilization to magnificent heights, but, if misused, can destroy the world.

We also face enormous stresses within American society—uneven distribution of wealth, large amounts of leisure for the upper and middle classes, and a work force excessive to our needs in most fields. The specter of unemployment, lack of fulfillment of individual goals, the breakdown of traditional family supports, and stresses which accompany the expectation of having to maintain a high standard of living hang over the heads of many people.

Those pressures are most pronounced on our young people. Because of good health they reach adolescence at an earlier age, and yet their entry into meaningful employment is delayed because of our increasingly large work force. Hence, their period of adolescence is prolonged and a sense of personal fulfillment curbed.

The environment in which we live, therefore, is a perfect setting for the abuse of substances in response to the stresses we face. Drugs, although a problem in themselves, have become a symptom of more deep-seated individual and societal problems and stresses. From history we can learn how civilizations can be destroyed by a collection of external and internal forces and changes. The introduction of opium to

124

China in the nineteenth century became a major factor in the decline of that civilization. In our own country there is the devastating effect of alcohol on the culture of native Americans.

A BRIEF REVIEW OF DRUG PROBLEMS IN THE UNITED STATES

Alcohol was not recognized as a major problem in the United States until the latter part of the nineteenth century, when our country received vast numbers of persons migrating from various parts of the world. Many of the immigrants were unprepared to join the predominantly farm-oriented American culture and were crowded into the growing cities. Along with these migrations came the marked increase in the use and abuse of alcohol that gave life to the temperance movement which sought to curb its use. That movement was supported by many religious groups, including Quakers. It is difficult to understand completely the religious fervor that was associated with that movement. But contributing factors may have included:

1. Alcohol, because it was associated with many of the problems of poverty and overpopulation in the cities, tended to be viewed as the cause of the problems, rather than as a symptom. Regardless, the abuse of alcohol seemed to exaggerate almost all of the evils of the crowded city societies.

2. A goal of many religious groups was to convert or to hold individuals within a godly society. Yet most individuals who suffered under the influence of alcohol, or any other substance, had very little interest in following any religious direction and were more concerned about the daily acquisition and consumption of alcohol than the improvement of a soul for an afterlife. Alcohol seemed to be tool of the devil, which prevented individuals from having the appropriate interest in furthering God's purpose. Quakers also had personal concerns. They believe that there is that of God in every person and that it is the individual's responsibility to continue to seek that God within. The use of alcohol or drugs tends to divert an individual from pursuing that goal and, in fact, contributes to an individual's loss of a sense of self-worth. That loss is characteristic of almost every person who abuses a substance. It is a powerful deterrent from seeking that of God within self and others.

The attention of the religious societies, including Friends, added to most Americans' belief that liquor was in itself a cause of poverty, crime, broken families, lost work, and immorality. The enormous power of the temperance movement ultimately led to the prohibition movement which resulted in the adoption of the eighteenth amendment to the United States Constitution in 1919. During that period the United States tried to deal with the problem of alcohol in an absolute fashion. There seemed to be no conceptual room for moderation. A simplistic viewpoint led to the imposition of standards which could not be enforced. The irony is that, in part, those supporting the temperance movement were correct. Even though absolute abstinence may not work for society as a whole, for certain individuals it is the only acceptable cure for a drug problem.

By the end of the nineteenth century, narcotics also were a major problem in the United States. Opium was easily imported and obtained. And in the latter part of the nineteenth century derivatives of opium, heroin, and morphine were created. Thus codeine was isolated in 1832, and although less addicting than morphine, it was widely used. Narcotics were not restricted in use until the early part of the twentieth century.

Cocoa leaves (cocaine) have been used for centuries by natives of South America, and by 1880 pure cocaine became easily available due to advances in manufacturing techniques. Its stimulant and euphoric properties were touted by athletes, workers, and students. It was bottled in popular soda drinks and easily obtained tonics. It was used as an over-the-counter remedy for hay fever and nasal catarrh in powder form.

Cannabis, or marihuana, was unfamiliar in the United States until this century, even though it was used historically throughout the Middle East. Its use did not become a problem in this country and was not restricted by federal laws until the 1920s and 1930s when Mexicans, who used this drug excessively, poured into the United States as farm laborers.

World War II brought non-alcoholic drug use, especially narcotics, to a low point. But by the 1950s drug use began to spread among the poor, especially within the Black population. In the 1960s, psychedelic substances appeared and marihuana use began to increase strikingly, as did other drugs like amphetamines and barbiturates. By the late 1960s, a "drug culture" developed which was linked by many people to the youth counter-culture. No longer was narcotics and alcohol use viewed predominantly as a problem of the poor and the lower socioeconomic class; it became and has continued to be a major problem throughout all levels of our society.

THE IMPACT OF ALCOHOL AND DRUG USE IN THE UNITED STATES

Without question, alcohol is a drug that has the most devastating effect on our society. Although it has been used for a long time and we have accepted its use, the problem of its abuse is increasing in intensity and in its destructive capabilities. Currently the average American adult consumes 2.65 gallons a year. In recent years, also, the age of alcoholics has declined, and alcoholism develops over a shorter period of drinking time than has been true in the past. There are an estimated three million adolescent alcoholics in the United States today, and six percent of all high school seniors drink alcohol daily. Add this to the availability of the automobile and it is not surprising that more than forty percent of the forty to fifty thousand highway deaths, and almost one million injuries a year, are related to alcohol. Abuse of women and children and interfamily violence also are largely associated with the use of alcohol. Additionally, it is almost impossible to measure the loss of productivity that results from the many untreated alcoholics in our society.

Cocaine abuse is a problem perhaps second only to alcohol. It is one of the most powerfully addictive and destructive substances known to humans. In the United States its use has increased fourfold in the past decade, producing increasingly serious health consequences. Nearly twenty-two million Americans report having used cocaine at least once, and that number is increasing. The power of its addiction comes not from the withdrawal symptoms, but rather from the self-stimulating or reward-seeking behaviors that become paramount in the victim's life.

Marihuana is used by about three million individuals daily and by about thirteen million occasionally. Many of those users take no other illegal drugs. Eleven percent of high school seniors use marihuana daily.

Heroin, although showing some decrease in usage in the past few years, is still a major problem. Of the approximately half million individuals in this country who are dependent on heroin, perhaps twenty percent are in prison and another twenty percent in treatment. The other sixty percent are neither in prison or in treatment but are driven to crime to support an increasingly expensive habit.

There are other drugs that are abused. Two to three percent of adults have used barbiturates illegally and some 280 thousand barbiturate users are abusers; a little less than half a million non-medical users of tranquilizers, such as valium and quaaludes, are abusers. About seven percent of junior and senior high school students have used solvents such as household cleaners and inhalents (model kit glue).

It is apparent that drug use is becoming an increasing problem within our society. It affects all socioeconomic groups. It consumes an enormous amount of our resources and enhances our trade deficit because many of the drugs are obtained outside of the United States. The cumulative use of all these drugs results in a marked increase in morbidity and mortality and a marked decrease in productivity. Therefore, from a Quaker standpoint, substance abuse is a major concern, regardless of whether it is a result or a cause of our societal ills.

SPECIFIC COMMENTS ABOUT INDIVIDUAL DRUGS

Alcohol. It is difficult to deal with alcohol in a nonemotional and logical manner. There is no question that there is a large societal abuse of it by occasional users who may not be termed alcoholics. This occasional use may lead to violence and death as a result of individual arguments and abuse, or its combination with driving. There is also the disease, alcoholism, which is associated with a great deal of mortality and morbidity.

Alcohol in small doses on a daily basis has been demonstrated to be beneficial. It may prolong life, decrease stress, and increase social interchange. On the other hand, when it is used excessively, either from acute overdose or because of long-term utilization, it can lead to brain damage, liver damage, loss of control over inhibitions, poor judgment, violence, and finally death. If it were possible to remove alcohol from our society, we would solve many problems. This was tried once and failed. So now we are left with the task of defining the line between the individual who uses alcohol occasionally and harmlessly, and the person for whom it is a major problem.

Although alcoholism is a disease that causes progressive physical damage, a specific cause for the disease has not been found. There are a host of primary symptoms which can characterize the alcoholic. Those symptoms include a high tolerance for alcohol, impaired nutrition due to poor eating habits, digestive problems, inflammation of the liver and pancreas, anemia, and impotence. Unfortunately, alcoholism is often not considered a medical diagnosis; instead it is considered a personal slur. If early-stage alcoholics are confronted, they will often deny the problem because they know that they can handle their drinking better than most and do not know that an early tolerance for alcohol is not a talent, but a symptom of the disease. Whether or not heavy drinking practices are responsible for this symptom or whether this tolerance for alcohol is an inherited metabolic characteristic is not known and is an area of current research.

It is known, however, that once alcoholism has been diagnosed, it requires confrontation and treatment. The only ultimately effective treatment is total and complete abstinence, since only a small percentage of diagnosed alcoholics can drink to moderation. The identification and treatment of alcoholism is a terribly complex subject. Alcoholism is often termed a "Merry-go-round Denial." This "Merry-go-round" involves many members of the immediate and extended family. When the family and the alcoholic come to grips with this disease and seek some form of help, treatment is possible. Many, however, feel that it is nearly impossible for an alcoholic to enter a treatment program until the pain of the alcoholism becomes greater than the pleasure. The group that has been most successful in treating alcoholics is Alcoholics Anonymous, with chapters and family support services throughout the United States. Sometimes treatment can be effected on an outpatient basis, but more than ever, alcoholics are treated within institutions where the individuals are removed from their environment, and both the family and the alcoholic can work on an intense program which can be followed up with outpatient therapy. Fortunately, throughout the United States employers are recognizing alcoholism as a disease and are developing employment policies for dealing with the alcoholic so that he or she can return to a productive life.

Cocaine. The abuse of cocaine continues to spread at an alarming rate. The drug can be lethal, particularly when it is smoked or injected intravenously. The most common route of administration is internasal. Cocaine is a central nervous system stimulant which is comparable to amphetamines (dexadrine-like compounds). The main effect of cocaine is to produce a euphoria (a sense of pleasure) similar to the subjective effect of amphetamines. Some users take the drug at ten 45-minute periods in order to maintain this stimulant effect. This can go on for several days, creating what is termed a "run." In time the user loses control of the frequency and duration of the binges, and the abuse worsens. After the binge, the user experiences a "crash," characterized by irritability and excessive sleeping which can last for hours or days.

Unlike withdrawal from opiates or alcohol, major physiological changes do occur with withdrawal from cocaine. Following a crash, however, cocaine users may have a moderate to severe depression and a decreased ability to experience pleasure. This can last for days or weeks and leads the user to return to the stimulation gained from using the drug. An overdose of cocaine can occur almost immediately after its absorption and is characterized by extreme anxiety, fever, convulsions, heart irregularities, and excessive body heat.

The number of deaths resulting from cocaine overdose is increasing. This is a drug that is used to an increasing degree by athletes, entertainers, and the affluent segment of society. Its use ultimately leads to a marked decrease in performance and to exhaustion, even though it provides a false sense of alertness and improved efficiency. It is a profoundly addictive and dangerous drug.

Marihuana. The use of marihuana is one of the most complicated problems we face. Its use now begins at a much earlier age than occurred a decade ago, and the drug is now more likely to be used frequently, rather than experimentally. One of the major paradoxes in the use of this drug is that although its use in high school is increasing, most members of all age groups continue to disapprove of its regular use and advocate some type of prohibition. In addition to the increased use of the drug, street marihuana has increased markedly in its potency over the past five years. The content of THC, the principal ingredient, has increased from less than one percent prior to 1975 to as high as five percent in the average "joint" in 1979.

The acute effects of marihuana are now generally agreed upon. It is a sedative, and intoxication interferes with immediate memory and a wide range of intellectual tasks in a manner that could be expected to impair classroom learning. There is also good evidence that marihuana interferes with driving skills.

While much is known about the acute effects, very little is known about the long-term effects of the drug except that it impairs lung function to a greater extent than tobacco does. The tar from marihuana is similar to that of cigarettes and is tumor-producing, although it is not clear whether this effect is as powerful as that of tobacco. There is no question that it increases the potential for chronic lung disease. One marihuana cigarette is equivalent to about fifteen regular cigarettes in lung function impairment. Whether daily use of marihuana will create a large population of individuals with chronic lung disease or create an increase in lung tumors is highly probable, but still not certain. There is no question that the effect of the combination of marihuana and cigarettes on the lungs is cumulative and devastating.

It is not certain whether marihuana has a long-term effect on learning skills, higher intellectual functions, and the developing brain. It is a fat-soluble substance and traces are found within the central nervous system for a long period after its use.

There are long-term effects of marihuana which have been demonstrated in some animal and human research, but it is not certain whether they have clinical significance. One is that heavy marihuana use may impair reproductive functioning; the other is that it may impair the body's principal defense against disease, the immune response.

Finally, the area of most uncertainty is the psychological effect of the drug. An acute panic anxiety is the most common adverse psychological reaction to the use of marihuana, especially when unexpectedly strong material is consumed. This has led to a caution against the use of marihuana by those with a history of serious psychological problems. An anti-motivation syndrome also has been described as characteristic of chronic marihuana users. There is a good possibility that one of the major attractive features of marihuana for users is its stress-relieving capabilities, which may lead to this seeming lack of motivation. The frequent use of marihuana by the young may impair the natural development of maturity in which individuals learn how to deal with stress-related problems without the use of mind-altering substances. It is hypothesized, but not proven, that the frequent use of marihuana delays the development of maturity, especially the abilities to deal with stress in a variety of different situations. On the other hand, many children and young adults may use marihuana as a form of self-medication in an effort to handle severely stressful situations which they are incapable of dealing with except through the use of the drug.

The choices are complex for a family or a parent faced with a family member who uses marihuana frequently. On the one hand, marihuana will certainly impair performance in school, and the fact that the individual cannot work up to self or parental expectations will lead to a continued sense of lack of self-worth, and in turn stimulate more use of marihuana. As with alcohol, many are able to function under the use of this drug as long as their performance meets internally or externally imposed demands. When performance cannot meet these demands, then the use of the drug becomes an increasingly apparent problem. Individuals who use marihuana regularly may not be capable of handling normal external stresses. Marihuana does not have the addicting effects of either cocaine or alcohol, but a tolerance to the drug develops and there may be psychological needs that stimulate repeated and frequent use. Therefore, a marihuana problem should be faced by the family collectively, as they would face an alcohol problem.

Other Drugs. There are many other substances that are abused: narcotics such as opium and its derivatives; stimulants such as amphetamines ("speed" and "dexies"); psychedelics, the mind-altering substances and halucinogens, including LSD, PCP; and several new, recently chemically synthesized drugs. It is not possible to do an in-depth review of these drugs except to say that many are commonly used, and it is important to know their effects. It is also important to recognize that there are now new mind-altering drugs which are prepared in the laboratory and which may be distributed to the population who use them experimentally. In none of these newly prepared drugs are the long-term or short-term effects well understood, but their potential is great.

HOW CAN QUAKERS ADDRESS THESE CONCERNS?

Before a Meeting approaches the concern of drug abuse, there are certain factors that should be recognized honestly. Among them are the following:

1. Many Meetings may tend to focus more on the problems of youth and adolescents, rather than the problems found generally throughout the Meeting. It is important for any Meeting to recognize that the abuse of drugs is probably more extensive in the adult population than among the youth or young adults. If a Meeting, therefore, has not addressed a drug problem among its older members, it has little chance of addressing the problem among its youth.

2. Direct education about drugs may be useful if done in a non-judgmental and non-paternalistic fashion, and if the education is provided by someone who is knowledgeable and respected.

3. Role models are probably one of the most powerful educational tools available. Not only can adults serve as models in general, but any individual who has been able to resolve a personal drug problem can be very effective in influencing the younger generation who constantly look to adults as individuals whom they should emulate.

4. The use of drugs by the younger generation is as much a form of rebellion as it is a manifestation of external or internal stress. There-fore, to the degree that a Meeting can allow the expression of individual variability and a recognition of the value of an individual's expression, the individual is less likely to turn to drugs as the only form of rebellion or self-expression available.

5. Parents and the stable family are the most important factors

in dealing with drug problems. A Meeting can provide support for family units and forums where families can identify problems and deal with them in a collective fashion. Such a strengthened family will be able to deal with this problem more effectively than a splintered family. Nevertheless, in all Meetings, as throughout our entire society, there are a growing number of single parents. Such persons who do not have an extended support group can find strength from the extended family within the Meeting.

6. It is not in the interest of any individuals to deny that problems exist. The more a Meeting can use its strengths to help identify and address the problems, the less likely it will be for individuals to find themselves on the "Merry-go-round Denial."

7. Meetings can be encouraged to seek wise counsel from individuals who are experts in the area of dealing with drug abuse. They can be encouraged to develop support groups that will enable individuals and family members to deal with these problems directly and openly. Drug abuse is not an evil which can be prayed away, denied, or exorcised.

Like most issues today, there are very few clear-cut responses to these concerns. This one especially, as is evident in the failure of the temperance movement, cannot be dealt with in an absolute fashion. Nevertheless, drug abuse problems cannot be denied, and in dealing with them a Meeting can strive to help its individual members draw upon internal and external resources for strength. In turn, the individual will become more dependent on his or her own internal resources which include regaining or developing communication with that of God within. This internal strength will provide more reward than increased dependence on the less reliable and hazardous support which comes from chemical substances.

SOME SUGGESTED READINGS

General

Julien, Robert M. *A Primer of Drug Action.* 4th edition. New York: Freedman and Company, 1985.

Lowinson, Joyce and Pedro Rutz, Eds. *Substance Abuse: Clinical Problems and Perspectives.* Baltimore: Williams and Wilkins, 1981.

National Directory of Drug Abuse and Alcoholism Treatment and Prevention Programs. National Institute of Drug Abuse and the National Institute on Alcohol Abuse and Alcoholism, 1984.

Richards, Louis G., Ed. *Demographic Trends and Drug Abuse.* National

Institute of Drug Abuse Monograph 35, 1985.

Alcohol

Meyer, Roger E., et al, Eds. *Evaluation of the Alcoholic: Implications for Research, Theory, and Treatment.* National Institute of Drug Abuse Research Monograph 4, 1981.

Secretary of Health and Human Services. *Alcohol and Health: Fifth Special Report to the U.S. Congress.* National Institute on Alcohol Abuse and Alcoholism, 1983.

Watterlord, Michael. "The Telltale Metabolism of Alcoholics." *Science 83* (June 1983):4,72.

Cocaine and Marihuana

_____ . *Adverse Effects of Cocaine Abuse.* The Medical Letter 26 (1984): 51.

Peterson, Robert C., Ed. *Marijuana Research Findings, 1980.* National Institute on Drug Abuse Monograph 31, 1980.

Excellent educational material on alcoholism and drug abuse can be obtained from:

Hazelden Foundation, Educational Materials, Box 176, Center City, Minnesota 55012.

National Institutes on Alcohol and Drug Abuse, Department of Health and Human Services, 5600 Fishers Lane, Rockville, Maryland 20857.

SOME QUESTIONS FOR DISCUSSION

1. Has your Meeting addressed the problem of alcohol and drug abuse affecting its members? If so, how successful were you? If not, what do you suggest?
2. What support groups are there in your Meeting for those with alcohol and drug problems? Have they been used? If so, how successful have they been? If not, how might they be made effective?
3. What support groups are there in your community? Are they being used? If so, how successfully? If not, how can they be used in the foreseeable future?
4. What is your Meeting doing to assist young people, single parents, and the elderly? What more might your Meeting do?

ABOUT THE AUTHOR

John Neff was born in Mexico of Congregational missionary parents.
He graduated from Pomona College and the Harvard Medical School.
For thirteen years he served on the faculty of the Johns Hopkins Medical School before moving to Seattle, Washington, where he has been
Medical Director of the Children's Orthopedic Hospital and Medical
Center, and Associate Dean and Professor of Pediatrics at the University
of Washington School of Medicine since 1981. During his lifetime he
has determined the extent of complications to smallpox vaccination in
the United States, started a program for foster children in Baltimore, and
served on the board of Broadmead, the Quaker retirement community.
He and his wife are members of the Seattle Friends Meeting.

Chapter 11

Sharing the Stewardship of Our Spaceship Earth

Ruth Lofgren

We humans are amazing people. Each of us is of two minds about the world in which we live. One mind holds our timeless, romantic view of the world, glories in "America the Beautiful" and songs like the "Hymn of Praise" in *A Hymnal for Friends:*

> The sun shines in splendor, and blue is the sky,
> The birds are all singing with joy as they fly;
> The rivers are winding between wooded shores;
> The whole world of nature its Maker adores.

This view has been put in perspective by photographs of the earth taken from outer space. We have seen our beautiful, blue, cloud-wreathed planet; how round and small it appears! The earth is truly our spaceship as we travel around the sun, our star, in this galaxy of a vast universe.

Our second view of the world grows out of the realities of our daily living in a competitive, industrialized world. As Wordsworth reminded us long ago,

> The world is too much with us; late and soon,
> Getting and spending, we lay waste our powers:
> Little we see in Nature that is ours;
> We have given our hearts away, a sordid boon!

The revolution in science and technology that began with Isaac Newton (1642–1727) resulted in massive changes in people's occupations and living conditions. Coincidentally, George Fox was

136

eighteen years old when Newton was born, so the Society of Friends had its beginnings during this early period of industrialization in England. Nearly a century later, Thomas Jefferson warned that if the United States developed its own system of manufacturing, the "fresh, health-giving, sunlit atmosphere of Virginia will be replaced by the dark, foul air of European cities." However, machines seemed to promise abundance. People could see the connection between technology, economic growth, and a higher standard of living, so an attitude congenial to a scientific and commercial age developed.

In the last half-century, the application of science and technology has resulted in more progress than had been made from the beginning of time up until World War II. For instance, a constantly growing list of drugs, vitamins, and hormones have revolutionized medicine, while fertilizers, pesticides, and herbicides have radically changed agricultural practices. The benefits of these and other changes have been evident to all; however, for decades we have been increasingly alarmed by the problems being created in our environment.

Let us examine some attitudes about the natural world, how human activities are influencing the environment, and ways in which we might share in the stewardship of the planet.

ATTITUDES ABOUT NATURE

Dominion vs. Stewardship. Humans have always been dependent upon plants and animals for food, shelter, and clothing, so it comes as no surprise to learn that each cultural group has its own attitudes toward its environment. Some people feel that human beings are a part of the natural world and should live in harmony with it, while others seek to be the masters of nature, attempting to dominate it for their own purposes. For instance, many Judeo-Christians have based their belief over the centuries upon the story of the Creation in the Book of Genesis in the Bible. Some people interpret "...and have dominion over the fish of the sea and over the birds of the air and over every living thing that moves upon the earth" to mean that everything is here for their use. Such an attitude can justify wasteful exploitation of natural resources. Others believe the passage from Genesis to mean that people have been put in charge of all living things—to have responsible stewardship over them. As King David declares in Psalm 24:1, "The earth is the Lord's, and the fullness thereof; the world, and they that dwell therein."

In *The Machine in the Garden*, Leo Marx explores the human

dilemma of possessing an idealized view of nature as a simple, rural paradise when the actual relationship we have with the natural world is basically technological (man the toolmaker). As Thomas Jefferson and many American writers realized, reconciling the dilemma will be difficult, given our commitment to technological progress.

"We have been through a great epoch of transition in the direction of natural explanations of things," Rufus M. Jones reminds us in *A Call to What Is Vital.* He urges the scholar and the Christian to share their contributions and wisdom: "We need a *sacramental view* of our world."

The Simple Life. Chief Seattle at a tribal assembly in Western Washington in 1854 said, "All things are connected like the blood which unites one family. The earth is precious to God and to harm the earth is to heap contempt on its Creator." In the *Washington Newsletter* of the Friends Committee on National Legislation for October 1985, a note on "Navajo—Hopi: Sharing Mother Earth" quotes Hopi leaders, "This land was granted to the Hopi by a power greater than man can explain. Title is vested in the whole make-up of Hopi life."

An Amish writer anticipated the environmentalists' view, "We didn't inherit the land from the parents; we are borrowing it from our children."

Science and Nature. In seventeenth century England there was a wide-spread spirit of inquiry, and the Quakers were a part of the movement. "Many early Friends were scientists by avocation, they were hobbyists, self-taught naturalists and natural philosophers without special academic training," Richard M. Sutton explained in his 1962 Ward Lecture at Guilford College on "Quaker Scientists."

As a boy, George Fox was very skillful in handling sheep and enjoyed the out-of-doors. His first visions came while he was in the mountains of Yorkshire. In his *Testimony Concerning George Fox* William Penn wrote,

> I have been surprised at his questions and answers in natural
> things, that whilst he is ignorant of useless and sophistical
> science, he had in him a foundation of useful and
> commendable knowledge and cherished it everywhere.

Scientists are seekers of truth concerning the natural world: the questioning, testing, and evaluating processes of science are similar in spirit to those of religious seekers like Rufus Jones. "Faith is not endangered by the advance of science. It is endangered by the stagnation of religious conceptions....let us not fetter science, let us rather *promote* religion," he said. Richard Sutton believes that most Quaker scientists

> find their careers a way toward science and usefulness, combined with the opportunity to explore Truth. They have high regard for Nature and Nature's God, and have held a high standard for themselves and others. For many, science has been the vehicle by which they have taught others. They have combined interest in their sciences with interest in people.

Is Stewardship Possible? Science and technology can indicate useful approaches to deal with the many and varied problems encountered in the environment today. However, economic considerations and the political climate in each jurisdiction will be critical in determining to what extent such helpful processes are employed.

Richard Sutton reports that currently the proportions of Quakers in science is significantly greater than that in the general population. Friends are among the many people of goodwill whose abiding concern for the environment and sustained efforts are bringing about changes here and there. Nevertheless, if our spaceship Earth is to be restored and protected, programs of on-going study and worldwide management and regulation of the uses of natural resources will be needed.

NATURE IN OPERATION

Millions of years before human beings became a significant force on the earth, living organisms had evolved systems of interdependence. As green plants harnessed the energy of the sun, they grew and provided food and shelter for the animals, including early humans. Dead plants and animals and their wastes were broken down by microorganisms as they converted organic materials to simple substances that the green plants used again. Actually, of course, the processes of photosynthesis and plant growth, animal activities, and the decomposition of dead organic matter all go on at the same time. "Food and feeder, eater and eaten, all depend on each other in a tangled complex web of life that includes the wind, the rain, the seasons," Paul B. Sears explains in *Ecology, the Intricate Web of Life.*

In the process of living—eating, sleeping, working, playing, traveling and socializing, reproducing, and keeping safe and warm—human beings have discovered how to use the resources in their environment and to organize their understanding of the natural world.

Ancient philosophers identified four elements: earth, air, fire, and water. If we use the terms *soil* for *earth* and *energy* in place of *fire*, we have useful modern categories. Let us see how human activities have affected the soil, water, air, and energy sources of our planet.

HUMAN USES OF NATURAL RESOURCES

Soil. Topsoil, a mixture of humus, minerals, water, air and organisms that supports the growth of plants, is an essential resource. In *So Human an Animal*, René Dubos reviews our actions:

> Increasingly, we cut down forests and flood deserts to create more farmland. On the other hand, we destroy fertile agricultural fields to build factories, highways, and housing developments, without regard to the natural and historical scenery. We first cleared the forests to make way for farms, then we cleared the farms to accommodate the cities and their suburbs. Almost everywhere, the land is being used not as a home, nor as an environment for the creation of human culture, but as a source of exploitation and speculation.

Cities and towns also use land for the disposal of trash. Some wastes are hazardous and toxic. Allen A. Boraiko reported in "Storing Up Trouble— Hazardous Waste" in the March 1985 *National Geographic* that "About 60% of all toxic waste legally disposed of in the U.S. is pumped down injection wells, to be imprisoned between layers of impermeable rock."

Effective programs of soil conservation, land use, and waste disposal are essential if the productivity of the earth is to be restored.

Water. In the early days of the Republic, the water in the lakes and rivers was generally clear and safe to drink. But as towns grew, they disposed of their sewage directly into the water. Epidemics of typhoid fever, dysentery, and cholera were common. As more and more fields were plowed, increasing amounts of topsoil washed into the lakes and rivers, adding to their pollution. Also, floods and droughts seemed to be more severe.

Today over half the people in the United States drink water that flows out of springs or is pumped out of wells. Two serious problems exist: the quantity of water is limited (it does not lie under all soil); also, groundwater may become polluted unless care is taken to protect it.

As sewage treatment plants are modernized, the treated water leaving them is of better quality; therefore, the quality of the water in the lakes and rivers will continue to improve.

Regulations that set standards for the quality of water in our lakes, streams, and wells need to be enforced.

Air. Air is a mixture of gases: nitrogen, oxygen, water vapor, carbon dioxide and a small amount of other gases. Most of the pollutants in the air are the result of burning. Smog and lead poisoning as well as the deadly carbon monoxide gas may result from the combustion of gasoline.

For millions of years green plants produced an abundance of oxygen. Now this abundance is threatened. Hugh Jernigan, Jr. discusses "Acid Rain and Wood Utilization" in Part II of a series on "Environmental Problems—Getting a Handle on Them" in the March 1982 *Quaker Life:* "Acid rain results mainly from the combustion of fossil fuels such as coal and oil, which in the process of being burned, give off the pollutants sulfur dioxide and nitric oxides." As rain washes them out of the air, two strong acids are formed that are doing tremendous damage worldwide. Forests are dying in Austria, Sweden, New England and across the Canadian border, where acid rain has been a growing problem since the 1950s. Just recently we have seen the first formal acknowledgment of acid rain as a problem across the U.S.-Canadian border.

If carbon dioxide were to build up in the atmosphere, more of the sun's energy would be retained, and the earth would get warmer. This greenhouse effect could melt the polar ice caps and result in the flooding of coastal areas over the entire planet.

Problems involving either the earth's atmosphere or the earth's oceans are worldwide and, therefore, require international cooperation if they are to be dealt with effectively.

Energy. Primitive peoples used the energy of their own bodies, the wind, the sun and where available, the tides and geothermal energy. Over many thousands of years domesticated animals were worked, wind power and water power were harnessed. With fossil fuels came the industrial revolution, and in this century nuclear power has become available.

"The nation has developed a relentless hunger for enormous amounts of electricity," Henry Still charges in "Energy: A Crisis in the Offing" in *As We Live and Breathe,* edited by G.M. Grosvenor. Today we generate eight times more electricity than we did thirty years ago. Expanding consumption, not population growth, accounts for almost all of that increase.

The pollution connected with fossil fuels and nuclear energy has created severe environmental problems. People are looking again at sources of clean energy; solar collectors, wind turbines, water power, and geothermal energy. This group of technologies may supply an increasing share of our energy needs in the future.

Conservation of energy is becoming an economic necessity. People prefer cars that get better mileage. Homes are being insulated and fitted with storm windows and weather stripping. Many Quaker Meetinghouses are old and drafty. Members of the Meeting might consider an energy audit of their Meetinghouse to identify where heat is being lost and what is needed to make it snug.

It is surprising how much more comfortable we are when ceiling fans are installed in rooms with high ceilings. Landscaping also makes a significant difference. Trees or vines can shade a building from the direct rays of the sun.

The Challenge. In *This Endangered Planet*, Richard A. Falk warns that "Man has an alarming capacity to adapt to conditions of persisting hazard without taking available steps to reduce or eliminate them." The crisis he foresees is caused in large part by modern technology, the demands that the rapidly increasing number of people on the planet make on its natural resources, and the consequences of dumping as a means of disposing of wastes. Let us develop strategies for rescuing our planet!

STEWARDSHIP OF THE PLANET

Four issues basic to stewardship of the earth are posed in Query 10: "The Environment" in the *Faith and Practice* of Philadelphia Yearly Meeting:

> Are you concerned that man's increasing power over nature should not be used irresponsibly but with reverence for life and with a sense of splendor of God's continuing creation?

> What are you doing to conserve natural resources for the welfare of future generations?

> Do you practice and encourage thoughtful family planning?

> What are you doing to assure adequate food, shelter, education and love for all people in all countries?

Consider this query with an open heart and determine which of our ongoing environmental problems is of greatest concern to you. Perhaps some of the following suggestions will stimulate you to develop your own strategies for sharing in the stewardship of the planet.

Identify Your Interest. If you have a strong empathy with the natural world, current accurate information is available to members of environmental organizations in their magazines and newspapers. Consider becoming a member of the Sierra Club (530 Bush Street, San Francisco, CA 94108), The Nature Conservancy (1800 North Kent Street, Arlington, VA 22209), or Friends of the Earth (1045 Sansome Street, San Francisco, CA 94111).

If your interests are more social and political, the publications and activities of the Friends Committee on National Legislation (245 Second Street NE, Washington, D.C. 20002), The League of Women Voters (1730 M Street NW, Washington, D.C. 20036), and Common Cause (2030 M Street NW, Washington, D.C. 20036) deal with a wide spectrum of subjects, environmental concerns among them.

Perhaps *your* concerns are best approached through service. If so, participation with the American Friends Service Committee (1501 Cherry Street, Philadelphia, PA 19102) and Friends World Committee for Consultation, Section of the Americas (1506 Race Street, Philadelphia, PA 19102) will be rewarding.

Share Your Concern. You may want to join with others who share your concern. Perhaps there is a local chapter of Common Cause or Sierra Club or some other group with which you can identify. A group can often be more effective in bringing about change, and many of us enjoy working with others of like mind.

Find Your Focus. As you understand a problem better, you may find *your* focus to be at the local level, or perhaps at the state or national level. An issue such as acid rain, for instance, requires an international focus. Choose the level of concern that suits your temperament and situation.

Make a Difference. When concerned citizens become involved in how agencies responsible for monitoring the quality of water and air are functioning, the quality of their performance often improves.

As your knowledge and commitment are recognized, you may be asked to serve on community advisory committees and other groups. Opportunities to inform the public of your concern occur as you accept invitations to speak at schools, clubs, and other groups.

When new laws or ordinances are needed or old ones need to be changed, sharing your views with the appropriate politicians may help

144

to initiate the change.

Sustain Your Interest. Many problems have existed for so long or are so complex that immediate success is not possible. An inspiring example of perseverence in the face of great odds is the work of Miriam and Sam Levering who as "Friends in Washington" began their decade-long mission to shape an international seabed mining system in 1972. Their efforts on behalf of the Law of the Sea Treaty were noted over the years in the Friends Committee on National Legislation (FCNL) *Washington Newsletter.* Their story, "Friends Who Made A Difference," by Florence Widutis, appeared in the December 1980 issue of the FCNL *Washington Newsletter.*

The United Nations adopted the Law of the Sea Treaty on April 30, 1982. But the United States, Venezuela, Israel, and Turkey opposed the treaty. It may take six or eight more years to obtain the ratification required to insure that the deep seas are treated as "the common heritage of mankind."

"WE SEEK AN EARTH RESTORED..."

In *The Defense of the Peaceable Kingdom,* Marshall Massey suggests that

> there are values and convictions built into our society and culture and, as Woolman would put it, well suited to our natural inclinations, that make it very difficult for us to believe that we could be so extremely dependent on so many different parts of the global ecosystem, or that the parts we depend on could be so much at our mercy.

Marshall Massey proposes that "we take up the cause of the environment—not merely as individuals, since many of us are already doing that—but as a group: as the Religious Society of Friends." He believes that the root causes of the worldwide environmental crisis are economic and egocentric and that they cannot be solved without the organized help of Quakers. "We Friends have, I think, a deeper understanding of, and a greater commitment to, Christ's nonviolent, transcendental politics than any other sect." An anti-environmental backlash could be disastrous. "If we don't teach the environmentalists, who will?"

Marshall Massey sees the nurturing of the helpless, respect for the interrelatedness of life, stewardship, and the cultivation of sanity to be central and basic to environmentalism. "All through the world, the tide of concern for the environment is on the rise," he says. He recognizes it in the "not in my back yard" syndrome and in instances of altruism and stewardship. He believes that Friends have an opportunity "to serve as a nucleus for something that's right on the edge of happening."

CONCLUSION

We have examined the problems and have heard the call to act in time to save Spaceship Earth. Let us seek the will to accept the responsibility to share in the restoration and preservation of our planet. As with any journey, it begins with a first step—by a Friend, by a Meeting, by the Religious Society of Friends.

SOME SUGGESTED READINGS

Boraikoo, Allen A. "Storing Up Trouble—Hazardous Waste." *National Geographic.* (March 1985), pp. 318–351.

Bryan, Ron and Wayne Anson. "The Stewardship of the Earth." *Quaker Life.* (June 1985), pp. 12–17.

Caldwell, Lynton K. *In Defense of Earth: International Protestation of the Biosphere.* Bloomington, IN: Indiana University Press, 1972.

Dubos, Rene, *So Human An Animal.* New York: Charles Scribner's Sons, 1968.

Falk, Richard A. *This Endangered Planet.* New York: Random House, 1971.

Massey, Marshall. *In Defense of the Peaceable Kingdom.* Pacific Yearly Meeting of the Religious Society of Friends (Friends Center, 2160 Lake Street, San Francisco, California 94121), 1985.

SOME QUESTIONS FOR DISCUSSION

1. When did you first become aware that plants and animals provide our food and much of our clothes and shelter?
2. If you could have changed it, how would you have enriched your childhood experiences with nature?
3. What is the source of the water you drink? What conservation measures do you think would be most effective where you live?
4. Which of our environmental problems concern you most; locally, nationally, internationally? How can you learn more about each problem?

5. Which decision-makers should hear what you have learned about the problem you selected for study, and what changes you recommend?

6. How can attitudes toward the stewardship of the earth be encouraged in ourselves? in others? in young people?

ABOUT THE AUTHOR

Ruth Lofgren was born in Utah to devout third-generation Mormon parents. She joined the faculty of the University of Michigan where her research with the electron microscope was in microbial cytology. When she was led to change fields, she taught biology and science education at Brooklyn College of the City University of New York. During this time she found her spiritual home with Friends and joined New York Monthly Meeting. She served on the Friends Schools Committee. Currently, she is active in San Antonio Monthly Meeting. She serves on the Wastewater Advisory Committee and the Industrial Wastewater Review Board for City Council and on the Utilities Task Force of the Physical Resources Council of Target '90/Goals for San Antonio.

The Slavery of Penal Servitude: Quaker Concerns about Prisons and Prisoners

Fay Honey Knopp and *Janet Lugo*

For a very long time Friends have been respected for their commitment to the abolition of all things oppressive and evil in the souls and institutions of humanity—oppressive and evil institutions that blight the human spirit and keep it in darkness and disunity with the source of life. Today, Friends testimonies are clear about such evil and oppressive institutions as war and slavery, but, as a Society, Friends are not clear about a growing, oppressive, and evil institution in our midst which blights the human spirit like no other and keeps it in abject darkness—the American prison.

Though Friends became clear eventually in our resistance to the model of slavery, and today are more clear in ways to resist the war model, we are less than clear about ways to resist modern penal oppression. We have not applied to prisons the searching light of our witness against violence and oppression.

FRIENDS AND THE WAR MODEL

As early as 1661, Friends were clear about the evil of war. In the Declaration to King Charles II of England, Friends advocated the abolition of the oppressive institution of war, clearly stating: "We

---

(This chapter is based on an article written by Fay Honey Knopp and Janet Lugo, "Too Late To Be An Abolitionist Now?," published by *Quaker Life*, April 1977. It was rewritten in 1986 by Fay Honey Knopp.)

utterly deny all outward wars and strife and fighting with outward weapons, for any end or under any pretense whatsoever. And this is our testimony to the whole world."

Generations of Quakers have suffered arrest, imprisonment, harassment, and distraint of goods for their opposition to this evil. Today, a query addressed to even the youngest of Friends about our peace testimony elicits a response that says in essence, "Quakers are against all wars." The testimony of Friends on the abolition of war of any kind is, and always has been, uncompromising, clear, and wholly acceptable to all but perhaps a very small number of Friends.

We fail, however, to see the similarities between the prison model and the war model.[1] The language and mentality of war have pervaded discussions of crimes in this country for decades. Discussions of both war and crimes often focus on identifying an alien "enemy" who is sharply different from us. The concepts of "good guys" (like us) and "bad guys" (like the others) often permit racial or ethnic stereotypes to permeate our images. Both criminal offenders and our international opponents are portrayed in ways which allow them to be seen as objects rather than persons, denying our belief that there is that of God in every human being. Moreover, from police to prisons, the social-industrial complex that feeds off the criminal justice system is the twin of the military-industrial complex. Scarce fiscal resources are poured into prisons and into techniques that manifest an overtly paramilitary response to problems of crime and disorder—problems that are in reality social and political and that can and should be solved by peaceful means.

As a Society, we have too easily accepted the perceptions of those who benefit from the prison and industrial complex to shape our Quaker views of crime, criminals, and imprisonment. Wastefully pouring billions of dollars into harsher punishments in pursuit of "domestic tranquility" is as futile as pouring billions of dollars down the bottomless hole called "national security." The punishment model has failed both internationally and domestically. We do not feel more secure in the world; we do not feel safer at home.

Allowing those who declare "war on crime" to shape our views of crime and criminals is tantamount to permitting Pentagon generals to shape our perceptions of war and politics. Unfortunately, their focus on fear and threats to our safety, and their unmet promises of crime deterrence through massive prison construction have not stirred our outrage or our imagination. Sadly, we do not "utterly deny" the war model of prison.

FRIENDS AND SLAVERY

Today, Friends will agree that slavery is as oppressive and evil an institution as human beings can experience. Friends were the first Christian group in America to see the evil of slaveholding and the first to renounce it within our own ranks, without regard to cost. Do we not now bask in the purity of Woolman's Light—that simple Quaker tailor from New Jersey—who, a century after the Declaration to King Charles, discerned the utter evil of the institution of slavery in a society where it was widely accepted, unexamined, and profitable?

Surprisingly, the testimony of Friends on the abolition of slavery was not quite so swift nor quite so sure as folk-telling would have it. The way was not easy. Generations of Quakers suffered the opposition and disapproval of their own people for their witness against slavery. John Woolman experienced, and often bemoaned, the pains of "singularity," by which he meant the loneliness, disdain, and social opprobrium which are the lot of those who witness against an evil that others cannot see, or seeing, are so involved with that they cannot face it. He died before he saw the fruit of his ministry—the abolition of slaveholding among Friends, completed by 1808.

Yet even then the fruit was not ripe. In the next generation the Grimke sisters, Quaker abolitionists laboring under the double handicap of being Southerners and women, were in the words of one of them "fairly ground to powder" in the Society of Friends, and ultimately disowned (in 1838) for their stubborn witness and outreach to others in the antislavery cause that was itself a Quaker testimony.[2]

Today, more than two hundred years after the death of John Woolman, few Friends realize that slavery, like war, is still not dead among us. The abolition of chattel slavery gave birth to another kind of slavery, equally evil and oppressive—the slavery of penal servitude.

Though the interrelationships between slavery and imprisonment can be demonstrated graphically by an examination of the conditions of imprisonment, it is underscored constitutionally, also. The Constitution did not, until 1865, make any mention of imprisonment as punishment for crime. The first mention came with the Thirteenth Amendment, which most of us remember as the amendment that abolished slavery and involuntary servitude in the United States.[3] What most Americans fail to realize is that it also *authorized* slavery and involuntary servitude *if used as punishment for crime.* As a result, the law concerning imprisonment began at the most primitive level—with the consideration of prisoners as slaves, and thus, as subhumans.

Prisoners, like slaves, are deprived of liberty, family, property, and self-autonomy and are often made to toil in prison factories, on chain gangs, or on prison farms. Many states pay nothing for prison labor, and in those that do, the rates usually range from two to fifty cents an hour. Prisoners are denied workmen's compensation, unemployment insurance, the right to organize, and other standard working benefits. Prison law is modern slave law, and the courts have served traditionally to uphold the legitimacy of the institution. As taxpayers, then, we are shareholders in the proceeds of captive prison labor. The prisons and jails of the United States today are direct descendents of the slave pens and the auction blocks of yesteryear, and they, too, must be abolished.

It is the religious duty of Friends today, as yesterday, to take up the cause of abolition—this time of penal slavery. To the query of Philadelphia Yearly Meeting of 1776, "Are Friends clear of...holding mankind [sic] as slaves?" we must reply with sorrow: Friends are still not clear. As long as we support imprisonment, leave unexamined the legitimacy of prisons, pay for prisons with our taxes, do not advocate alternatives to imprisonment, do not demand constitutional and human rights for prisoners—we are slaveholders still.

YESTERYEAR: VOICES OF ABOLITION

> The spirit of the Lord is upon me because He has annointed me; He has sent me to announce good news to the poor, TO PROCLAIM RELEASE FOR PRISONERS and recovery of sight for the blind; to let the broken victims go free, to proclaim the year of the Lord's favor.
> (Jesus as quoted in NEB Luke 4:18-19, emphasis added)

The powerful testimony of Jesus to the necessity of bringing an end to the caging of human beings precedes other fervent calls for prison abolition. The following voices represent a wide spectrum of Americans calling for abolition.[4]

As reported in the minutes of the 1870 Congress of the American Prison Association and American Correctional Association:

> Judge Carter, of Ohio, avowed himself a radical on prison discipline. He favored the abolishment of prisons, and the use of greater efforts for the prevention of crime. He believed they would come to that point yet....Any system of imprisonment or punishment was degradation and could not reform a man. He would abolish all prison walls and release all confined within them....

Clarence Darrow, in a 1902 address to the prisoners in the Cook County Jail in Chicago, Illinois, said:

> There ought to be no jails; and if it were not for the fact that the people on the outside are so grasping and heartless in their dealings with the people on the inside, there would be no such institutions as jails....The only way in the world to abolish crime and criminals is to abolish the big ones and the little ones together. Make fair conditions of life....Nobody would steal if he could get something of his own some easier way. Nobody will commit burglary when he has a house full. The only way to cure these conditions is by equality. There should be no jails. They do not accomplish what they pretend to accomplish. If you would wipe them out, there would be no more criminals than now. They terrorize nobody. They are a blot upon any civilization, and a jail is an evidence of the lack of charity of the people on the outside who make the jails and fill them with the victims of their greed.

Ralph Banay, formerly in charge of the psychiatric clinic at the Sing Sing Prison, said in January 1955:

> The prison, as now tolerated, is a constant threat to everyone's security. An anachronistic relic of medieval concepts of crime and punishment, it not only does not cure the crime problem; it perpetuates and multiplies it. We profess to rely upon the prison for our safety; yet it is directly responsible for much of the damage that society suffers at the hands of offenders. On the basis of my own experience, I am convinced that prisons must be abolished.

In 1971, after a single night at the Nevada State Prison where twenty-three judges from all over the United States were locked in cages as a social experiment, Kansas Judge E. Newton Vickers summed up his experience in this way: "I felt like an animal in a cage. Ten years in there must be like 100, or maybe 200. Send two bulldozers out there and tear the damn thing to the ground."

In *Morales vs. Schmidt: 340 Federal Supplement* (W.D. Wis. 1972) Western District of Wisconsin Federal Judge James Doyle wrote in his legal decision:

> I am persuaded that the institutions of prison probably must end. In many respects it is as intolerable in the United States as was the institution of slavery, equally brutalizing

to all involved, equally toxic to the social system, equally subversive of the brotherhood of man, even more costly by some standards, and probably less rational.

The voices of those who have experienced American prisons are the ones that are least heard but provide powerful testimonies to the potential for ending imprisonment. A resolution passed by the Ex-Con Caucus, Second Annual Northeast Prisoners' Association Meeting, in Franconia, New Hampshire in 1975, stated:

> We are working for a society in which the worth and the preservation of dignity of all people is of the first priority. Prisons are a major obstacle to a realization of such a society....We believe that the primary task of the prisoner movement at this time is to organize and educate in the communities, work places, and prisons to develop the mass support needed to abolish the prison system.

THE ABOLITION OF PRISONS

Just as superficial reforms could not alter the cruelty of the slave system, so with its modern equivalent—the prison system. The oppressive situation of prisoners can only be relieved by abolishing the cage and with it the notion of prison punishment as we know it today.[5]

As in yesteryear the way will not be easy to abolish these modern institutions of oppression. Misled by the unexamined assumptions of the society around us, we have only just begun to perceive, dimly as yet, the need for resistance to the prison model. Thus it is encouraging to examine the action taken by the National Board of Directors of the American Friends Service Committee (AFSC). Mindful of constitutional, humane, and spiritual considerations, they adopted the following three Minutes in January 1978:

> *The AFSC's Approach to Prison Construction Moratorium.* The American Friends Service Committee, believing prisons to be dehumanizing and destructive institutions, commits itself to support a moratorium on the construction of jails and prisons in order to prevent the expansion of the capacity of our country to hold people behind bars. It also commits itself to working for humane and socially constructive alternatives to prison.

The Abolition of Imprisonment. The American Friends Service Committee rejects imprisonment as punishment for those whose behavior may be considered criminal. Constructive and creative means of addressing criminal behavior should be employed. This stand is based on our belief in the dignity of all human beings. It does not address issues regarding other forms of restraint as a response to destructive behavior. We are aware that the abolition of prisons cannot be immediately realized but commit ourselves to working toward this goal.

The Revision of the Thirteenth Amendment. The American Friends Service Committee totally rejects the concept of slavery and involuntary servitude. Therefore we support amendment of the Thirteenth Amendment to the United States Constitution which now reads:

Neither slavery nor involuntary servitude, EXCEPT AS A PUNISHMENT FOR CRIME WHEREOF THE PARTY SHALL HAVE BEEN DULY CONVICTED, shall exist within the United States, or any place subject to their jurisdiction.

The exception clause should be deleted so that the Thirteenth Amendment would prohibit all slavery and involuntary servitude within the U.S. and its jurisdictions.

Though the 1978 Minutes of the AFSC begin to open the way for Friends to move forward and resist the prison model, the path ahead is not easy. For the vast majority of members of the Religious Society of Friends, primarily white and middle class, prisons remain but a metaphor, distant and strange, evil to be sure, but somehow "necessary."

Yet, to say that prisons should be abolished does not say that no one in our communities requires restraint in order to protect society. There are some individuals who exhibit patterns of behavior dangerous enough to require a safe, secure environment for as long as such patterns exist. Such setting need not be oppressive but can offer opportunities to reshape and reconstruct lifestyles and behavior patterns.[6]

To say that prisons should be abolished, *does* say that:

1. Prisons are damaging and pain-creating institutions that do not solve the problems of the victim, the offender, or the community.[7]
2. The pain of punishment is counterproductive and cruel.

3. The majority of prisoners are persons who have already been punished by life situations, racism, and injustice.
4. The vast majority of persons imprisoned currently are overrepresentative of people of color, ethnicity, and the poorer class.[8]
5. The vast majority of people imprisoned do not represent a threat to other persons and alternative responses to their offenses are known, have been practiced in some jurisdictions, and could be available to all jurisdictions if such practices became public policy.

Above all, as abolitionists we are saying that the existence of a small group of persons who represent a threat to society must no longer be used as a justification for penal servitude, either for them or for the vast majority of others for whom restraint is not necessary for society's protection. What we utterly deny is the validity of prisons as we know them, based on the doubly oppressive concept of slavery plus punishment. Both prongs of that concept are destructive and wrong and disagreeable to the truth. For, notwithstanding this small group in need of restraint, the connection between crime prevention and prisons is all but nonexistent. In the long range, prisons do not prevent, control, or deter crimes, and they contain only a tiny fraction of those who commit crimes.

Ever since the building of the first American prison—an experiment that failed—those who have populated our prisons have been primarily the poor, the racial minorities, immigrants, foreigners, the young, and the powerless. It would seem clear that this overrepresentation reflects deliberate social choices since there have always been alternatives to prison available to lawbreakers from the middle and wealthy classes. For "folks like us" there are good lawyers, special schools for "exceptional youth who are unreachable by conventional educational methods" (for which, if you are poor, read "juvenile delinquents"); psychiatric services; sex-offender programs; drying-out hospitals; counseling; parenting programs; mediation services; crisis intervention services; and a range of other helping strategies. And there are alternatives extended by the courts, mostly to "folks like us," such as bail, suspended sentences, fines, alternative sentences, probation, and opportunities to do community service and make restitution.

Underlying all of these alternatives is the fact that, from the very beginning of our lives, "folks like us" are accepted into, encouraged to participate in, and expected to succeed in basic social institutions: educational, financial, vocational, and social. On the other hand, "those folks" who go to prison are very often viewed from the very beginning of their lives, because of race or class or labeling, as alien, different, suspect, even dangerous. For the most part, they remain outside the institutions which channel "folks like us" into lives of relative comfort and success.

Perhaps the one institution "those folks" need not struggle to get into is the prison. Many are led there through poverty and racism, and through police, prosecutorial, and judicial discretion.[9] The prison thus serves as a warehouse for the portion of our population that is targeted and programmed for failure.

A QUAKER ROLE: ABOLITIONISTS STILL

We believe with John Woolman that we still have the power, if we have the heart, to "labour for a perfect redemption" from the spirit of oppression that threatens to swamp us all, and to live in that life and power that takes away the occasion for crime and prisons. *But we need to begin!* We need to challenge and resist the continued life and growth of the penal institutions that hurt, dehumanize, and destroy. We need to say *no* to human cages as we say *no* to war and slavery. We need to move toward a social reality that speaks to the yearnings for a true and caring community, with real liberty and real justice—economic, social, and political—for all; a reality that seeks to restore both the wrongdoer and the wronged to full humanity, to lives of integrity and dignity *in the community:* a reality that embodies the Christian principle of loving kindness toward every neighbor, including the wrongdoer; the Muslim principle of oneness in the community; the Jewish principle of *chesed* or steadfast love binding the community; a reality that manifests the Quaker principle of the Christ within.

We have leadings and strategies on how to do this.[10] We have no finished blueprint, nor do we need one. Prison abolition, like complete disarmament, is a struggle and an unending process. Each generation must make its own contribution in the light of its own understanding. But we, like Friends before us, must ultimately be willing to renounce an evil *because it is evil,* without counting the cost.

NOTES

1. For further information on the war model of prisons, see F.H. Knopp, et al., *Instead of Prisons: A Handbook for Abolitionists* (Syracuse, NY: Safer Society Press, 1976). Also see R. Gross, F.H. Knopp, and H. Zehr, "Crime Is a Peace Issue: A New Call to Justice Making," in the

156

Friends Journal (March 1, 1982).

2. See G. Lerner, *The Grimke Sisters from South Carolina* (New York: Shocken Books, 1971).

3. See F.H. Knopp, et al., *Instead of Prisons*. Also see B. Esposito and L. Wood, *Prison Slavery*. (Washington, D.C.: Committee to Abolish Prison Slavery, 1982). See also T. Sellin, *Slavery and the Penal System* (New York: Elsevier Scientific Publishing Company, Inc., 1976).

4. See also F.H. Knopp, et al., *Instead of Prisons*.

5. Ibid.

6. For examples of such alternative settings for sex offenders, see F.H. Knopp, *Retraining Adult Sex Offenders: Methods and Models*, (Syracuse, NY: Safer Society Press, 1984) and *Remedial Intervention in Adolescent Sex Offenses: Nine Program Descriptions* (Syracuse, NY: Safer Society Press, 1982).

7. See N. Christine, *Limits to Pain* (New York: Columbia University Press, 1981).

8. See "What Color Are America's Prisons? Incarceration Rates by Race/Ethnic Groups—1980," *Jericho* (Summer, 1983).

9. See the American Friends Service Committee, *Struggle for Justice* (New York: Hill and Wang, 1971).

10. See F.H. Knopp, et al., *Instead of Prisons*.

SOME QUESTIONS FOR DISCUSSION

1. How do you react to the authors contention about "the slavery of penal servitude?" How do you view their contention that concern for prisons is a part of a broad concern for abolition?
2. What is said in your Yearly Meeting *Discipline* on this subject? Is that statement vague or does it include some specific suggestions for individual and/or group action?
3. What alternatives to incarceration are there for many offenders?
4. How cognizant are the members and attenders of your Meeting of local prisons and prisoners? How concerned are they? What could be done about this dismal aspect of society?

ABOUT THE AUTHORS

Fay Honey Knopp is a member of the Middlebury (VT) Monthly Meeting of New England Yearly Meeting. She is a recorded minister. For thirty years she has been an active Quaker "abolitionist" concerned about men and women in federal and state prisons. She was the founder and the coordinator of The Safer Society Program of PREAP (Prison Research Education/Action Project), a nationwide program of the New York State Council of Churches. As such, she serves as a consultant to many states and counties regarding sex offender and victim treatment. She has written widely, as indicated in the notes included in this essay. She has received several honors, such as the Karl Menninger Award, the Martin Luther King, Jr. Award, and a citation as an Outstanding Woman of Connecticut.

Janet Lugo is a member of the 15th Street Meeting in New York City and a long-time member of the Prison Concerns Committee of New York Yearly Meeting. She was at one time a staff member of the Quaker Information Center in Syracuse, New York, on criminal justice and one of the founders of the program on Alternatives to Violence in New York state institutions.

Chapter 13

Quakers and Government: Can We Make a Difference?

Edward F. Snyder

There are only 125 thousand Quakers in the United States today. That is .05 percent of the U.S. population of 240 million. In the world as a whole, there are only 250 thousand Quakers out of a total population of approximately five billion people. Based on numbers alone, it is nearly inconceivable that Friends could have any significant impact on national and international events.

Furthermore, the concentrations of money and power in industry and in the military, the vast influence of the mass media, and the seemingly insoluble nature of the problems confronting the world all combine to make us feel we are helpless victims of circumstances beyond our control.

Why, then, should we bother to try to speak out? Why should we spend precious time and energy on what appears to be a futile effort to influence the course of events? And if we do speak out, will anybody listen?

There are several reasons why we *must* speak out:

We Really Have No Choice. The historic testimonies of the Religious Society of Friends are made for this hour. Surprisingly, this is not a self-evident statement. Over the past decade a number of Friends Meetings have seriously considered laying down their peace committees. Recently I was asked to make the case for "the relevance of the peace testimony in today's world" because a number of people in a very active Meeting had serious doubts that it was indeed relevant. Yet, with several nations having the power through the use of nuclear weapons to extinguish civilization and with leaders of the Catholic, Episcopal, and other churches making far-reaching peace statements, it seems absolutely clear that the Quaker peace testimony has never been more relevant.

Furthermore, our testimony against injustice and oppression and in favor of human rights has never been more needed than at this time when internal chaos threatens our cities, South Africa, and the Middle East. Our belief in the right sharing of the world's resources is desperately needed in a hungry world where the gap between the haves and the have-nots continues to grow. Our testimony on simplicity has never been more relevant than in this time when pollution and overconsumption threaten to damage irreversibly our beautiful world.

If we really believe that our testimonies are an integral part of, and grow out of, our religious faith, then words and acts which are consistent with them should follow naturally and inevitably. Who are we to judge whether our efforts bear fruit? If we act in a spirit of humility and informed goodwill, we should be very slow to draw conclusions about cause and effect. The test is not whether an act is effective by the world's standards, but whether it is rightly motivated. George Washington said: "Let us raise a standard to which the wise and honest can repair; the event is in the hands of God."

The Doors to the Offices of Decision–Makers Are Open to Us. Decisions about crucial life and death issues in modern society are made in significant measure, though not exclusively, through governmental processes. The idea of "government" creates problems for some Friends. Some have "dropped out" of any active involvement in public affairs because they are deeply frustrated by what they feel is the unresponsive nature of government. Some other Friends take a principled "anarchist" stand against any form of government because of its coercive nature and ultimate commitment to violence. Others just object in general because of its high taxes and interference in what are viewed as private matters.

By and large, Friends have accepted the need for government that is just and humane, and many would even echo William Penn's statement that "Government seems to me a part of religion itself, a thing sacred in its institutions and ends."

Regardless of theories, Friends from the earliest times have been quite astute in recognizing where decision-making powers lay in different societies and have sought to bring a Friendly influence to bear on it. Sometimes that was done as a matter of survival of the Society—to establish or to protect the principle of religious freedom. Sometimes Friends acted in the interests of peace and justice generally.

The history of audacious peacemaking missions by early Friends to Sultans, Czars, and governors has been told many times. But the organized lobbying efforts of Friends in the early days in England are not nearly so well known. Frederick Tolles, a Quaker historian, pointed out in the 1956 Ward Lecture at Guilford College that:

> Quakers have been engaged in lobbying—that is to say—in seeking to influence legislators by personal visits—ever since 1656 when a hundred and sixty-five Friends went to Westminster Hall and sent into the House of Commons a paper offering to lie "body for body" in jail in place of their imprisoned and suffering fellow Quakers. But after 1675 they intensified their legislative activity, seeking acts for the release of prisoners and the ending of persecution. The Meeting for Sufferings coordinated the work. The weightiest Friends in England, including George Fox and William Penn, busied themselves buttonholing members of Parliament and appearing at committee hearings. The yearly meeting even rented a room in a coffeehouse hard by the Houses of Parliament for a headquarters—a kind of Friends Committee on National Legislation office.…The legislative struggle for religious liberty was substantially won in 1689 with the passage of the great Toleration Act, but the lobbying efforts went on until Friends were finally granted the right to substitute a simple affirmation for a formal oath in 1722. From time to time in the course of this campaign the Meeting for Sufferings urged Friends to write their Parliament-men on the subject. If anyone thinks the techniques of the FCNL are a modern innovation, he knows little of Quaker history.

Indeed, a British historian, N.C. Hunt, notes that Quakers were the earliest political association to focus on the House of Commons. They exercised the kind of strong, central control in their campaigns that the FCNL would not dream of today. To assure a coordinated Quaker position, local Friends were urged to send their letters to members of Parliament in care of the Meeting for Sufferings in London, where a subcommittee was appointed to "consider which of them are fit to be delivered to the MPs and which not." Hunt views these Quaker "techniques of regular, constant, and peaceful political agitation" as the first organized effort to influence the embryonic parliamentary system in Britain and suggests that Friends made "a very real contribution to our peaceful constitutional evolution."

Today, Friends in the United States have a special opportunity and responsibility to work for peace and justice. We live in a political system where individual citizen action is expected, encouraged, and can be effective. Our nation is one of the two superpowers, wielding nearly incredible military, economic, and political power. The United States is in a superlative position to provide courageous leadership toward a world of peace and justice, and we, as citizens, have a tremendous responsibility to those in other countries and to those of future generations.

It is difficult for many of us in the United States to realize how powerless people in smaller countries feel. Crucial decisions affecting their future regarding war and peace, prosperity or depression, are often made in elections in the United States or in legislation passed by a Congress which is very far away and beyond their influence. People in Western and Eastern Europe watch the political moods and trends in the United States with intense interest because their future, in many ways, lies in our hands. The people in developing countries are even more vulnerable as we dispense arms and development funds or trade preferences to countries in need. I was in Malaysia in the late 1960s when the funds they were expecting to use for economic development for a year were wiped out by an "inconsequential" United States release of stockpiled rubber, thereby reducing the world price paid for the Malaysian rubber crop. In 1985 the FCNL circulated a communication opposing the MX missile to members of the United States House of Representatives from a newly-elected Quaker Senator in Australia, Jo Vallentine. She recognized that the decision in Washington would have a far-reaching impact on her nation halfway around the world.

Fortunately, the views of Friends are often well received by policy-makers because of the compassion, intellectual effort, and good judgment of Quakers who have gone before us. We have a responsibility to maintain that reservoir of goodwill for future Friends. Part of the esteem of which we are the beneficiaries also results from the fact that, while Friends have sought to protect their own interests through support for religious liberty, conscientious objection to military service and to war taxes, Friends are also known to act on behalf of the disadvantaged, the poor, and the oppressed everywhere. Often we are told on Capitol Hill: "It is a pleasure to talk with someone who is trying to see the broader picture and not just out to get something for themselves."

FRIENDS: POLICYMAKERS OR LOBBYISTS?

Friends have entered into the crucible of politics and decision making throughout their history. William Penn's "Holy Experiment" in Pennsylvania found Quakers in control there from 1682 until the middle of the next century, when compromises involving support for war finally forced the end of Quaker control. Three other American colonies had Quaker governors—Rhode Island, West New Jersey, and North Carolina. Since then Friends have served in many state legislatures. And in the United States Congress, Friends who were elected officials have maintained an open door to representatives of Quaker organizations even if they did not agree with them. Two of the most controversial of U.S. Presidents in the twentieth century have also been Friends—Herbert Hoover and Richard Nixon.

In Great Britain Friends have served in Parliament for more than 150 years. The best known is probably John Bright, the nineteenth-century reformer; the most consistent was probably T. Edmund Harvey, who maintained his Quaker pacifism while holding his seat in Parliament during both World Wars.

Quaker historian Frederick Tolles concluded in his Ward Lecture that "in the long run, lobbying for Friends was a more congenial method of influencing politics than electioneering." Friends who lobby are one step removed from actual decision making. They can thus avoid some of the most difficult challenges to conscience faced by policymakers who must vote for or against specific propositions and answer to their constituents and to their party leadership for their acts. But this provides small solace for lobbyists. Any person who acts in the political arena must deal with the question of compromise, and lobbyists are no exception. As lobbyists consider how to present their best case, they must constantly consider questions such as: how long can one call for the most desirable but least likely solution without losing all credibility? Yet, at what point do Quaker lobbyists betray their cause by asking for too little?

Quaker educators, publicists, and journalists are close allies of Quaker lobbyists. No significant or far-reaching change in public policy can be achieved unless there is a solid base of support for it among significant segments of the public. The role of the lobbyist is to focus that desire for change on key policymakers. First and most essential, however, is the need to build support for new and creative policies by education through the churches, the press, academic institutions, and private organizations. In New England, the American Friends Service Committee played a crucial role in creating public momentum for a nuclear freeze. In Michigan, Kenneth Boulding helped to organize the first "teach-in" against the Vietnam War. The churches played a leading role in opposing that war and in focusing on the need to reverse the arms race. Quaker doctors in New England formed the nucleus of Physicians for Social Responsibility, a precursor of the Nobel Prize-winning International Physicians for the Prevention of Nuclear War. Individual Quaker scientists, educators, and journalists across the United States have used their talents to persuade their colleagues in various organizations to consider Quaker perspectives on public policy.

We live in a period of increasingly rapid social change. Most of us very much enjoy the benefits of modern technology and medicine, but in other ways we yearn to go back to "the good old days." We want simple solutions to complex problems and ambiguous situations. We want leaders who will tell us that they have the answers. Yet, those who study or travel widely, and experience deeply, understand that nuclear weapons, international anarchy, the population explosion, world hunger, and oppression require revolutionary changes in the world's political and economic order. The old ways are no longer adequate. Indeed, revolutionary changes are essential if we are to build a society worth living in. There is a massive educational job waiting to be done. Friends who have faith in our historic testimonies have a crucial responsibility now to narrow the gap in understanding between those who long for the old order—which is passing away—and those who would welcome the new order—which is waiting to be born.

THREE ENCOURAGING THOUGHTS FOR FRIENDS
ENTERING THE PUBLIC ARENA

Do Not Be Discouraged by the Numbers. Although you are only one of 240 million people in this country, your influence is far greater than that—if you are politically active. Some people estimate that only about five percent of U.S. citizens participate actively in public policy decision making—and that means people all across the political spectrum from left to center to right. Consider the members of your family, your neighbors, and your acquaintances. What percentage of them do more than absorb national and international affairs through television or the newspapers, gripe about politics, and vote on election day? How many go beyond that to write letters to their member of Congress and/or to the editor of the local newspaper, to organize and/or speak at public meetings, to be active in local politics, and to educate Friends and other groups on policy issues?

Whatever your figure, it surely indicates a dramatic increase in your potential influence if you are one of those activists. The strength and appeal of those various contending activist groups within that active five percent largely determine the future of the remaining politically inactive citizenry.

Never underestimate the influence of committed lives. I think of six persons among many who are inspirations to us all. Sam and Miriam Levering, whose remarkable work to help bring the Law of the Sea Treaty into being is still inadequately understood; Stuart Innerst, who carried on what seemed to be a losing battle for many years before he saw the United States recognize the People's Republic of China; Dorothy Hutchinson, whose incisive mind and beautiful spirit provided leadership for the FCNL, the World Federalists, and the Women's International League for Peace and Freedom for many years; Chester Graham, whose effective peace work in the Midwest spanned more than half a century; and Raymond Wilson, who helped set the goal of world disarmament on the agenda of the United States, the Soviet Union, and the United Nations, and who used his persuasive voice to fight world hunger and encourage the creative use of U.S. agricultural abundance.

Work with Like-Minded People. Friends are not alone in this struggle. Indeed, we often rely on leadership supplied by people in other churches, in other peace groups, and in political life. There is strength in united action—through coalitions, and through councils of churches.

As I look around our society for the groups which can do the critically important public education needed to reverse the arms race and build a world of peace and justice, I focus on the churches. While they have often in the past failed to fulfill their prophetic role, the churches have great strength and even greater potential. The churches

1. Share a vision of a world of peace, with justice;
2. Have a policy for dealing with "enemies" (love them, feed them, understand them, forgive them);
3. Offer hope and faith to counter the widespread sense of despair, frustration, and failure;
4. Have loyalties beyond and above a particular nation-state;
5. Are international, cross-cultural, and multiracial, reflecting the diversity of the whole world. They can thus provide information and insights beyond those which are filtered through official channels;
6. Have staying power because they are institutionalized, through their educational programs they can transmit values from generation to generation;
7. Can bring to bear on human affairs the spiritual dimension of existence and the focused power of God working in individual lives;

8. Have congregations in cities, suburbs, small towns, and rural areas, touching the lives of every social and economic class, through which education and action can take place.

Working with other churches and coalitions has advantages and disadvantages. It is certainly true that when one works closely with people from other traditions, cultures, or political perspectives, we may find problems and misunderstandings as well as creative insights. Personality "quirks" and people on "power trips" can create deep frustrations and make it difficult to remember the advantages of united action. At those times, it may be helpful to recall a sign which hangs in the office of one of the most effective staff people I know on Capitol Hill. It reads: "There is no limit to the amount of good that you can do if you don't care who gets the credit." That is good advice in any endeavor. It can be especially empowering in groups working for peace and justice where struggles are intense and immediate rewards and results may be sparse.

You Have Friends on Capitol Hill. There is no question that government is complex, the federal budget is enormous, the bureaucracy is a labyrinth, and Congress is a puzzle, but you don't have to understand it all before you can be effective. There is rhythm to public policy formation, and there are established procedures and channels for making decisions. To be effective you need to know what decisions are being considered, who will make the decisions, and when they will do it.

Nothing is sadder than to see groups get excited about an issue *after* the decision has been made, without their input. Nothing is more exciting than to see how a few well-placed phone calls to a Senator's local office on a particular morning can help influence a very important decision.

One of the most effective citizen acts you can take is to thank Senators and Representatives for making a courageous speech or casting a difficult vote on a controversial issue. You can be sure they will receive critical comments from constituents, editorial writers, their colleagues, and perhaps their party's leadership. There are many members of Congress and others on Capitol Hill who value moral support and who need to receive more of it. I am often asked whether it is worthwhile writing to anybody in Congress other than one's own Representative and Senators. My answer is that if you want to criticize a vote or recommend a policy position, confine your letters to those who directly represent you. But if you write in praise or appreciation, there are 535 eligible members of Congress. No one I know on Capitol Hill has rejected or thrown away or failed to read such a communication.

The Friends Committee on National Legislation is located directly across the street from the new Hart Senate Office Building on Capitol Hill. Its staff keeps track of issues, of committee assignments of members of the House and Senate, of important hearings, and voting records of the members of Congress. Its purpose is to help Friends to be knowledgeable about the issues and to be aware of when decisions are being made and who the key players are. A monthly newsletter, weekly telephone tape-recorded messages (202/547–4343) and periodic background papers supply crucial information. The FCNL aspires to have a "Meeting contact" in every Monthly Meeting in the United States. Its General Committee of about 230 Friends, appointed from most Yearly Meetings in the United States, makes its policy and sets its legislative priorities. This assures that the FCNL is responsive to the needs of Friends across the country. The FCNL also publishes a series of "How-Tos" with useful information on writing and visiting members of Congress, writing the President, working in politics, writing to editors, and "adopting" a member of Congress.

THE ENCOUNTER

Sooner or later, if we are to have an impact on public policy, we must go beyond reading about public issues and complaining to family and friends. At some point we must seek out and "encounter" people who are involved in the policymaking process. Those people may be members of Congress, editors, local business leaders, or political party activists. A personal interview is best. A phone call may be possible. A written communication can express your ideas most exactly, but you miss the opportunity for reaction and response. Whatever the format, this encounter, this exchange, provides the occasion for mutual learning and growth.

It is helpful to remember that however exalted the position of the "Proper Person in Power" (as early Friends referred to the object of their entreaties), even the highest officials are fallible human beings. Do not be overawed. In some cases the person you go to visit may be more apprehensive than you are. In many cases, if you have done your homework properly, you will be surprised to realize that you know more about the subject than the official.

Here is a small check list for your encounter, whether you go alone or with a group:

1. Have you given adequate time for prayer and reflection as you prepare for your interview? Much of what we call synchronicity and serendipity may in reality be God at work in the world, speaking, writing, and acting through faithful men and women who have prepared themselves to follow Divine leading.
2. Have you sought to understand how the world looks from the other person's perspective—his or her hopes, fears, and past history? You do not have to agree with the other's views, but it is important to appreciate where other people have been on their life's journey as you try to relate to them.
3. Have you found a comfortable "place to stand," where you do not feel yourself hemmed in and committed to defend particular narrow perspectives based on partisan politics or narrow national, class, profession, or racial loyalties? Finding a place to stand which gives first place to a Divine perspective is especially important when discussing important foreign policy issues. It helps us to see the strengths and weaknesses of all systems and confounds those who seek to put us in a narrow pigeonhole, for or against one particular nation.
4. "Where there is no vision, the people perish" (Prov. 29:18). Are you prepared to communicate a vision which might become a reality if enough people worked for it? At its best, Friends impact on public affairs does not consist of providing one more needed vote for a particular measure, no matter how important. The major contribution of Friends is to offer a new, more hopeful vision of the future, to raise people's sights, to create a new agenda. Our task is to communicate a deeper level of reality to jaded policymakers; to give wholehearted support to those who are providing courageous leadership, to seek out and encourage all those who are genuinely dedicated to building a world of peace and justice.

Trite but true, it is still important to remind ourselves that the world is now passing through a narrow and dark valley with shadows of death everywhere. We are privileged to live in this time of great challenge and decision making. If we are true to our Quaker heritage and testimony and our own God-given talents, we may even play some small, constructive part in helping humanity make safe passage toward a peaceful and humane world whose outlines we can only dimly perceive from our present desperate perspective.

168

SOME SUGGESTED READINGS

Alderson, George and Everett Sentman. *How You Can Influence Congress.* New York: E.P. Dutton, 1979.

Barone, Michael and Grant Ujifusa. *The Almanac of American Politics.* National Journal, published annually.

· Wilson, E. Raymond. *Uphill for Peace.* Richmond, IN: Friends United Press, 1975.

SOME QUESTIONS FOR DISCUSSION

1. Do you agree with the author that "only about five percent of the people participate actively in public policy decision making"? What is the percentage in your community? What group are you in? Why?
2. Which is the most important question to ask when deciding on a course of action? Will it work? Is it right? What will the neighbors say?
3. Do you agree with the author that "the churches have great strength and even greater potential" for influencing public policy? Why or why not?
4. What have been your experiences in talking with "decisionmakers?" What did you find were the most effective ways of communicating? What were the least effective ones?
5. On what issue (or issues) before Congress currently are the members of your Friends Meeting in substantial agreement? What have you done about this (or these) issue(s)? What else could you do?

ABOUT THE AUTHOR

Edward Snyder was born in Iowa, reared in Maine, and worked in a Connecticut law firm before joining the staff of the Friends Committee on National Legislation in 1955 as legislative secretary. He became executive secretary in 1962, a post he still holds. As a registered lobbyist he has testified before Congressional committees on a variety of subjects, including the creation of a peace corps; more funds for arms control and disarmament, the United Nations and other international agencies, and American Indian health programs; the military draft and the Vietnam War. He believes strongly in coalitions of like-minded people and has helped found or lead groups to stop funding of the Vietnam War, for a new foreign policy, for international development, and for civil liberties. He spent two years heading the Quaker

International Conference office in Singapore in 1967–1969 and traveled extensively in that region. He has also visited the Soviet Union and Eastern Europe. He and his wife are members of Adelphi Monthly Meeting in Maryland.

Chapter 14

Pay Thy Taxes
as Long as Thou Canst

Wallace Collett

There is a wonderful and illuminating account from the seventeenth century of how our conscience should direct our actions. It may be apocryphal, but it is so characteristic of the persons involved that it seems authentic.

Young William Penn, a gentleman of high social status, had heard Quakers preach and had experienced an opening of the Spirit in his own life. After a few months he had the opportunity of meeting George Fox, the inspiring leader of the Religious Society of Friends. Penn was obviously troubled in his conscience about following the custom of his class of wearing a sword. So he asked Fox, "How long should I wear my sword?" Fox replied in the Quaker language of that day, "Wear thy sword as long as thou canst."

THE USE OF CONSCIENCE

For many years Carrie Collett and I have been troubled in our consciences as we paid our income taxes, knowing that a large proportion of our money would go to the military budget. But we are responsible, law-abiding citizens and remained obedient to the civil law. We worked for peace in many ways, both in actions and in financial contributions. At tax time, however, the voice of conscience was not stilled by those good deeds. We knew, inwardly, that our tax payments placed us in complicity with the military system.

Conscience seldom issues a clarion call. Rather it moves through the subterranean channels of one's spirit and emerges at some unanticipated time as a clear understanding, a "leading." There came a time in 1982

170

when Carrie and I knew that we would no longer pay voluntarily that portion of our federal income taxes that would be used for the preparation for war. Thus, our action of war tax refusal the following April was not a difficult decision, nor did it require courage or the weighing of possible consequences. We had an inner assurance that this was what we must do.

OUR FIRST TAX REFUSAL ACTION

We searched for sources of information about war tax refusal and prepared ourselves as best we could to make a useful, credible witness of opposition to war. That search was not as easy as I had thought it would be. We did not locate readily available advice and information in Quaker publications on war tax resistance. However, we did find a useful handbook published by the War Resisters League.

That search showed us how important it would be for the Religious Society of Friends to consider the concern of war taxes as a corporate body and supported the creation in 1985 of the Friends Committee on War Tax Concerns.

We also consulted with our tax accountants and law firm as to tax code and legal implications. Those consultations were the first of many opportunities our action has opened for discussion with others about the evils of the war system and the necessity to establish peace. Our contacts with friends and acquaintances, and with bankers and various business people, have shown an initial reaction of surprise and disbelief. Then, as we have described our motivation, they have come to understand our position of religious belief and humanitarian concern. They have told us, however, that our action is not rational, since the Internal Revenue Service (IRS) will forcibly collect our refused taxes plus interest and penalty, thus providing even more funds for the defense budget. Our response to this sincere advice is that the important, critical issue is the witness against war and that the interest and penalty collections are insignificant in relation to the enormity of the evil. In fact, they will not even pay the cost of the red button that controls the firing of an atomic missile.

What we did in April 1983, and have done in each of the following years, was to refuse to pay one-third of our federal income tax, judging that to be roughly the amount of the federal budget that is allocated to present military expenditures. According to the Friends Committee on National Legislation (FCNL), that figure is now up to thirty-six or thirty-seven percent, and some war tax refusers include the cost of past wars in their refusal action, taking the figure to over sixty percent. We have our accountants prepare our return in accordance with the tax code, in typewritten form, and have it show alongside the final figure the amount we will pay, in ink, along with a note: "See Statement Attached." We have sent the amount refused to the American Friends Service Committee, to be used in its peace program, and have so advised the IRS.

FORMS OF WAR TAX RESISTANCE

What we have done has seemed appropriate to us in the light of our conscience and of our financial situation. However, there are a number of ways of engaging in war tax resistance. Some resisters refuse to pay a special federal tax on their telephone bills that was levied for military use. Some include a letter opposing war taxes with their tax payments, and send copies to their Congresspersons. Some are led to file a tax return but refuse to pay any of the amount. Others resist all cooperation with the tax and do not file a return. Some purposely order their lives so that their income does not subject them to federal tax. A few Friends have even moved to other countries to avoid any complicity with war taxes. Information about these and some other modes of war tax resistance will be found in literature listed at the end of this article. The legal implications of these actions are also described therein.

As to what course is correct for any of us, we should realize that there are two messages in Fox's admonition to Penn. The first is that we should continue to wear the sword, to follow the custom of the law, until we have clarity, a sense of compulsion, a concern to take a contrary action. Such action must be based on a firm conviction of conscience.

The second message is that we should discard the sword if and when we find it is at odds with our belief. Action must follow belief. We must no longer comply with custom or even with civil law if our belief brings us under the authority of a higher law. In our case our war tax refusal is an act of civil disobedience required of us by our conscience and our faith.

ACTIONS AGAINST WAR TAX REFUSALS

The Internal Revenue Service reacted quickly after we filed our tax return in April 1983. Three weeks later we were assessed a $500 penalty for having filed what they claimed to be "a frivolous return." That was a newly enacted provision in the tax code and was assessed against many war resisters in 1983. We contested the penalty, finding it contrary to the principles of religious freedom and the right of free speech embodied in the First Amendment to the United States Constitution, as well as faulty in other aspects. We also realized that this penalty, added on top of existing provision for penalties, would be a severe financial problem for many conscientious war tax resisters. We engaged legal counsel and entered a complaint in the Federal District Court.

The pleadings of the government, written by the Department of Justice in Washington, were both interesting and disconcerting. The government recognized the constitutional problems of the "frivolous penalty" and accepted our contention that we have a right to express our opposition to war in connection with our tax filing. They also had to agree that the new "frivolous return penalty" cannot be assessed merely for refusing to pay a portion of our tax. But the court held on limited technical grounds that our tax return for the year 1982 was "frivolous" because of the entries we made on the face of the return, adding that we would not have been "frivolous" had we conveyed that information only in a statement attached to the return.

We took the case to the Circuit Court of Appeals and had a most unsatisfactory and summary treatment there of what we consider to be a serious, substantive issue. We do feel, however, that the legal challenges to the new "frivolous" penalty of the tax code made by us and a number of other tax resisters have forced the IRS to accept some of the constitutional arguments we have presented against our subsequent tax returns, when we have followed the same war tax refusal action but have placed our explanation and objection in an attached statement.

This legal action has provided several opportunities for the presentation of our stand on war taxes to the public. The news conferences called when we filed the case in federal court resulted in television and radio coverage, in well-written articles in the papers, and in many cases, chances to talk with individuals. All of the news reports and articles included Carrie's response as to why she is taking this action—"so our eleven grandchildren can live and grow up." We continue to have opportunities to speak on radio talk shows, to talk to groups, and to engage in deep discussion with individuals.

These contacts inform us as to the deeply-felt concern everyone has about the imminence of war, particularly of nuclear war. Many persons screen this concern with arguments of a communist menace, statements that "mankind has always fought and always will," "we must defend our nation and our freedom," and other justifications for war. But, as the discussion proceeds, we find underneath the argument an understanding that the violent ways of the past are suicidal in our time, and that we must be courageous and determined in creating a system without war.

That first year the action of the Internal Revenue Service to collect our refused taxes was delayed for several months. Finally they began sending the usual computer-prepared collection letters, then invaded one of our accounts and took the amount we had refused, plus some interest and late payment penalty. In the following two years that action has come much sooner. We have used their letters, phone calls, and visits as opportunities for discussing the basis for our war tax resistance. We note that many people are fearful of the IRS. It is wise to deal with their personnel in an open but firm manner and to realize that the penalties are mostly civil rather than criminal. Perhaps Quakers should fill the jails now in protest against war as they did the seventeenth century. But, as of now, refusing to pay this tax is in itself not a criminal jail offense.

QUAKER HISTORY OF WAR TAX RESISTANCE

There has been concern about war taxes from the beginning of Quakerism in the seventeenth century. Many individual Friends and Friends Meetings have recognized that both the use of weapons and payments for weapons are contrary to the substance of our peace testimony. In 1711 William Penn stated the basis for the civil disobedience of war tax refusal, saying:

> Our civil disobedience is only due to Christ, not to confound the things of God's with Caesar's. For no man can be true to Him that's false to his own conscience, nor can he extort from it a tribute to carry on any war, nor ought true Christians to pay it.

On numerous occasions early Friends in America resisted war taxes. For example, the Quaker-dominated Assembly of the Pennsylvania Colony refused in 1709 to appropriate a requested four thousand pounds for an expedition into Canada. The explanation given to the Governor was: "It was contrary to their religious principle to hire men to kill one another."

A very clear-cut statement on this issue comes from the *Book of Discipline* of New England Yearly Meeting of 1785. It says:

> It is the concern of this Meeting to recommend to the several Monthly Meetings that they, consistent with our ancient testimony, refuse the payment of all taxes expressly or specifically for the support of war whether called for in money, possessions, or otherwise, and that such Friends as do actively pay such taxes be dealt with as disorderly walkers.

There is also a poignant chapter in John Woolman's *Journal* in which he describes his conscience-driven decision to refuse to pay war taxes and his queries with Friends and with his Monthly and Yearly Meeting about the issue. He was as persistent on this subject as he was on slavery.

In our time, and especially in the last twenty years, there has been an upsurge in the attention paid to this concern by individual Friends and by Meetings. Excerpts from documents of three Yearly Meetings will illustrate the positions that are being taken.

The *Faith and Practice* of my Yearly Meeting, Wilmington, has advice as to the relationship between the civil government and the conscience, stating that "Friends do not see their governmental rulers as having unlimited authority, but give their ultimate allegiance to God." Then the Yearly Meeting comments on Friends and conscription by stating that "The Society of Friends holds all its members in prayerful concern, feeling that this decision is up to the individual conscience" (not the disorderly walker treatment). Furthermore, in regard to war issues beyond conscription, it says: "Friends who are not subject to military service must also search their lives to avoid practices that contribute, however subtly, to the war system." Similar statements appear in the books of faith and practice of almost all Yearly Meetings.

There are now a growing number of specific advices on war tax resistance as a part of the peace witness of Friends. A Baltimore Yearly Meeting Minute for 1982 on the subject of war tax refusal says:

> The Yearly Meeting finds that such actions are consistent with Friends testimonies for over 300 years that God's love "will never move us to fight and war against anyone with outward weapons." [and continues] The Yearly Meeting stands in loving support of those moved by conscience to witness against making war and preparation for war, including those who refuse to pay military taxes voluntarily.

And lastly, from Philadelphia Yearly Meeting in 1984:

> In this nuclear age with its stress on sophisticated weapons systems, guided missiles, and push-button war, fewer people are required to operate the military machine. Thus the conscription of our money has superceded in part the conscription of people in supporting modern militarism.

The minute then continues with strong support for war tax resistance.

In the past several decades the Religious Society of Friends has given more attention to concern about conscription for military service than about conscription of our money for military purposes. Thus there were major Friends conferences on draft issues in 1948 and in 1968, sponsored by the Friends Coordinating Committee for Peace. Each conference issued declarations that have given needed guidance to Meetings and individuals. A guidebook, *Quakers and the Draft,* was mandated by the 1968 conference. Friends were also at the center of the creation of two national organizations that work on draft issues: The Central Committee for Conscientious Objectors (CCCO) and the National Interreligious Service Board for Conscientious Objectors (NISBO).

THE FRIENDS COMMITTEE ON WAR TAX CONCERNS

Now, similar attention is being focused on the concern of paying for war. In the fall of 1984, after discussions with many Friends across the country, the Friends World Committee for Consultation, Section of the Americas (FWCC), called representatives of eleven major Quaker organizations to a consultation on war taxes. That group noted that whereas the military draft impinges only on young men of draft age, the draft of our tax money to pay for war preparations applies to almost all of us. It was decided that an on-going committee should be formed. As a result, the Friends Committee on War Tax Concerns (FCWTC) began its work early in 1985. The Friends World Committee for Consultation affirmed sponsorship of that new group at its annual meeting in March, saying at the close of the Minute on sponsorship:

> Most important in our difficult concerns over war taxes is our finding God's will for us in this witness, and the resulting strong unity for our witness. That quality in the start of FCWTC has real promise for all of us.

Visiting Friends from other countries expressed urgent interest in the concern and a desire to cooperate with the FWCC.

The Friends Committee on War Tax Concerns has three programs under way. Study papers are being prepared on the various issues of war tax resistance that will be published in the same format and will constitute a guide book to be used for study and consultation. The subjects will cover war tax resistance's biblical background, Friends history, and spiritual and rational bases; and also legal and tax information and implications, the positions of other denominations, a bibliography on the concern, and some other topics.

Regional conferences are planned for in-depth exploration of the concern and for seeking for right leading as individuals and as a Society.

The third program relates to how this concern of conscience affects a Quaker organization in its function as an employer. It is required by law to withhold taxes on its employees' salaries, and it is placed in a quandary when some of its employees are religiously motivated war tax refusers who request their employer not to collect and pay war taxes. Almost all the Quaker organizations are struggling with this and many have determined to resist the onerous tax collection requirement. The FCWTC plans to hold a conference for employers, in co-sponsorship with the New Call to Peacemaking, thus involving the Brethren and the Mennonites. Thus, the FCWTC could become a clearinghouse for the sharing of experiences and information among the various peace employers on this important witness.

There are also several secular organizations that are performing useful services in the field of war tax resistance. Some are shown in the appendix to this article. The bibliography being published by the FCWTC lists all such organizations that we know of, as well as the description of their services and activities. Friends will be especially interested in the program of the National Campaign for a Peace Fund Tax. A number of legislators in both the Senate and the House are sponsoring a bill for conscientious objector status for tax money that has similarities to the C.O. provision in the Selective Service codes. When passed into law, this bill will allow the taxpayer to assign a portion of her or his taxes to programs for attaining peace rather than for military purposes.

FOUR PRINCIPLES OF WAR TAX RESISTANCE

For what reasons do war tax resisters take the civil disobedience action of refusing to pay taxes voluntarily for war preparation? I suggest there are four main pillars that support the basis of this witness.

1. The prime and controlling motivation for war tax resistance is a conscience-guided determination to refuse complicity with the evil of the war system. In the Richmond Declaration of Faith in 1887 is this statement:

> We feel bound explicitly to avow our unshaken persuasion that all war is utterly incompatible with the plain precepts of our divine Lord and Law-Giver, and the whole spirit of His Gospel, and that no plea of necessity or policy, however urgent and peculiar, can avail to release individuals or nations from the paramount allegiance which they owe to Him who hath said, "Love your enemies."

As an example of a contemporary expression, here is how Carrie and I began our first message to the IRS:

> Under the clear guidance of our conscience, and directed by our religious faith, we have come to the time when we can no longer pay that portion of our federal income tax that is used for military purpose—for the preparation for war and killing. As Christians and as members of the Religious Society of Friends we refuse to lend any support to the evil that is war.

2. The war preparations of our country and of other countries are illegal under international law, and we as citizens are guilty if we support the activity. May I again quote from our personal statement to the IRS:

> We believe that we are enjoined by international law from paying for the military budget that produces nuclear bombs which when used will kill millions of civilians and will destroy cities and vast areas of our earth. The indiscriminate destruction of cities which results from modern war is prima facie proof of war crimes, as defined by Principle VI of the Nuremberg Charter, and of crimes against humanity as defined in the Charter. Article VII provides that the individual is not free from responsibility for crimes of this type just because he was acting under orders from his government.

The United Nations by unanimous action adopted the Nuremberg Charter as proposed by the United States. Article VI of our Constitution established the primacy of international agreements in U.S. law. Other international treaties signed by the United States also prohibit the kind of war preparations in which our nation is engaged.

3. The insanity of the arms race is in itself a sufficient basis for taking civil disobedience action to oppose it. The staggering budget requests of the Pentagon are clothed in the gilt and tinsel of defense, but we know, in our innermost knowing, that weapons once built are ultimately used and that the arms race is a race to war. We and all humanity are living in the greatest insecurity, the most serious jeopardy, of all history. If radical changes are not made soon in international relationships, a major war will break out at some unplanned time and will escalate into a holocaust that destroys civilization. Our "defense" policies are irrational and insane as well as immoral. We must abolish war, not pay for it.

4. War tax resistance can be an effective method of opposing war. The military industrial complex that President Dwight Eisenhower warned about is sustained by and relies on our income tax payments. Patriots took tax resistance action at the founding of our nation when they staged the Boston Tea Party. The "defense establishment's" greatest vulnerability is its reliance on a continuous flow of income tax payments made by the "self-assessment" of citizens. The firm protest of the million war tax resisters now can overcome the dominance of the military in our nation's policies and set us and all the world on a new course.

A growing number of people of all faiths are coming to understand that war is a blasphemy against the divine will and a criminal act within human society. Each of us must struggle with the conscience question: "How long should I pay taxes that are used for war preparation?" In a paraphrase of Fox, the applicable response is, "Pay thy war taxes as long as thou canst."

SOME ORGANIZATIONS ON WAR TAX CONCERNS

Friends Committee on War Tax Concerns (FCWTC), P.O. Box 6441, Washington, D.C. 20009. 202–387–7635.
National Campaign for a Peace Tax Fund (NCPTF), Box 2121, Decatur Place, NW, Washington, D.C. 20008. 202–483–3751.
National War Tax Resistance Coordinating Committee (NWTRCC), Box 2236, East Patchogue, New York 11772. 516–654–8227.

War Resisters League (WRL)–East, 339 Lafayette, New York, NY 10012. 212–288–0540.

SOME SUGGESTED READINGS.

Durland, William, Ed. *People Pay for Peace: A Military Tax Refusal Guide*. Center on Law and Pacifism, Box 308, Cokedale, CO 81032.

Hedemann, Ed. *Guide to War Tax Resistance*. War Resisters League. See address above.

Kaufman, Donald. *The Tax Dilemma: Praying for Peace*. Scottdale, PA: Herald Press. The Mennonite approach.

MacKenzie, Fiona, Ed. *Paying for Peace: Conscientious Objection to Military Taxation*. Quaker Council for European Affairs, through the Friends Book Stores.

The Friends Committee on War Tax Concerns will have a series of pamphlets on war tax issues available in 1987.

SOME QUESTIONS FOR DISCUSSION

1. Do you feel that it is valid to claim that paying for the military system and its weapons is of a similar nature to serving in the military system and using its weapons? Why or why not?

2. How can we balance our responsibilities as citizens to pay our taxes for the beneficial services provided by the government with our responsibilities as people of faith to resist complicity with violence and war preparations?

3. How do you react to the quotation from *Faith and Practice:* "Friends do not see their governmental rulers as having unlimited authority, but give their ultimate allegiance to God"?

4. What experience (or experiences) have you had of coming into clarity on a concern of conscience and then being able to follow the guidance of that conscience in a changed course of action? Are you willing to share such an experience with others?

5. Are we willing to ask ourselves: "How long should we cooperate with the war system by paying taxes that are used for war preparation?"

ABOUT THE AUTHOR

Wallace Collett lives in Cincinnati and is a member of the Community Friends Meeting which is affiliated with both Wilmington and Ohio Valley Yearly Meetings. After teaching high school for a few years, he entered business. He is one of the founders of the Servomation Corporation, a national food service organization, and was chairman of its executive committee until his retirement in 1980. He is member of the Board of Haverford College, on the Board of Advisers of the Earlham School of Religion, and chair of the General Board of Pendle Hill. He was chair of the Wilmington College Board for ten years and of the American Friends Service Committee for eight years. He is active in organizations in his community and operates a farm near Wilmington. Currently he is clerk of the Friends Committee on War Tax Concerns.

Chapter 15

Sufferings and Sanctuary: Individual and Corporate Opportunities for Costly Discipleship

Peter Blood-Patterson

In his book on *The Cost of Discipleship*, Dietrich Bonhoeffer, the renowned German theologian executed by the Nazis, condemned faith which is based on cheap grace. To him cheap grace meant assuming that you will be saved if you believe in the right doctrines, worship in the right way, or are a member of the right religious group—without having to risk or sacrifice anything major in your day-to-day life. Paul communicated the same idea in Romans 12:2. "Adapt yourselves no longer to the pattern of this world, but let your minds be remade and your whole nature thus transformed. Then you will be able to discern the will of God, and to know what is good, acceptable, and perfect."

We do not have to be living in Nazi Germany or the Roman Empire to recognize that many things in the world around us are not according to God's plan. Any community that commits itself to trying to be totally obedient to God's hopes will find itself frequently in conflict with the culture and powers of this world. People of faith are continually forced to choose where their loyalty will ultimately lie: with worldly success, comfort, and authority—or with the authority of Christ and the Holy Spirit. Again and again throughout history communities of believers have had to face ridicule, ostracism, loss of property or advancement, imprisonment, exile, and even death for their efforts to live their lives in accordance with their beliefs.

HOLY OBEDIENCE IN HISTORY

The messages brought by the prophets of the Old Testament to the society they lived in were rarely welcomed. Many of those visionaries were severely persecuted for their courage in speaking the truth as they heard it. Those true prophets were explicitly contrasted with the false prophets who merely reassured those in power with words they wanted to hear.

Early Christians were separated from the communities around them by the economic sharing they practiced, their refusal to bear arms, their "unusual religious beliefs and practices" (there were rumors that they practiced cannibalism), and above all their refusal to participate in the Roman state religion. Putting "a pinch of incense on an altar to Caesar" was the ancient equivalent of a loyalty oath to the U.S. Constitution or pledging allegiance to the flag. The refusal of most Christians to carry out symbolic acts of loyalty to the secular rulers of the day was considered treasonous and led to the deaths of thousands of Christians in the Roman arenas.

Jesus himself was executed by the Roman state authorities on political rather than religious charges. If he had been prosecuted on religious grounds, his trial and punishment would have been left to Jewish religious leaders without Roman involvement, and the sentence would have been death by stoning rather than crucifixion. Both the Jewish religious establishment and the Roman government were right in considering the message of Jesus, Peter, and Paul to be revolutionary in its scope. The fact that the Emperor Constantine's policy of co-opting succeeded to a far greater extent than three centuries of repression and mass execution in destroying that message is a major tragedy for the Christian church to this day.

QUAKER SUFFERINGS IN THE PAST

The first generation of Quakers were persecuted for a variety of stands they felt compelled to take. Friends held open "nonconformist" worship services (that is, worship outside the established Anglican Church) when that was specifically prohibited by Parliament. They refused to pay tithes which were primitive income taxes used primarily to support the state church. They were also persecuted or prosecuted for blasphemy, refusing oaths (both loyalty oaths and oaths in court), refusing to pay "hat honor" to judges and other authorities, plain speech (refusing to use "honorifics" in addressing authorities or "social superiors"), interrupting religious services, and refusing to bear arms. Those actions led to loss of property and social position, imprisonment under conditions that led to thousands of deaths, and, in a very few cases, to the death penalty.

After 1688 the persecution of Friends sharply decreased. Since that time Friends have been much more likely to face ridicule or economic loss than imprisonment for their peculiar beliefs, and in many periods Friends have faced few such consequences. They have run afoul of the law or community standards primarily during times of war (e.g., if they refused to hire a substitute to the draft during the Civil War) or of major social conflict over an ethical issue, such as slavery. Although modern Friends take pride in our forebears' early opposition to slavery, it is significant that only a small minority of Quakers were involved in abolitionist work or the Underground Railroad, and that such Friends were more often criticized or merely tolerated for those stands than supported by the wider community of Quakers at that time.

In this century American Quakers have served prison sentences mainly for violating conscription laws. No provisions were made for conscientious objection during World War I. A few of the first Friends "called up" during that conflict were inducted into the army against their will and initially threatened with being shot when they refused to carry out any duties in their army units. That provided one rare instance where being told you were being sent to prison could (and was) considered good news.

In World War II the Peace Churches succeeded in convincing Congress to exempt religious pacifists from military service. Hence, conscientious objectors were sent to work in isolated Civilian Public Service (CPS) camps. Some draft-age Friends felt that the very system of conscription and CPS camps was so involved in war-making that they could not in conscience participate in it. Nearly all the hundred or so Friends taking that position spent several years in federal prisons. That was a difficult position to take since many Quakers viewed those "non-cooperators" as embarrassing extremists who endangered the newly won concession for Friends of exemption from the military.

A number of Quakers, most of them students at William Penn College in Iowa, similarly refused to register when the first peacetime draft was instituted in 1948. During the 1950s and 1960s most Friends felt comfortable cooperating with the draft law. During the Vietnamese war, however, the moral implications of any complicity with the military hit much harder. Many Quaker young men ended up, as a result, joining the draft resistance movement, returning their draft cards to the government and refusing alternative service. Although many more Friends took that position than during World War I, only a hundred or so were ever imprisoned at that time, due to much lower prosecution rates.

SUFFERINGS AMONG FRIENDS TODAY

Some young Friends today are facing imprisonment for refusing to register under the U.S. draft law. A new cost of this stand has been the loss of federal loans for higher education. Some Quaker colleges and yearly meetings have made special provisions to assist such young men caught in a bind between their consciences and their thirst for learning.

A similar stand taken by a much larger and growing number of Friends is war tax resistance. These Quakers feel that they are unable in conscience to pay part or all of their federal income or phone taxes because the major portion of those taxes go to preparation for war. That position is similar to the opposition of early Friends to paying tithes. In almost all cases such tax refusal has led to the seizure of bank accounts, salaries, or property rather than imprisonment. Many Yearly Meetings have minuted their support for those taking this stand.

Many Friends work hard to change government policies they feel are contrary to Quaker beliefs. Many, of course, work for such changes through legal means. Some Friends, however, have felt called to carry out acts of civil disobedience because of their sense of urgency in ending policies they feel are deeply wrong. An example would be the holding of a sit-in or a pray-in at a plant manufacturing nuclear warheads. Friends usually insist on the need to participate in such actions peacefully, openly, with a friendly spirit toward those being "opposed" (or, more accurately, being reached out toward), and with a willingness to pay the legal consequences for their actions. Those are basic principles of nonviolent, direct action developed by Gandhi, Dorothy Day, Martin Luther King, Jr., Cesar Chavez, and others.

Children, too, are often presented with difficult decisions because of their beliefs. School-age Friends have often been subjected to ostracism for refusing to pledge allegiance to the flag, to purchase war bonds, to participate in civil defense drills, to take part in lotteries, or to join in racial or ethnic putdowns or harassments. A child can be ridiculed by peers for simple acts of faith and for differences in Quaker practice. As they think over their basic beliefs, some Quaker children decide that it is wrong to eat meat; or they may come to other conclusions which may seem strange to their parents. When children are wrestling with questions of this kind, they deserve tenderness and support from their families and Meetings in their efforts to hear and obey God's voice.

INDIVIDUAL VERSUS CORPORATE OBEDIENCE

Is the kind of faithfulness that leads people into conflict with the surrounding society ultimately an individual concern or an issue with which Quaker groups as a whole need to wrestle? That has been a major source of controversy in many Monthly Meetings, Yearly Meetings, and Quaker organizations in recent years. Some Friends suggest that because of our belief in the Inward Light (the direct inspiration of God in each person's heart), matters in this area must be left to individual conscience.

Clearly, powerful witness to the world begins, inside and outside the Religious Society of Friends, with individual leadings. A central idea, however, in our Judeo-Christian tradition has been the recognition that God speaks and acts through gathered communities of believers rather than simply through individuals in isolation. The leadings of individual Friends have always been tested on the threshing floor of the local Meeting, with some callings supported and others rejected by the group, either explicitly or informally. That was in fact a major reason why our structure of Monthly, Quarterly, and Yearly Meetings was established originally. Some concerns which began with individuals have eventually been adopted by Yearly Meetings as expectations for all members. For example, John Woolman's personal belief that Friends should not hold slaves was eventually incorporated into the *Disciplines* of virtually every Yearly Meeting.

In fact, no person engaged in acts of costly discipleship can survive long without the active love and support of a community. It is in the community of believers that we receive affirmation that we are not crazy or foolish or self-destructive in what we are doing—affirmation from those we love and respect that we are, instead, acting courageously to push forward the frontiers of God's kingdom in this world. Only communities acting together will have the staying power and wisdom to be able to bring about major changes where evil still holds sway over the political, economic, or cultural institutions around us.

MEETING SUPPORT FOR INDIVIDUAL ACTIONS

The group in London Yearly Meeting responsible for making decisions between annual sessions (called Representative Meeting in many Yearly Meetings in the United States) is known still as the Meeting for Sufferings. As the name implies, that group was originally set up to collect information and to organize support for Friends suffering, imprisonment, or other hardships for acts of conscience. Fox's entire structure of church government was organized in large part to assist in such support, as well as to test the individual leadings of Friends. A third key function of that structure was to uphold certain standards of separateness from the world in individual action, including areas such as mixed marriages, plain dress, and service in the military.

There are many ways in which a Monthly Meeting or a Yearly

Meeting can support the leadings of its members. Those include:

1. *Forming a clearness committee* to meet with a Friend or a family and provide confirmation that a leading is "from God." Meetings may at times ask all of their members facing a certain ethical challenge, such as the draft or war taxes, to meet with a Meeting committee and search together for what is right.
2. *Writing a Minute of support* which can be forwarded to other Friends groups, government leaders, judges, the Internal Revenue Service, and the mass media.
3. *Giving moral and spiritual support* can be especially critical for Friends in prison whose emotional staying power relies heavily on hearing clearly the message that "You are not alone; we are with you in our hearts."
4. *Providing practical and financial help,* including food, childcare, and other assistance when a member is imprisoned, suffering economic hardship for his/her actions, or away from home carrying out a leading. Some Yearly Meetings have special Suffering Funds which assist with bail, legal fees, and other expenses associated with acts of conscience.
5. *"Releasing" a Friend* where a Monthly, Quarterly, or Yearly Meeting decides to raise funds to enable a member to pursue full-time a particular leading on behalf of the Meeting.

CORPORATE ACTION BY THE MEETING

The boundary line between Meeting support for individuals and corporate action by the Meeting is not a sharp one. In the past, particular stands that a Meeting felt strongly about led to counseling ("eldering") or even expulsion ("disownment") for members who refused to follow the Meeting's guidance. Today Meetings are usually reluctant to act this forcefully, even on such clear-cut and basic principles as participation in the military. Many Quakers, however, feel that the pendulum has swung too far towards individualism and that our corporate life and witness as Meetings has been weakened as a result.

Merely advocating a position or supporting individual action may in some periods be illegal. Some English Friends were arrested during World War II for public efforts urging men to consider being conscientious objectors. Some Minutes of Support have been worded to express the Meeting's feeling that its member is acting "on their behalf" in an act of civil disobedience, implying shared complicity of the group in such conscientious lawbreaking.

Some Yearly Meetings and Quaker organizations have decided they cannot honor IRS liens on the salaries of employees who are war tax evaders. In some cases that position had been extended to ceasing income tax withholding for employees who request that for reasons of conscience. Taking the latter action represents an act of civil disobedience by the entire employing group.

Yearly and Monthly Meetings have officially endorsed public witnesses on many occasions. For instance, the American Friends Service Committee and several Yearly Meetings participated in sending humanitarian aid to all sides in the Vietnam War, even though that was against United States law. In theory such corporate acts of civil disobedience could lead to prosecution of the clerk or other officers of the Meeting, seizure of group property, or even loss of tax-exempt status. To my knowledge, none of those has occurred to Quaker groups in modern times.

Furthermore, many Quaker groups have wrestled with the ethical implications of investments owned by the group. That has frequently led to decisions to divest of holdings which are felt to be contrary to the beliefs of Friends, such as investments in companies which carry out military research or arms production, sell or promote alcohol or tobacco, or carry on operations in South Africa.

In the last several years many Monthly Meetings have wrestled with a new form of corporate response to wrong—declaring sanctuary for Central American refugees. That particular form of corporate witness is explored in more detail below.

THE HISTORICAL AND BIBLICAL ROOTS OF SANCTUARY

The idea of offering shelter or protection to the persecuted is firmly rooted in both biblical and Quaker history. The prophet Isaiah admonished the people of Israel to "Shelter the homeless, do not betray the fugitives; let the homeless people of Moab find refuge among you; hide them from the despoiler" (Isa. 16:3–4). Jesus affirmed this call with the words, "I was a stranger and you welcomed me" (Matt. 25:35).

Over the centuries Friends have taken those admonitions seriously. Penn's "Holy Experiment" in Pennsylvania was established in large part to provide a safe haven for people persecuted for their beliefs, a majority of whom were not Quakers. Then and since then, Friends have frequently attempted to intervene with the U.S. government to prevent wrongdoing toward native Americans. Later, many individual Friends sheltered and transported runaway slaves even though that action involved disobeying federal law and the risk of imprisonment. In the

1930s and 1940s Quakers sought, largely unsuccessfully, to intervene with Hitler on behalf of Jews in Germany and in the territories overrun by his armed forces. In that same period individual Friends in Europe hid and aided Jews covertly.

During the Vietnam War some Friends Meetings declared themselves "sanctuaries" as a symbolic expression of support for young men facing arrest and trial for draft refusal. Friends in Canada were actively involved in welcoming and supporting U.S. emigres who fled from imprisonment in the United States for refusal to fight in Vietnam.

Recently, a number of Friends have risked their lives by traveling to rural areas of Nicaragua with an ecumenical group called Witness for Peace. Their hope has been that the physical presence of North Americans in those villages would lessen the number of attacks there by U.S.-backed guerillas.

THE REFUGEES "AT OUR DOOR"

In recent years over half a million Salvadorans and Guatemalans have fled to the United States from the violent civil wars going on in their homelands, which include the indiscriminate bombing of civilian areas and the widespread operation of death squads. The U.S. Immigration and Naturalization Service claims that those people are here for economic reasons alone and rejects nearly all asylum applications from countries friendly with our federal government.

Even a few minutes spent with a refugee living in Sanctuary at a Friends Meeting elicits convincing, spine-chilling, heartrending testimony of the terror which many refugees feel at the possibility of deportation. Most such refugees living in Sanctuaries have had close friends and family members murdered by death squads, personal torture experiences, near brushes with death, or all of the above. Death squads are paramilitary groups closely associated with the state security apparatus who have killed thousands of church workers, literacy educators, community activists, union leaders, and other people in El Salvador and Guatemala considered as indirect threats to those in power. Many refugees fled their countries only after their names appeared on death lists or their immediate co-workers were murdered.

The U.S. Refugee Act of 1980 was specifically passed to prevent the deportation of refugees from this country in just such situations. People involved in the sanctuary movement feel that our government is flagrantly violating its own laws in this respect for political reasons—i.e., reluctance to acknowledge publicly the widespread human rights violations in countries allied with our government. These

Friends, and others, therefore feel that they are not only obeying God's requirements of them as they understand them, but U.S. law as well. In spite of this, Friends involved in the sanctuary movement can be charged with "harboring illegal aliens." Jim Corbett of the Pima Friends Meeting in Arizona was tried with ten others in Tucson in 1986 for such charges, and eventually acquitted.

SANCTUARY AS CORPORATE SHELTER FOR THE PERSECUTED

Corbett has defined Sanctuary as a "congregationally-declared protective community with people whose basic human rights are being violated by government officials." That means that a Church or a Friends Meeting acts corporately to provide physical and symbolic shelter to individuals and/or families whose lives are in danger because of our government's policies.

The current "Sanctuary Movement" began in 1982 in Tucson, Arizona. Quakers there have been heavily involved from the beginning. People who had been assisting large numbers of refugees privately for some time felt the need to take action in a public way and as congregations. Among the over three hundred congregations in the United States which have declared Sanctuary as of June 1986, Quaker and Catholic groups are the most numerous, with about forty-five to fifty each.

It is clear that Sanctuary stands squarely in the Quaker tradition of shelter and concern for the persecuted. The biggest difference between Sanctuary and most of the actions described earlier is that it represents a uniquely corporate response of a Monthly Meeting as a whole. That is true even though the bulk of the day-to-day work, financial support, and legal risks are sure to be carried more by some than by others in a Monthly Meeting. It is also an unusual witness to the extent to which it combines personal religious response to individuals in danger with public witness to alter government policies which threaten these and many others in the first place.

Since Sanctuary is a corporate action by its very nature, it can only be taken with the support of the entire Meeting. Some Meetings have taken up to two years to reach unity on this action. Obviously such an issue can evoke strong convictions and feelings on both sides. Great patience and tenderness has often been required in the process of attempting to hear what God is asking a Meeting to do.

Once unity is reached, welcoming a refugee or a family into the lives of the Meeting takes a substantial commitment of financial support, caring, and, above all, time. Since the refugees may be arrested at any moment, it is crucial to the concept of a sheltering community for a member of the Meeting (or of a supportive neighboring congregation) to be physically present with them at all times.

On the other hand, Meetings which have taken this stand describe the rich impact of their action on the life of the Meetings. That impact includes a deepened sense of community and connectedness within the group, a fresh and powerful vocal ministry, the attraction of new members and attenders, and the sense of hope and challenge gained from growing close to the refugees. Friends have also discovered deep new bonds with members of other faiths in their area.

Here is a typical Minute of a Monthly Meeting on Sanctuary for refugees. It was recorded in October 1985 by the Concord Monthly Meeting of Philadelphia Yearly Meeting and reads as follows:

> Concord Monthly Meeting of the Religious Society of Friends offers sanctuary for refugees who are fleeing death or persecution in their native countries.
>
> We extend this offer in order that our actions come into better harmony with the teachings of Jesus of Nazareth, with Friends traditional beliefs and practices, and with our own consciences.
>
> At this time we intend to join with the Sanctuary Movement to aid Central American refugees.
>
> We mean by this action to honor the United States Refugee Act of 1980, and we call upon our government to honor its own law and to make our whole country a sanctuary.
>
> Our Meetinghouse stands upon the main line of the Underground Railroad of slavery days and we are proud of the part that our earlier members played in carrying slaves to freedom. We hope to find within ourselves the courage and energy to play a similar role today.
>
> We are conscious of our smallness of numbers and we invite our neighbors of all religious faiths, or of none, to assist us in carrying out this commitment to justice and freedom.
>
> Because we believe that all places on earth are equally holy, our sanctuary will comprise not only our Meetinghouse, but also the homes of our members and of any who may join us in this witness.

Penn's statement, "No cross, no crown," applies to faith communities as well as to individuals. We must be prepared to offer something real, something substantial of ourselves as a Meeting, to be willing to sacrifice and risk in major ways, if we are to continue growing and flourishing as a people of God. Offering Sanctuary is one way many Monthly Meetings can begin to do this.

SOME SUGGESTED READINGS

MacEoin, Gary, *Sanctuary:A Resource Guide for Understanding and Participation in the Central American Refugees Struggle.* Harper and Row, 1985.

Meltzer, Milton. *Ain't Gonna Study War No More: The Story of America's Peace Seekers.* Harper and Row, 1985.

Selley, Robert. *Handbook of Nonviolence.* Lawrence Hill, Lakeville Press, 1986.

Sider, Ronald and Richard Taylor. *Nuclear Holocaust and Christian Hope.* Intervarsity Press, 1982.

War Resisters League. *Guide to War Tax Resistance.* War Resisters League, 1981.

SOME QUESTIONS FOR DISCUSSION

1. What powerful winds of faith led thousands of people freely to join the ranks of early Christians, Anabaptists, and Friends, knowing that that decision would lead to certain persecution and very possible death?
2. What stories of struggles and faithfulness strike the deepest chord in you?
3. What things that are happening in your local community, state, or the wider world seem to you to be deeply in conflict with God's hopes? Are you in some ways responsible for, involved in, or benefiting from such wrongs?
4. What members of your Monthly Meeting or Yearly Meeting are involved in acts of costly discipleship? How does what they are doing make you feel? Are they being supported by your Meeting? If so, how? If not, why not?
5. Does your Meeting make difficult decisions through prayerful waiting for God's voice? What issue would it take to challenge your Meeting into corporate action: a request to submit the names of Meeting members of Jewish ancestry to the Nazis? a demand that the picture of a dictator be hung on the Meetinghouse wall?

6. Who is "the stranger at the door" or "the least of these" in your community that Jesus is talking about in Matthew 25:40? How is your Meeting a shelter for the persecuted?
7. What effect might it have on your monthly meeting to carry out a major act of costly discipleship as a Meeting community?

ABOUT THE AUTHOR

Peter Blood-Patterson grew up in the Lake Erie Yearly Meeting and is currently a member of the Media Monthly Meeting of Philadelphia Yearly Meeting—a Meeting which declared Sanctuary in June 1986. Peter is a nurse and family therapist, currently attending a training program in spiritual guidance at the Shalem Institute for Spiritual Formation, in Washington, D.C. He is a song leader and the editor of two popular group-singing songbooks—*Winds of the People* and *Rise Up Singing*. The Ann Arbor, Michigan Monthly Meeting held a sanctuary for him at the time of his arrest for refusing alternative service during the Vietnam War. A collection of letters and questionnaires he received from many Quaker draft resisters is in the archives of the Peace Collection of the Swarthmore College Library.

Chapter 16

Toward a More Just and Humane United States Society

Jim Lenhart and *Asia Bennett*

...If these pure principles have their place in us and are brought forth by faithfulness, by obedience, [and] by practice, the difficulties and doubts that we may have to surmount will be easily conquered. There will be a power greater than these. Let it be called the Great Spirit of the Indian, the Quaker "inward light" of George Fox, the "Blessed Mary, mother of Jesus" of the Catholic, or "Brahma—the Hindu's God"; they will all be one and there will come to be such faith and such liberty as shall redeem the world.[1]

It has been more than one hundred years since Lucretia Mott interpreted the spiritual basis of her work for equal rights for women, blacks, and others in the eloquent passage quoted above, showing the connection between the life of the Spirit and the efforts Friends and others were making in the late nineteenth century to achieve a more just and humane society in the United States, and, in the process, helping to "redeem the world."

A century later, the roots of war and injustice still remain intertwined with the American way of life, and workers for peace and justice are as misunderstood, mistrusted, and maligned as was Lucretia Mott. Yet who among us can doubt, even in the shadow of nuclear destruction and national dehumanization, that at least some progress has been made on some fronts of human endeavor.

SOME EXAMPLES OF PROGRESS IN RECENT DECADES

Among the many examples of progress in recent decades in creating a more just and humane society in the United States are the following:

1. Racism as an institution has been greatly weakened, if not eliminated, and blacks and other minorities have made real economic, political, and educational gains. Much remains to be done, but much has also been accomplished.
2. Sexism, in all its ramifications and permutations, is being exposed through the courage and faithfulness of a relatively small number of American women crusaders, including many Friends. Their efforts need more understanding, acceptance, and support before true and lasting equality between the sexes will be achieved, but we are closer to it today than we have ever been.
3. Elimination of war and the achievement of a truly peaceful society are being envisioned and seriously discussed among small groups of concerned people who are specifying what practical steps must be taken now to get us to a warless world in, say, fifty years. To quote Lao-tze, "The journey of three thousand miles begins with a single step."
4. The American work place is now safer and workers better protected by health, safety, unemployment, and collective bargaining provisions than heretofore. Child labor has been eliminated and the connection between decent work and wages and the overall health and well-being of U.S. society is being clearly seen and articulated by economists, social planners, and others.
5. The level of health and wellness among U.S. citizens is among the highest in the world. Medical science and modern sanitation and disease prevention practices have eliminated many illnesses and extended the lives of millions.
6. More and better education is available for more people—at all ages and levels of development. Our era of high technology and computerization offer both great challenge and great opportunity for the education of the whole person, throughout a whole lifetime.

These are only a few examples of progress made during the past several decades. Others include an emerging concern for our natural environment, accompanied by steps to restore a deep and nurturing respect for and relationship with Mother Earth; higher standards of living in all aspects of life for more Americans; and greater sensitivity to and more provisions for those among us who are mentally, emotionally, or physically handicapped.

SOME CURRENT PROBLEMS IN THE UNITED STATES

George Fox saw "an ocean of light" flowing over "an ocean of darkness" that he had seen in his own experience, and we American

Friends certainly can see both light and dark in our own individual, group, and national lives. Alongside the gains and progress we have made stand enormous and difficult problems:

1. Incredible and pervasive poverty exists in the midst of plenty. While the number of millionaires and the income levels of most U.S. citizens increase steadily, some 35 million people in our country (most of them women and children) live below the poverty level and have little effective way of rising above it. Linked to pervasive poverty is hunger, malnutrition, high child mortality, and spiritual deprivation suffered by millions because of the nightmare reality of life in the United States.
2. Deep trouble is being experienced by the basic unit of our society—the family. Half of all marriages end in divorce, millions of children are being raised in single-parent situations, and the combinations of guilt, anger, grief, and emotional trauma experienced by many members of broken families has an unseen but powerful effect on all levels of society.
3. Increased use of alcohol, drugs, and other mind-altering substances, and an often related increase in crime of all kinds in all levels and sectors of American society, are approaching a crisis level. The complexity, cost, and consequences of this growing national dilemma and the bulging prisons, ruined lives, and loss of human energies and potentials that result from drugs and crime are truly a national tragedy. They amount to a war against ourselves.
4. Urban problems such as housing, schools, employment and declining tax bases vie for national attention with a steady decline in that most basic of all American institutions—the family farm.

Deepening and complicating all these problems, and adding many of its own, is the ongoing and increasing U.S. expenditure for weapons, armaments and other means, methods, and materials for achieving "peace through strength." Perhaps as a recent college graduate student said in her commencement speech, "We look back on historical periods and are amazed because people then were afraid of darkness itself. We think they were ignorant and primitive. I have a hope that some day people will look back on our period of history and be amazed because we are in fear of one another. I hope some day that such fear is seen as primitive."[2]

HOPE NOURISHED BY MILLIONS

Yet Friends continue to follow the vow of the Psalmist to "hope continually." Like Albert Camus, we believe that hope "is awakened, revived, nourished by millions of solitary individuals whose deeds and works every day negate frontiers and the crudest implications of history. As a result, there shines forth fleetingly the ever threatened truth that each and every man, on the foundation of his own sufferings and joys, builds for all."[3]

The history of American Quakerism and American life is filled with examples of individuals taking action in response to their inner concerns or promptings and making a difference in the lives of their fellow human beings. Sometimes that difference becomes immense. Jim Corbett's act of taking Central American refugees into his home in Tucson, Arizona, has helped lead to the creation of the modern Underground Railroad, the growing nationwide sanctuary movement, and the safe passage of thousands of men, women, and children to freedom and new lives in Canada.

Similarly, the concerns of John Woolman and Anthony Benezet and the actions they took in the mid 1700s to convince Friends that slavery was wrong led a hundred years later to the Emancipation Proclamation. And Lucretia Mott's pioneering work in the 1800s helped start the still-continuing struggle to open American society for the full participation of women.

Such examples are exceptions, however, to the general work of Friends, which tends to take place in smaller, less historic, but no less important dimensions. It is in the home and family, in the neighborhood and school, the Church and Meeting, where most Friends focus their energies and activities. And it is there they become, in Harold Goddard's words, "leaveners." As he wrote when he was professor of English at Swarthmore College, "Leaveners are in a secret conspiracy of goodness against existing society." The beauty of it, as Goddard went on to point out, is that "Everyone, anyone, can enlist in this conspiracy" and help transform society—and themselves.[4]

SOME QUERIES FOR INDIVIDUALS

As part of this transformation process, some Friends have examined their personal lifestyles, eating and buying habits and patterns, family budget and general priorities, and have decided to make some changes. Is this something you, your family or friends might consider doing?

Many Friends have long been involved in education, both public and private. Are there things you could be doing to help the school system with which you are most concerned to better educate its students in regard to some of the problems in the United States?

Are you helping your children and/or grandchildren envision and help prepare to create a more just and humane society through their educational, vocational, and social activities? Are barriers and divisions between races and classes of people being lowered or eliminated by the way you and your family are living and relating to others?

Are you witnessing to your concerns for a more just, humane, and peaceful society in whatever ways are appropriate for you? Are you communicating with others so that the "conspiracy of goodness" gains more recruits and not more opponents?

Are you involving Friends and your Church or Meeting in these and other areas of your personal life and witness?

That last query focuses on the link between individual and corporate action that has been an important part of Quaker social concerns since the first days of our religious society. The Meeting for Worship and the Meeting for Business once were the testing grounds where personal concerns were brought forward and shared, and if the Meeting united in support, the individual Friend acted on his or her concern; if not, no action was taken.

TOWARD A RENEWING RELATIONSHIP

That testing process and the benefits it produces for both individual Friends and the Meeting have been greatly modified through the years, and Friends now channel many of their activities and find collective support in many other ways and means. Yet the potential remains great for Friends and their Church or Meeting to nurture, deepen, and strengthen both their own relationship and the effectiveness of their actions through a process which always holds the promise of creating between the individual and the group what Thomas Kelly called "The Blessed Community." In that community horizontal relationships between people are combined and transformed into vertical relationships with the Divine, a relationship which at its center renews, in Kelly's words and in the experiences of many Friends and other religious people, "our life and courage and commitment and love."[5] The work among and between Friends, their Churches and Meetings, and the outside world takes many forms, but at its best it is rooted in a sense that Something or Someone greater is working through us, through others, and through time itself to continue the very process of creation.

The practical result of this process may be the use of the Meeting-house or Church by various groups. Or it may require the Meeting to examine whether it is part of the problem or the solution to such things as racism, sexism, apartheid, the military-industrial complex, discrimination against minorities, or the appropriate use of energy, money, or time. These are not easy questions to face, to discuss clearly and sensitively, and on which to reach consensus. Yet they challenge us in our day, as they challenged Lucretia Mott, to bring forth "pure principles" by "faithfulness, by obedience, by practice...."

This combination of faithfulness, obedience, and practice produces an amazing variety of responses. Some Friends Churches in California, for example, have gained a large percentage of Hispanic or Southeast Asian members and attenders as Friends reach out to their communities. In New York and other urban areas, Meetinghouses and Churches become soup kitchens, homes and shelters for the homeless, or places of sanctuary for refugees. What are some Meetings or Churches in your area doing for others?

Larger groups and associations of Quakers likewise respond in various ways to human needs. The Evangelical Friends Alliance has formed an emergency relief unit to aid victims of disasters. The Friends United Meeting has developed a series of volunteer service projects. Other Friends and Quaker groups have joined in the Habitat for Humanity, the Heifer Project, and many other efforts to provide better housing and living conditions in the United States and abroad. What are some other efforts that you and your Quaker group could consider supporting?

"TO TRY WHAT LOVE WILL DO"

The largest and best known group effort by Friends and others to work effectively for a more just, humane, and peaceful society in the United States and throughout the world has been and remains the American Friends Service Committee (AFSC). Formed in 1917 to provide "a service of love in wartime," the AFSC has been for almost seventy-five years a collective, constructive, sometimes controversial, and always conscientious, attempt, in William Penn's words, "to try what Love will do."

At the heart of the AFSC's philosophy and program is

> ...a belief in this infinite worth and equality of each human being. This belief leads the AFSC to search for creative ways to challenge injustice and war. In communities throughout the country, the AFSC works with people to bring an end to poverty, exclusion, and denial of recognition and rights.[6]

By its very nature, this work sometimes produces controversy and confrontation between the AFSC and those who hold economic, political, social, and even religious power. This matter of controversy should come as no surprise to Friends, whose founder was beaten, imprisoned, and almost killed; or to other Christians whose founder *was* killed for putting his faith into practice. At its heart, that is what the AFSC is—faith put into practice:

1. Faith in a basic and inherent sense of justice puts AFSC staff people into the fields and farms of southern California to work with and support migrant workers and their families. Many of those people have crossed the U.S. border from Mexico without proper documents and are willing to put up with often incredible living conditions so they can remain hidden and invisible while making a small amount of money to have a slightly better life. An important aspect of the AFSC's work is to increase public understanding and awareness of the causes and nature of Mexican migration northward. A question for Friends to ponder might be whether there is any fundamental difference between what motivates Mexicans and what motivated early Americans to come to, explore, and open our country.

2. Faith in the hope and desire of all peoples to live in peace and to resolve differences puts AFSC people into a program to bring citizens of the United States and the Soviet Union together for seminars, discussions, visits, and friendly, open exchanges. The goal is to defuse hostility and promote reconciliation by helping individuals in the United States and the USSR and other Eastern Bloc countries to understand each other's perspectives and to appreciate and respect each other as people. The AFSC's East-West program also provides educational materials and resources for Americans who are interested in learning more about the Soviet Union or who want to reach out to the Soviet people in other ways. Would you and your Quaker group benefit by discussing what you really know about the Soviet Union and its various ethnic peoples?

3. Faith in the abilities of local people to be able to identify and deal with their own problems, if they have access to adequate resources, has put the AFSC into the programs which address housing and safe haven in communities from Maine to Florida and from the Canadian border to the Rio Grande. Native Americans in South Dakota, the Pacific Northwest, and Maine are helping to deal with problems ranging from poor nutrition to a life expectancy of only forty-five years. Working side by side with Native Americans and learning to understand and respect their values, culture, way of life, and spirituality is a Quaker experience that goes back to William

Penn and John Woolman, and today is being carried on by Friends in Iowa, Oklahoma, Philadelphia, and other places, as well as through AFSC programs. Do you and other Friends know what life is really like for most Native Americans?

4. Faith in the willingness and ability of the American people to respond and correct injustices once they understand them, puts AFSC people into programs that raise the level of awareness of what is happening:

— to undocumented and other farm workers in Florida and elsewhere in the United States.

— to mistreated Haitian refugees regarding what they need to improve their lives and how Friends can help them empower themselves.

— to the Kanjobal Indian people who have fled to Florida from Guatemala and who need to be defined and treated as political refugees and given asylum.

— generally to most poor and powerless people in the United States, and why it is absolutely right and essential for the AFSC and other Friends to continue "to speak truth to power" on their behalf.

Some of these AFSC programs are relatively new, but many have roots in the 1940s and 1950s and demonstrate the commitment of the Service Committee "to stay with people and concerns for a long term and to work on projects even where quick solutions are not apparent." What other Quaker work over the years provides examples that some problems of peace and justice are long-term but eventually can be solved?

THE SEEDS OF WAR

A concern behind the work of AFSC and many other Friends over the years is to identify and deal with root causes of problems. Thus John Woolman challenged Friends in the 1700s to examine their holdings and possessions to see whether the seeds of war had their roots in these material things. That connection between economics and the social and political order which flows from and supports the material values on which American society is based continues to challenge and inspire Friends to seek alternative ways of living.

Some Friends and the AFSC, for example, were instrumental in starting such intentional communities as Celo in North Carolina and the Movement for a New Society in Philadelphia and other U.S. cities. A Quaker Society for Economic Democracy has recently emerged in the

United States, patterned after a similar group in London Yearly Meeting. From time to time working parties in Yearly Meetings attempt to help Friends clarify issues and reach decisions about more equitable ways to handle economic and material questions. Often those attempts stretch Friends to uncomfortable limits before they are ready or able to respond adequately and appropriately.

On a more personal level, many individual Friends have tried to examine their own lives, to involve their Meetings in looking into matters and questions of economics, and to carry forward what the Friends World Committee for Consultation calls the Right Sharing of World Resources.

This area of life, along with the ongoing problems of peace, justice, and making the United States a more humane society, will provide Friends with stimulation, challenge, and opportunity aplenty, to say nothing of "doubts and difficulties"—to last into the twenty-first century and beyond.

As Friends continue to try to create a more just and humane U.S. society, may we heed Thomas Kelly's call of "living by a vow of perpetual obedience to the Inner Voice, in the world—yet not of the world—ready to go the second mile, obedient as a shadow, sensitive as a shadow, selfless as a shadow." Such bands of humble prophets can recreate the Religious Society of Friends and the Christian church and "shake the countryside for ten miles around."[7]

It is those "solitary individuals," to use Camus' image, "whose deeds and works every day negate frontiers and the crudest implications of history," as well as the "bands of humble prophets" among us who are creating a more just and humane society by the way they live and move and have their being. It is to them, most of whom will never be mentioned in any book, any time, that this chapter is dedicated. May they continue to find hope, strength, and courage, to persevere by knowing from their own experience that:

> Religion is the core and fabric of life. It is not a creed; it has nothing to do with churches and gatherings and doctrines and sanctity....It is the quality of our life's texture; it is the spontaneity and disciplines of grace; the way we let somebody pass us in a crowded bus; the force of our affirmation.[8]

And may they—and we—have this kind of faith:

> The world can't be made over in a day. Why can't it? Owing to something in the nature of man? Yes. And what is that

something? More than anything else, I venture to say it is the belief that the world cannot be made over in a day—a belief the evidence for which, to any one man, consists in the general prevalence of that belief among other men. Justification by —unfaith! If the world were inhabited by men and women who had faith to believe that the world could be made over—with poverty and war, for instance, eradicated—if not in a day, then in a decade, or even in a dozen decades, who can doubt that it would be made over in that time?...How much more in keeping with the spirit of Jesus it would be to affirm with William James, as he speaks of the faith that creates its own verification: "This world *is* good, we must say, since it is what we make it—and we shall make it good."9

NOTES

1. Margaret Hope Bacon, *Lucretia Mott Speaking* (Wallingford, PA: Pendle Hill, 1980), pp. 26-27.

2. Meaning Ilene Lenhart, Unpublished speech (Northhampton MA: Smith College School of Social Work, 1987).

3. Albert Camus, *Resistance, Rebellion, and Death* (New York: Random House, 1974), p. 272.

4. Harold Clark Goddard, *Alphabet of the Imagination* (Atlantic Highlands, NJ: Humanities Press. 1974), pp. 10-11.

5. Thomas R. Kelly, *A Testament of Devotion* (New York: Harper and Row, 1941), p. 87.

6. _____, *Eyes on the Border* (Philadelphia, PA: American Friends Service Committee, 1985), p. 8.

7. Kelly, p. 73.

8. John P. Hogan. *One Man's Joy* (London: Friends Home Service Committee, 1975), p. 15.

9. Goddard, pp. 39-40.

SOME SUGGESTED READINGS

Bryn, Severyn. *Quaker Testimonies and Economic Alternatives.* Wallingford, PA: Pendle Hill, 1980.

Garver, Newton. *Jesus, Jefferson, and the Task of Friends.* Wallingford, PA: Pendle Hill, 1980.

Swayne, Kingdom W. *Stewardship of Wealth.* Wallingford, PA: Pendle Hill, 1982.

Wattenberg, Ben. *The Good News Is the Bad News Is Wrong.* New York: Simon and Schuster, 1984.

Write to the following organizations for their annual reports and other pertinent materials:

The American Friends Service Committee (AFSC), 1501 Cherry Street, Philadelphia, PA 19102.
The Friends Committee on National Legislation (FCNL), 245 Second Street NE, Washington, D.C. 20002.
Movement for a New Society, Box 1922, Cambridge, MA 02238.
Quaker Society for Economic Democracy, 321 Sterling Place, Brooklyn, NY 11238.

SOME QUESTIONS FOR DISCUSSION

1. What other improvements in U.S. society in recent years would you add to those mentioned in this chapter?
2. Which three problems would you select as the most important facing the United States today? Why?
3. What has your Quaker Church or Meeting done in recent years to contribute to a more just and humane U.S. society? What more might you do now?
4. What work of the American Friends Service Committee or other Quaker organizations is most relevant to the concerns of Friends in your Meeting or Church? How can you do more in carrying that work forward?

ABOUT THE AUTHORS

Jim Lenhart is a former editor of the *Friends Journal* and Associate Executive Secretary for Information and Interpretation of the American Friends Service Committee. He lives in western North Carolina, continues his membership in the Celo Friends Meeting, and tries to work toward simplifying his life in both spiritual and material ways.

Asia Bennett is the Executive Secretary of the American Friends Service Committee. She has served previously as Personnel Secretary and as Regional Executive Secretary in the Pacific Northwest. The mother of three grown children, she spent a number of years working with young children before coming to the AFSC. She is a member of the Swarthmore Monthly Meeting of Philadelphia Yearly Meeting.

Chapter 17

Friends and a Planetary Perspective: Helping to Create a Peaceful, Just, and Humane World Society

Leonard S. Kenworthy

The world into which many of us were born and in which we were reared no longer exists. It has been shattered by such widely divergent factors as radio and television, airplanes and spaceships, the atomic bomb, multinational corporations, and the participation of millions of people in many parts of our planet in a Revolution of Rising Expectations. Remnants of our former world remain, but One World is rapidly becoming a reality, even though most people (including Quakers) are not really prepared to understand it, to live effectively in it, and to contribute creatively to it.

The form our emerging world society will eventually take is unclear, but we are gradually becoming aware that it is already an increasingly interdependent world of five billion human beings with diverse ways of living—and it may be a world of eleven billion or more inhabitants before we reach zero population growth. Furthermore, it is a world of new nations and of new or emerging world powers, an urban world, and a world of more and more regional and international organizations. It is also a world torn by tensions over religious beliefs, over forms of economic and political organization, and over resources and trade. It is also a world plagued by other problems, including thermonuclear and biological warfare, the pollution of our planet, and the alarming gap between the rich and the poor.

But we know, too, that a better world is possible. As Alvin Toffler concluded in his recent provocative book, *The Third Wave*, "...with intelligence and a modicum of luck, the emergent civilization can be more sane, sensible, and sustainable, more decent and democratic, than any we have ever known." Because it is a world in the making, we have an unparalleled opportunity to help mold it into something resembling

205

the world we want. Quakers are an infinitesimally small group, but size is not always what matters. In the past, Friends have often had a powerful impact on the world of their day, and we can do so now and in the future, acting as architects and change-agents for a new world society.

Quakers have long been known for their concern for peace. Now we need to couple that with a concern for equality and justice for all the passengers on Spaceship Earth. To be effective in carrying out those twin concerns, we will all have to reeducate or educate ourselves, substituting a cockpit or spaceship view of the world for the porthole glimpse so many of us now have. We will need to become citizens of the world as well as of our local communities and nations. We will need to understand diversity and eventually to welcome it, for the global society we should help construct must be a pluralistic world, and we must become people with a planetary perspective.

SOME CAUSES FOR OPTIMISM

Confused by the pace of change, by the continuing crises in many parts of our planet, and by the conflicting views about solutions to our global problems, many people become discouraged, disillusioned, and even cynical. Some retreat into the past with the hope of restoring it, even though their picture of the past may be only a figment of their imagination.

True, the changes in our day are numerous, the crises far-flung, and the conflicting ideas for solutions baffling at times. Nevertheless we need not abandon hope. Undergirded by our religious beliefs, we can maintain our faith in a better tomorrow. And by looking back from time to time, we can gain strength from seeing how often human beings have overcome obstacles which once seemed insurmountable. Sometimes it has taken centuries, but human sacrifice has been abandoned, human slavery abolished, dueling dropped, and lynchings largely discontinued.

Despite setbacks in recent decades, there have been gains in many movements and causes worldwide. For example:

1. A large part of the world's people have gained their political independence and been organized into over a hundred new nations in the last forty years, with at least some self-rule.
2. Population control has finally been accepted by most nations and many are now exerting strenuous efforts to curb the number of births in their lands.

3. Several diseases have been drastically curbed or eliminated (such as smallpox, malaria, leprosy, yaws, polio, river blindness, and tuberculosis) and thousands of doctors, nurses, and paraprofessionals have been added all over the globe.

4. New implements such as small plows for rice paddies have been developed and the food supply of the world vastly increased.

5. Concern has grown internationally over the destruction and pollution of our environment, and action has been taken in many places to restore various areas, such as the Mediterranean Sea.

6. Through the use of the mass media millions of people now have more access to news about the world than heretofore; we are truly "a wired world."

7. High-speed trains, airplanes, giant tankers, and subways have helped to shrink our world and to transport people and goods.

8. Some liberation of women has taken place in almost every country, with phenomenal gains in some places.

9. Experts in psychology, psychiatry, anthropology, and allied fields have revealed much about human beings and groups.

10. Several regional organizations (such as the European Community and the Organization for African Unity) have been formed, and the United Nations and its agencies have contributed much to the world.

11. Millions of people are now enjoying the creativity of people from other parts of the world in literature, art, music, dance, sculpture, and other art forms as we have found increased ways of sharing the beauty formed in so many different ways by the people on our planet.

In many respects, then, our earth is—or can be—a rich treasure house, a busy workshop, a vast scientific laboratory, an enormous stage, a giant concert hall, a mammoth museum, a large art gallery, an enormous playground, and a global human relations laboratory. Take heart, friends, with these and other causes for optimism.

SOME CAUSES FOR CONCERN

Even though our planet is in many ways a fantastic place, it is also plagued with problems. Some are easily seen; others are less apparent. Most are worldwide, taking different forms in various cultures and countries. Nearly all are complex and deep-seated, defying easy solutions. Here are a few of them; readers will certainly be able to add others:

1. War is certainly our number one world enemy, with the threat of extinction by nuclear weapons hovering over us constantly. The cost of war amounts to nearly 900 billion dollars annually—money diverted from pressing human needs. And we are now facing the possibility of wars in space!

2. Poverty comes close to war as our basic world problem. It is staggering to compare or contrast the $7,000 per person income of U.S. citizens with the $800 income of people in seventy other countries and the $150 per person in thirty-six poverty-stricken lands. Such stark figures should stagger our imagination and help us to realize that a large part of the world's people live in the Third or Fourth Worlds and that many of them are ill-housed, ill-fed, illiterate, and ill.

3. Closely allied with the foregoing point is the ill-health of much of the world's population, whether in rural areas or in the slums and shantytowns of the world's cities.

4. Belatedly, and often reluctantly, we are facing up to the fact that overpopulation is a basic world problem, exacerbating many others and preventing millions of people from sharing in the good things of life.

5. Despite recent gains in food production globally, famines persist and increase, and malnutrition cripples millions of people, even causing blindness and mental retardation. Yet the problem is more one of distribution than of production.

6. In recent decades many of the new nations have allocated large percentages of their national budgets to education. Yet the growth of the world's population has meant an actual increase in the number of illiterates globally.

7. For centuries human beings have plundered our planet, squandered our resources, poisoned our waterways, polluted our skies, and scarred our land. Consequently, we live on a planet in peril. Surely our cry should be "SOS"—Save Our Spaceship!

8. Complicating our global crisis are the competing ideologies—political, economic, and religious—and the fanaticism of many of their followers.

9. Scattered over the face of our earth are millions of refugees (perhaps as many as fifty million since World War II) whose plight is often unbelievable.

10. Adding to the sickness of the world society is the lack of strong support for the United Nations and its specialized agencies, as well as other international organizations. The UN serves many useful purposes but how much more it could do with adequate support.

11. Finally, there is so little done to educate children, young people, and adults about world affairs and to develop world-minded citizens, concerned with the fate of all the inhabitants on Planet Earth.

So, in many respects this is a beautiful and fabulous world. But in other ways ours is an ugly, perplexed, and disturbed global society.

QUAKER CONCERNS ABOUT THE WORLD IN THE PAST AND AT PRESENT

Since almost the beginning of the Quaker movement there has been an international dimension to many of the concerns of Friends. Thus, despite the extreme difficulties of travel, some early Friends visited parts of Europe, Turkey, Russia, the islands of the Caribbean, and the American colonies, taking with them their messages of personal salvation, and sometimes their messages of social salvation. And when they could not travel, they often sent messages to the rulers of the world, such as George Fox's Epistle of 1656 addressed "to all nations."

Their earliest relief work was carried on for their own members who were being persecuted. But in 1690 Quakers became concerned about food and clothing for the prisoners of war in the Irish Revolution. Similar work has been carried on ever since that day and in many parts of the world, sometimes on a large scale.

Some Friends also began decades ago to try to help avert wars and to foster reconciliation. Examples include the efforts of Rhode Island Friends to avert the King Philip's War in 1675, the work of John Fothergill and David Barclay in trying to prevent the American Revolution in the 1770s, the attempts of Joseph Sturge to mediate the conflict between Germany and Denmark in 1854 over Schleswig-Holstein, and John Bright's endeavors to prevent war between England and Russia in 1853. Such work has also continued intermittently for nearly three centuries, including our day.

Individual Friends also have been pioneers in urging the establishment of international organizations, starting with William Penn's remarkable *Essay Towards the Present and Future Peace of Europe* (1693) and John Beller's *Some Reasons for a European State* (1710), and coming on down to recent times, with the part played in the League of Nations and the United Nations by Inazo Nitobe, Philip Noel-Baker, the Pickards, Sydney Bailey, and others. Wherever Friends have settled in the world or developed Yearly Meetings, they have been concerned about such testimonies and concerns as education, peace, women's rights, the fair treatment of minorities (or majorities), and care of prisoners and the mentally disturbed. In the twentieth century much of the work of Friends around the world has been organized and administered by the Friends Service Council (British) and the American Friends Service Committee (AFSC). Here we will mention only a few of the activities of the AFSC over the seventy years of its existence.

After World War I there was the extensive feeding of children and famine relief work of American Friends in Germany, Austria, and the Soviet Union. In 1943 similar work was carried on in India.

During and after World War I there was the relief and reconstruction work in France and other parts of Europe. And similar activities were carried out in Korea in 1952; in Nigeria, Mali, and Zambia in the 1970s; in Cambodia and Lebanon in the 1980s.

Food production was a primary concern of the AFSC in Kampuchea in the late 1970s and medical work in China in 1941, in Southeast Asia in 1966, in Central American and Zimbabwe in the 1980s.

Emigrés and refugees have frequently been a major concern of the AFSC, such as in Spain in 1937, in Germany in the late 1930s, in the Gaza strip in the Middle East in 1949, in Hong Kong in 1959, in South Africa in 1976, and in Thailand in the 1980s.

Other forms of international activity have included the international work camps of the AFSC, the seminars for young diplomats, the International Institutes for public education in the United States, the Peace Caravans, and the (international) School Affiliation Service.

Over the more than forty years of its existence, the Friends Committee on National Legislation has pressed vigorously for legislation in the United States on international as well as national issues. Among the measures it has supported have been initiatives for disarmament and the abolition of atomic weapons, the restoration of diplomatic relations with China, the formation of an international peace corps, opposition to the war in Indochina, multilateral agencies for the distribution of foreign aid, the passage of the UN Treaty on the Law of the Sea, measures to prevent hunger and poverty around the world, and the stewardship of the world's resources.

High on the list of the efforts of the Friends World Committee for Consultation have been the support, with the AFSC, of the Quaker Program at the United Nations and the self-imposed one percent tax by individuals for the Right Sharing of World Resources.

Individual Friends have also contributed greatly to the furtherance of the better world; as in the efforts of Victor Paschkis in founding the Society for the Social Responsibility of Scientists and of Eric Baker, an English Friend who was the co-founder of Amnesty International.

International recognition of the role of Friends certainly reached its height in 1947 when the Nobel Peace Prize was awarded jointly to the

American Friends Service Committee and the Friends Service Council for the spirit of reconciliation which has always inspired their relief work.

Yet censure has sometimes been mixed with praise both from within and without the Religious Society of Friends for our international activities.

Some Quakers feel that the Society of Friends has become primarily a service organization or a Quaker Red Cross rather than primarily a religious group. And/or they believe that "concerns" originate too often in the offices of the AFSC rather than in local Friends Meetings.

Some have also said that whereas many service organizations enlist persons of skill without adequate spirit, Quakers tend to enlist persons of spirit without adequate skills. Of course, the ideal is persons with both qualifications.

Some say, too, that Quakers are often prophets of gloom and doom, frequently seeking and talking about the problems of the world and seldom about the progress in alleviating such problems. But the opposite criticism is sometimes made of Quakers—that they are unrealistic idealists with their heads in the clouds and without their feet on the ground.

Two other criticisms are even more harsh. One is made especially by those outside our Society when they ask how Quakers can be such ardent proponents for peace and yet have so many divisions and so much misunderstanding, and even hostility, within their own group. The other is the question as to whether Quakers are specialists in applying band-aids or sedatives when they should be social surgeons. Where, some people ask, are the dramatic and provocative statements by Quakers on the world social and economic order comparable to their powerful pronouncements on peace? Answers to such questions cannot be given in this brief essay, but they are certainly worth pondering seriously. To them can be added a few overall comments.

In his book on *The Meaning of the 20th Century*, Kenneth Boulding asserted that:

> If I were to nominate the activity which is now open to mankind and which would increase most dramatically the probability of his survival, I would nominate a massive intellectual effort in peace research—that is, in the application of the social sciences to the study of conflict

systems and especially the conflict systems in their international aspect.

How do you react to that proposal?

In times past the American Friends Service Committee has been especially creative in introducing innovative programs, such as their international work camps, their seminars for young international diplomats, and their institutes of international relations. What innovative programs would you urge them to introduce or pursue?

In an essay which was printed posthumously in *The Testament of Devotion*, Thomas Kelly wrote: "Would that we could love the whole world! But a special fragment is placed before us in the temporal now which puts a special responsibility for our present upon us." To which of the many world problems posed in the first part of this chapter would you give top priority for Friends in the United States today?

What next steps do you suggest for better understanding among the various groups of Quakers in the United States so that we might practice in our own "family" what we espouse as advocates of peace internationally?

As wealthy individuals in terms of world standards, have the members of your Meeting or Yearly Meeting ever wrestled with the question of whether Quakers in the United States today should be calling for more radical measures than they have ever proposed in order to bring about a more peaceful, just, equal, and humane international society? Could you? Should you?

HOW INDIVIDUALS AND FAMILIES CAN HELP PROMOTE A BETTER WORLD

Since the dimensions of the topic dealt with in this essay are enormous and the space is limited, it may be helpful at this point to concentrate on what individuals and families, and local Meetings, can do to promote the kind of world about which we have been writing. In telegraphic style, here are some suggestions for readers in terms of individuals and/or families. You will undoubtedly think of others. In each instance you might well think in terms of whether (A) you are carrying on that activity relatively well, (B) whether you could improve your performance on that activity, (C) whether you might add it as a new activity, or (D) whether it does not appeal to you at the present time. Here, then, are fifteen suggestions:

1. Add to your background on some aspect of world affairs.
2. Combat the idea that world peace is unattainable and a better world

impossible. Discuss this with your friends and others.
3. Probe one of your international prejudices.
4. Get acquainted with some person from abroad who is now in the United States. Share your family life with him or her.
5. Become a specialist on some aspect of world affairs in the months or years ahead.
6. Occasionally discuss world affairs at the family dinner table.
7. Visit museums and/or art galleries with your older children to enjoy the creative work of people from abroad. Also eat in "foreign" restaurants.
8. Purchase up-to-date books for yourself and your children on various aspects of the world.
9. Inform yourself on the global dimensions of the curriculum of the school your children attend and urge a strengthening of such programs.
10. Contribute in some way to the international dimension of an organization or institution of which you are a member.
11. Take part in the one-percent program of the Friends World Committee for the Right Sharing of World Resources.
12. Study, work, or travel abroad.
13. Advocate legislation in Congress on world affairs, keeping in touch with the Friends Committee on National Legislation.
14. Support candidates who favor effective world affairs legislation.
15. Take part in a demonstration on some aspect of world affairs.

HOW LOCAL FRIENDS MEETINGS CAN HELP PROMOTE A BETTER WORLD

Since most readers will be able to do their most effective work through the local Quaker Meeting or Friends Church, we will suggest a few programs for enhancing the international awareness and action of such groups. Here are some for your consideration:

1. Make sure that the Peace and Social Action Committee is concerned about the international dimensions of its work and encourage them in that regard.
2. Examine the curriculum materials for children and young people used in your First-Day School or Sunday School to make certain that international concerns are included in them.
3. Arrange for programs in your adult class or adult forum on world topics.
4. Plan a meeting or series of meetings on the Society of Friends around the world.

5. Arrange a fun program or series of such programs on the food, music, and dances of people in other countries.
6. Plan celebrations around various international days and/or weeks, such as UNICEF Week and UN Day or Week.
7. Increase and update the books in your Meeting library on the world, including the children's section.
8. Plan a bulletin board on world affairs and/or urge the editor of your Meeting newsletter to include material on the world in that publication.
9. Make your Meetinghouse or Friends Church available to local groups interested in world affairs and/or cooperate with other groups in sponsoring forums on world issues.
10. Entertain a group of students from abroad who are studying in a nearby college or university.
11. Include contributions to the American Friends Service Committee, the Friends Committee on National Legislation, and the Friends World Committee for Consultation in your annual budget.
12. Urge the local library to update and extend its books and pamphlets on world affairs, and/or urge your local newspaper and radio and television station to increase and improve their coverage of world events.
13. Consider declaring your Meetinghouse or Friends Church a "sanctuary" for refugees and/or adopting a refugee family.
14. Plan a simple meal from which the profits will go to support people in a famine area of the world.
15. Arrange with other groups for a public demonstration on some pressing world problem, such as world hunger or disarmament.

NATIONAL AND INTERNATIONAL QUAKER GROUPS
AND THEIR CONCERN FOR THE WORLD

For many decades Yearly Meetings have shown concern for the problems of the world. In their annual sessions and through various committees, commissions, and publications they have endeavored to contribute to the alleviation of some of the world's ills—always using peaceful means and always trying to retain the religious basis of their concerns.

In their annual gatherings Yearly Meetings often have visiting Friends from Quaker groups from abroad. Frequently they have speakers from abroad or speakers on international topics. They have issued statements on global concerns. Usually they have had study groups on some aspects of world affairs. Many Yearly Meetings have been active in missions in various parts of the world—carrying out the injunction of Jesus, "Go ye, therefore, into all the world, proclaiming the Gospel."

Fifty years ago the Friends World Committee on Consultation was formed, and gradually it has grown in strength and influence. Today it includes regional groups—Europe and the Near East, the Americas, Africa, and the Asia-West Pacific sections. Through its triennial meetings, held in various parts of the globe, it has fostered understanding and friendship among Friends and contributed to world peace and to a more just and humane world society. Through offices in New York, Geneva, and Brussels it has sought to have an impact on the European Community and on the United Nations. And through encouraging Friends to travel, through conferences, and through its publications, it has contributed to a better world.

CONCLUSION

In his book *One World in the Making,* Ralph Barton Perry said: "People live in a greater world, embracing the whole of earth and its inhabitants, and their lives must be organized in the same proportions." Certainly as Friends we need to reorganize or organize our lives so that we become Friends with a planetary perspective. We need to translate into action the words of the Lord's Prayer that "Thy kingdom come on earth as it is in heaven." We may not be able to do much, but every effort we make should be satisfying to us and helpful to others.

SOME SUGGESTED READINGS

Boulding, Kenneth. *Mending the World.* Pendle Hill Pamphlet 266, 1986.

Goldstein, Eleanor and Joseph Newman. "What Citizens Need to Know About World Affairs." *U.S. News and World Report,* 1983 (revised edition).

Muller, Robert. *New Genesis: Shaping a Global Spirituality.* Doubleday and Company Image Books, 1984.

Yarrow, C.H. Mike. *Quaker Experiences in International Cooperation.* Yale University Press, 1978.

You can also obtain materials from the American Friends Service Committee, the Friends Committee on National Legislation, and the Friends World Committee for Consultation on their international work.

SOME QUESTIONS FOR DISCUSSION

1. What aspect (or aspects) of this chapter struck you as new or different? Why?

2. What changes would you suggest in the section on Some Causes for Optimism? Why?
3. What changes would you suggest for the section on Some Causes for Concern? Why?
4. How do you react to the criticisms of some Quaker work? Why?
5. On what point or points mentioned in this chapter could you and/or your family act now?
6. On what point or points mentioned in this chapter could your Meeting work now?

ABOUT THE AUTHOR

Leonard S. Kenworthy is a birthright and convinced Friend, long active in world affairs. He has traveled in eighty-eight countries and lived in five outside the United States for sizeable periods. In 1940–1941 he was the Director of the Quaker International Center in Berlin for the American Friends Service Committee. After World War II he was a member of the Planning Commission for UNESCO and its first Director of Education for International Understanding. Vocationally, he has spent most of his life in teacher education, specializing in social studies and international education. He has written widely for children, teachers, Quakers, and others.

Chapter 18

Friends Outreach: Mission and Service United

Kara Cole

Jesus said, "Go into all the world and preach the Gospel to every living creature"; George Fox said, "Let all nations hear the sound by word and writing....Be patterns, be examples in all countries,...that your carriage and life may preach among all sorts of people; then you will come to walk cheerfully over the world, answering that of God in everyone."

What canst thou say?

OUTREACH EQUALS MISSION AND SERVICE UNITED

What canst thou say, indeed.

The question haunts Quaker bureaucrats and local Meeting members alike. In answering, there are overwhelming temptations to call upon our glorious history, to settle into polite arguments (called discussions) about whether we are doing "mission" or "service," and which is more in the Quaker tradition, about those we know who have done one or the other in ways of which we do not approve, about how much it will cost, about how it should be done, plus other considerations.

Even so, the extent and excellence of Friends outreach (whether we call it "mission" or "service") in our time is impressive. It is clear that Quakers see it as their mandate to carry on the tradition, and that many Friends in our day are being called for that special ministry which has gone by various names over our history. It is also clear that the nature of our outreach is as varied as ever, and the basis upon which we are called is probably even more varied—sometimes causing discomfort on the part of Friends from all segments of the family of Friends.

It is important always to be in the process of looking at what we are doing and why. Some Friends need to be asked to practice what they preach, and others need to be reminded to preach what they practice. Mission and service are inseparable if we are to be obedient to our Christian calling and to our Quaker tradition. To do mission (in the traditional sense of "preaching the gospel") without serving the needs of those whose spiritual and physical condition must change is to carry an empty, hypocritical gospel. Conversely, to meet physical needs as if persons were only physical is to deny the power of God's spirit to meet deep longings for relationship with the creator of the universe.

A word about mission. The word itself is a flag among many Friends. For some, it is a battle flag, and one is told that it dare not be flown. For others, it is the flag to which loyalty must be affirmed—without which there can be no trust. I am unwilling to lose the word from the vocabulary of Friends. Therefore, I must be clear that I use it in its traditional and dictionary meaning—*sent*. I would plead that we learn to use it much more broadly, that we give it a fresh and positive definition by the lives we live as "missionaries" wherever we are (even to those next door), that we be strong in not allowing those who define the word inappropriately with their lives to continue to do so, that we do what Quakers have done with so many things so often in the past—set the standard for "mission" and "missionaries" and be bold and forward-looking in doing so.

GOD'S LOVE COMPELS US

The basis for Friends outreach has always been, and continues to be, the love of God. In the knowledge and experience of God's overwhelming love for us, we feel compelled and called to share that love with any who will listen and/or receive. The ways that we share, reach out, serve—the ways we work in mission, are as varied as the individuals in the Religious Society of Friends. God calls us as we are and empowers us to fulfill those callings beyond anything that we can imagine in our finiteness. If that is difficult to believe, take a look at some of the ways in which the outreach of Friends is being accomplished in our time.

ANNOUNCING GOOD NEWS

There is no indication that Jesus meant only the "poor in spirit," though he certainly did mean that as well. In the United States and in many other countries of the world, the announcement of the Gospel continues to be made. From George Fox and Margaret Fell to the present day, Friends have been exceptional preachers of the Gospel, and there is nothing in present day conditions or Friends belief that would herald any change. Jesus was clear that the primary audience for the Gospel is the poor. We are often reminded that the present condition of the world is such that the rich are getting richer and the poor are getting poorer; that the "middle class" as we have come to know it, is disappearing. Therefore, the Good News of Jesus is even more relevant, particularly when we understand that the Good News includes both word and deed, both mission and service.

Thus, in our day we find:

1. The work of the Fellowship of Friends in Chicago's Cabrini-Green district—a multifaceted urban outreach work which includes education, evangelism, youth advocacy in the legal system, sharing of food and clothing resources, athletics, tutoring—attempts to meet the social, spiritual, mental, and physical needs of those in that community.

2. The work of the American Friends Service Committee in many communities in the United States—collecting, sorting, and redistributing clothing to those who are cold and often homeless. This ministry provides fulfillment to those who do the collecting and distributing as well as to those who receive the clothing.

3. The work of many local Meetings and Churches in providing day care for the children of working parents (many of whom are single mothers with severely limited incomes). Ministry to children (and from children) has been a consistent concern of Friends, even though the forms of that ministry have changed over the years. Today, many children find stability and love through the care and education provided them in Meeting day-care centers.

4. The work of many local and Yearly Meetings to provide care and sometimes sanctuary for refugees from all over the world. Friends engage in that outreach in the belief that all persons are created and loved equally by God. As recipients of that love we share it with those who are rejected by their own countries or governments. That outreach is not without risk in our time. It is certainly not without cost. Nor was it in the days when American slaves were aided by Quakers to find places of freedom.

5. The work of many local Meetings, often in cooperation with other faith communities, in feeding the poor in their communities. As American governments—local and national—have diverted more of their resources to military purposes, there has been a great increase in the number of persons who are both hungry and homeless (a fact largely unnoticed by the mass media). Feeding programs vary in their frequency, of course, but people of faith have worked hard to

step in and fill the need. Food is, indeed, good news to the hungry.

6. The general commitment of Friends in working with and for the elderly. Some of that work is not for the poor; for example, housing in retirement centers which are costly but do fill a need. But there are, as well, projects which link young and old in caring relationships, which provide low-cost housing and medical care, which provide day-care for elderly people who have relatives to care for them evenings and weekends, which provide social gatherings and educational experiences, and fun for elderly people who would otherwise have few such opportunities.

7. The cooperation of Friends from all segments of our Society, working together as the Associated Committee of Friends on Indian Affairs. Native Americans continue to struggle to find their place and legitimacy in the United States. The financial support, food, clothing, and workers which this committee has generated comprise a dramatic story. There are now five Native American centers with Meetings, schools, and a wide range of activities which can only be described as fulfilling Jesus' mandate to carry the Good News to the poor.

8. The work of Friends Meetings, Yearly Meetings, and groups to provide housing for those who cannot afford it. Two examples come to mind immediately—the work of Friends in Florida to stimulate and guide the building of houses for Haitians who would otherwise not have adequate housing, and the work of Friends in Virginia Beach to secure funding and oversee the building of a low-cost housing community near the Meetinghouse. In most cases housing projects require long, hard work and considerable expertise on the part of a few who are willing to sort through the bureaucracies to secure all of the required licenses and funding. But it continues to be a concern that must be met if we are to be faithful to our outreach concerns.

This list is incomplete, of course. No doubt one of your favorite outreach ministries is missing. But the list gives strong evidence that Friends are still committed to announcing the Good News to the poor in whatever ways they are called to do so.

RELEASING THE PRISONERS

We know from reading the New Testament that Jesus meant to release both the physical and spiritual prisoners; nothing in his life and ministry would indicate that our intention and calling should be less.

Throughout our history, outreach to prisoners has been a central calling; Elizabeth Fry set an example which has challenged all generations of Friends in prison ministry. Quakers have led various movements for prison reform, for programs which provide reorientation for recently released prisoners, and for programs which provide care to the families of prisoners.

Today there are programs in several local and Yearly Meetings for prison visitation. Aspects of the visitation program include sharing in the Meeting for Worship, taking in appropriate literature (both religious and otherwise), becoming acquainted with the families, helping to seek appropriate and helpful legal advice, and linking with, if not providing, half-way house support for released prisoners.

Proclaiming release for the prisoners, as Jesus commanded, includes finding ways to freedom from spiritual bondage, too. The seeds of social alienation which cause illegal behavior can be rooted out by a fresh infilling of God's love and forgiveness. It is hard work, and the failures are heartbreaking, but Friends persist, as they are called.

RECOVERY OF SIGHT FOR THE BLIND

It is a fascinating study to find how many times "sight" images were used by Jesus to illuminate a spiritual truth. To some extent each of us suffers from impairment of our spiritual sight—Jesus was clear that announcing recovery of sight to the blind was at the center of his ministry. He was referring, of course, to both physical and spiritual sight. I think that it could be argued that sight in this reference in some sense stands for handicaps. Jesus not only healed blind people and offered spiritual sight to them at the same time, He also cast out demons, healed lameness, and even restored life. In all cases the physical healing was accompanied by spiritual healing as well.

Friends today are involved, out of concern and calling, in various forms of medical work, in spiritual healing groups, and in service which includes becoming "eyes" for those who cannot see. It is often noted that the proportion of Friends whose livelihood is earned in the "helping professions" is much greater than in other groups. In fact, people sometimes comment wryly that it is a good thing our predecessors were more interested in being in business, as we can "afford" today to be helpers as we live off the profits of our business heritage! Nonetheless, many Friends do serve in vocations which are not particularly lucrative out of a real sense of mission and service to those who are needy in various ways.

TO LET THE BROKEN VICTIMS GO FREE

There is probably no human being who has ever lived who has not experienced being a victim at some time or another. Whether we are victims of another person, a system, our own insecurity—whatever it might be—we have personal experience to bring to those who seem broken in their victim role. What good news it is to those persons that there is a way to be set free! Again, that freedom is both spiritual and physical.

I think under this mandate comes the splendid work of Friends for justice. In the States, all Friends share in various ways in the Friends Committee on National Legislation (FCNL), a registered religious lobby which has for more than forty years kept alive the testimony for peace in the halls of the federal government. The dedication and expertise with which this work functions is remarkable. The FCNL also provides each year for the training and experience of a limited number of young people who are considering careers which might put them in positions of political influence.

The involvement of local Friends in various peace movements, in local lobbying, in United Nations work, in various demonstrations, in shelters for the battered, in child protection programs, and in other endeavors, aids the broken victims directly as they "mend" and find freedom. Such activities are varied and numerous.

MISSION AND SERVICE OVERSEAS

Thus far, most of the examples have been of outreach within the United States. Yet it may well be that the work of Friends has been most dramatically successful abroad. Perhaps all of the examples of the kind of work that Quakers have done at home are duplicated overseas.

There can be no question that the work of early Friends missionaries in Kenya and Burundi, Bolivia and Peru, China and Taiwan, India, Central America, Jamaica, Cuba, and the Middle East have extended the Gospel in ways and places that the missionaries themselves could not have imagined. They were simply being obedient.

It needs to be emphasized that in all cases Friends set out to do mission work with a broad and enlightened perspective. Early missionaries did educational, medical, agricultural, and developmental work from the very beginning, along with and as a part of the whole Gospel which they felt called to share. While not perfect, to be sure, the story of Quaker mission work is one of which all Friends today can be justifiably proud. It is one which we should study openly, helping us to understand why the work was so successful and why the message was accepted and spread with enthusiasm.

In fact, "we" have been so successful that we must now go through the difficult emotional task of realizing that English is no longer the first language of a majority of Friends, that the majority of Quakers worldwide are not white, and that it may be time for those Friends around the world to send "missionaries" to us.

But it is not only missionary work which has flourished abroad. The American Friends Service Committee (AFSC) has done outstanding work in relief through its history. It is chiefly remembered by people outside Quaker circles for its relief and rehabilitation work during and after the World Wars, but the excellence of that work is its standard. One of the things which has marked the AFSC is its policy of helping victims of oppression and need, regardless of their political or ideological orientations. That policy has made the organization unpopular and even suspect at times, even among Friends, yet the overall results of its work made it the recipient of the Nobel Peace Prize in 1947, jointly with the Friends Service Council of London Yearly Meeting.

WHAT WAY FORWARD?

In looking ahead we must first look to and learn about our faith life. One good way to have a feel for the future is to look at the past. Friends are certainly not the oldest faith community, yet our more than three hundred years of experience highlight some patterns which we ignore at our peril.

There will always be human need, fostered by the complex workings of governments and by natural causes. Because that need will be greater than Friends can meet, it is vitally important to look to our faith community for support as we (individuals and groups) await discernment concerning specific leadings and urgings to go about the work of outreach. Affirmation of our leading in the local Meeting is a strong and important practice of Friends—it is central to obedience and effectiveness.

Hence, looking to our faith life is the first element, and the second is closely linked with it—looking to the world in which we are living that life. There can be little doubt that our educational efforts must be both inward and outward.

We must constantly claim, study, and understand our Quaker and Christian history, without worshipping it. The Bible tells the story of God, who is the rightful recipient of our worship. George Fox is not Jesus Christ, but pointed the way to that One who can speak to our condition. Silence is not the basis of our worship; our relationship to and dependence upon God is. Preaching—excellent and effective preaching—is a part of our heritage and of our mandate. Our testimony on equality arises out of our understanding that each person is uniquely created by God and deserving of respect. We eschew hierarchical structures because God is our leader, our authority in all matters.

Our second educational task is to learn all we can about the world in which we are attempting to be faithful to God's call. It is not enough to affirm with wringing hands that the world is a terrible place and we are the ones who know what to do to remake it. There are excellent materials available regarding development, missions, economics, the efforts of other denominations, and the world in general. While it would be something of a waste for the Meeting to become only a study group, there is much to be said for being efficient and knowledgeable about our outreach. It is even more true that the world is changing rapidly, behooving us to keep up-to-date on a wide range of issues and developments which really are our concern.

We say, as Quakers, that we believe in "letting our lives speak." That concept certainly was given strong affirmation by Jesus when he prayed that the whole world may know God because people love one another so much (John 17:21). It is a constant challenge to us to live what we believe. It is certainly that kind of love which causes curiosity in those who experience it—curiosity which in many cases compels belief and a strong desire to experience that kind of faith community.

GETTING AND KEEPING IT ALL TOGETHER

Outreach after the manner of Friends is the marriage of mission and service, the action which results from individual and corporate leadings. It is the work to which we are called by the God whose love sends us to do that wonderful work in our world. Outreach takes prayer, waiting, work, and resources. We have proved that we are able to take on the task; let us pray together for the strength and guidance to live up to our reputation and our calling.

SOME SUGGESTED READINGS

Cattell, Everett. *Christian Mission*. Richmond, IN: Friends United Press, 1983.

Friends World Committee for Consultation. *Vocations of Friends in the Modern World*. Study Book 1 for the 1952 Friends World Conference.

Hodgkin, Henry T. *The Missionary Spirit and the Present Opportunity*. The 1916 Swarthmore Lecture of London Yearly Meeting.

Rowntree, Joshua. "Missionary Spirit of Early Friends." An address of the conference of the Friends Home Mission and Extension Committee, June 1908, published by the Yorkshire 1905 Committee.

SOME QUESTIONS FOR DISCUSSION

1. As you read this chapter, did you find some prejudices within yourself regarding the concepts of mission and service? What were they? How do you explain your misgivings or prejudices?
2. What favorite outreach efforts of yours were not discussed in this chapter? Why do you think they are important and should be highlighted?
3. Is your Meeting involved in a specific outreach project? Is it local, regional, national, or international? In what ways does your Meeting talk about this work?
4. Is it possible for you to think of yourself as a "missionary"?
5. What future do you see for Quaker outreach as defined in this chapter? Are there particular projects which you think are uniquely suited to Quakers? If so, what are they and how can we go about doing them?

ABOUT THE AUTHOR

Kara Cole is a convinced Friend who has had many opportunities in recent years to experience the mission and service work of Friends first-hand. From 1979 through 1986 she was Administrative Secretary of Friends United Meeting, having come to that position from a background in education and in business. She always has been active in her local and Yearly Meetings, first in Northwest Yearly Meeting and more recently in Indiana Yearly Meeting. Her articles and reflections are often published in Quaker journals and she has had broad ecumenical experiences as well. Her membership at present is in the West Richmond Friends Meeting in Richmond, Indiana. She and Wayne Cole are the parents of four grown children.

Chapter 19

Gray on Gray: Quaker Concerns on Aging in the United States

Michael Allen

One of the most dramatic and dynamic changes in the twentieth century in the United States has been the aging of our population. At the turn of the century, four percent of our people, numbering around four million, had reached their sixty-fifth birthdays or more. Today the percentage of our people who are sixty-five or older is nearly triple that number, constituting 11.9 percent of our people or a total of twenty-eight million men and women. That is the equivalent of the total population of Canada, and it means that each day 1,500 individuals reach their sixty-fifth birthday!

And what are the trends projected for the future? Between 1946 and 1964, the "baby boom" occurred, with 76,400,000 children born. That "baby boom" generation will continue to cause strains and stresses in our social institutions. The schools were among the first to feel the impact of that phenomenon, then the job market. Next will be pension plans, social security, medical and social care–and later–the Churches. The critical years for that generation will be around 2010. By 2030 there probably will be over fifty million retirees, or nearly twice the number of persons over sixty-five, than there are today. Whereas the proportion of the elderly in the total population now is one in nine, the proportion in the next half century will probably be one in five.

Unfortunately in our American society today the word "aging" has largely negative interpretations or connotations. "Ageism" is considered the systematic discrimination against old people which occurs in many ways and which affects males and females, the physically fit as well as the ill, the people who are married, divorced, single, or widowed.

Too often such a system of unequal treatment is based upon a general belief that older adults constitute a homogeneous group of individuals

226

who are inferior, due to their existence in the losing stage of life. Lamentable, also, is the fact that the losses in physical and mental skills, capabilities, and the ability to contribute to society are often exaggerated. As Robert Butler, a former director of the National Institute of Mental Health, has stated:

> At best the living old are treated as though they were already half-dead....In America, childhood is romanticized, youth is idolized, middle age does the work, wields the power, and pays the bills, and old age...is a period of despair, deprivation, desolation.

QUAKER MEETINGS AND FRIENDS CHURCHES AND THE AGING

Historically Friends have been concerned with the elderly as important members of any Quaker group—integral members of caring fellowships or religious societies of Friends. But care of the elderly was not a major concern; there were not many old people, and those were usually taken care of by their families.

But currently societal changes are affecting Friends as well as other groups. There are more elderly people in our Meetings today than in the past—and often a higher percentage than in the population as a whole. Families live in smaller quarters than in the past and do not always see their way to taking in older people. Often sons and daughters live at a distance, even abroad in some cases.

Hence attention to older people is a growing concern among all Quaker groups. We are turning our attention to the needs of older persons in the local community and in our nation and to the members and attenders of our local Quaker Meetings and Churches. Perhaps a basic question before all Quaker groups is whether we provide an alternative to or a haven from the societal tendency to depreciate and devalue older people.

Surely the Quaker tradition and belief system of respect for the dignity and worth of every human being as a child of God enhances the possibility that Friends in their local Meetings, in their Yearly Meetings, and in their national and international organizations will not *conform* but *transform* societal negativism to a positive view of aging (Rom. 12:2). Certainly Friends should be in the forefront of those who view older adults as individuals who are diverse in personality traits and capabilities and as people who are in the process of growing spiritually, socially, and psychologically, even though they often sustain losses in their physical capabilities.

What, then, are some of the ways in which Friends can counterbalance the negative impact of aging? One consideration should be a careful review of the use of prepositions when discussing and developing aging ministries. Use of the words "to" or "for" are sometimes acceptable if they are used in the sense of providing services to older adults. But the overuse of such words may foster the dependency of aging members and attenders. Such words may also represent a patronizing attitude on the part of those rendering such services.

Ministries with the emphasis of "by" often encourage the independence of older persons and their ability to contribute constructively to varied groups. Yet such an emphasis on independence may lead to age-segregated efforts.

More acceptable to Friends should be the frequent use of ministries "with," which stress the interdependent relationships that enhance mutual understanding and grant a greater degree of dignity to older people. To Quakers the concept of "with" should be central. It should encourage cooperation among various age groups and enhance the search for consensus or "the sense of the Meeting."

One example of such intergenerational cooperation is the Third Age Committee of the Newberg, Oregon, Friends Meeting. Formed in 1976, it is composed of persons from various age groups from teenagers to the elderly. Based on their experience, here are some tasks which any similar Quaker group might undertake:

1. Survey community resources for the elderly, such as Meals on Wheels, a daily telephone contact, and homemaker services.
2. Seek the inclusion of various age groups in Sunday School or First Day School classes, Bible and issue-centered study groups, projects, committees, and activities.
3. Initiate and/or sponsor community-wide day care centers for the elderly and assistance to older adults to keep them in their own homes and apartments as long as possible.
4. Encourage and assist the children of elderly parents to strengthen family ties and sometimes arrange for the construction of special apartments on sections of their homes for the semi- independence of their older members.
5. Encourage the use of the Meetinghouse for the use of such groups as the Gray Panthers, Councils on Aging, units of the American Association of Retired Persons, and meal-site programs.
6. Provide retirement planning classes and programs, especially for those under sixty-five.
7. Include older people in as many of the on-going committees of the local group as possible.

8. Arrange for visits to elderly shut-ins by Meeting members.
9. Build a local Meeting collection of publications of value to older Friends and encourage the use of such materials.
10. Develop discretionary funds for emergency aid to elderly Friends where needed.

HOUSING AND HEALTH CARE FOR FRIENDS

For many older people housing is not a major problem for a time. Actually seventy-five percent of the older adult population of the Untied States own their own homes. But as the maintenance of such homes becomes more burdensome; due to declining health or reduced income, there is an increasing need for retirement housing, often with health care and social services.

As long ago as the end of the nineteenth century, Friends in various parts of the United States arranged special boarding houses for older Quakers. Among them were several facilities in the neighborhood of Philadelphia. But there were similar homes then or shortly thereafter in such places as Amesbury, Massachusetts; Baltimore, Maryland; Barnesville and Waynesville, Ohio; and Richmond, Indiana.

Reflecting changes in our society in the last few years, several retirement homes and retirement communities have been built in the last few years. Some are simple and not expensive but do not provide full health-care facilities; others are more elaborate and expensive with separate apartments and life-care.

Counting the earlier established Friends boarding homes, there are now forty-four Quaker-sponsored facilities for older people across the United States. They are located as follows: California, two; Florida, one; Idaho, one; Indiana, three; Maryland, two; Massachusetts, two; New Jersey, eight; North Carolina, one; Ohio, eight; Oregon, one; and Pennsylvania, fifteen. Some of them are under the care of local Monthly Meetings, some of Quarterly Meetings, and a few of Yearly Meetings. A few are under the care of nonprofit corporations whose membership is all or partly Quaker.

There also has been the development of adult day-care facilities which provide housing, health, and social services during the day to enhance the quality of life for older people and provide respite service for caregivers. Such programs are especially helpful to families with an Alzheimer's relative. Lambert House Adult Care Center, established in 1974 in Portland, Oregon, under the care of the Reedwood Friends Meeting, is an example of such a facility.

Such services probably will be increasingly in demand because of the burgeoning of our adult population and the increasing governmental practice of "privatizing" more and more social and health responsibilities. In addition, recent public health regulations known as DRG (diagnostic related groups) have reduced patient-care-days in hospitals and placed increasing burdens on alternative, community-based, private health care.

EDUCATION AND THE AGING

Quaker tradition is rich in stressing the importance of education in sharpening the tools and enhancing the gifts of various kinds of ministry. Two quotations selected from London Yearly Meeting's *Christian Faith and Practice in the Experience of the Society of Friends* typify Quaker concern on this point.

The first is taken from a statement by Joseph John Gurney in 1831:

> We shall never thrive on ignorance. Our Creator would have us cultivate our understandings in matters of a religious as well as a civil nature. The great rule is that all should be subordinated to the highest object, all...for the glory of God.

The second is one of the current General Advices which stresses the importance of education as a lifelong process. It says:

> Seek for your children that full development of God's gifts which true education can bring. Remember that the service to which we are called needs healthy bodies, well-trained minds, high ideals, and understanding of the laws and purposes of God. Give your best to the study of the Bible and the understanding of the Christian Faith. Be open-minded, ready constantly to receive new light. Be zealous that education may be continued *throughout life* and that its privileges may be shared by *all*.

Such a strong emphasis on education about aging needs to be incorporated in the life of Friends at all levels of their organization from the local Meetings to the Friends World Committee for Consultation. Such programs should include at least three purposes:
1. To develop enlightened attitudes, values, and understandings which reduce ageism and negative stereotypes of people about the aging process and about the elderly.
2. To sponsor programs which will help prepare professionals to serve with the older, adult population.

3. To promote research and publications which will reinforce and support the quality of life and the ministries of older members of the Religious Society of Friends.

The first objective may be enhanced by examining closely the age-based Sunday School or First-Day School classes. For younger children there are certainly advantages in some grouping by age. But with young people and adults there are merits in having intergenerational groups from time to time to consider topics of common interest and bringing varied experiences to bear on them. Several Meetings in Oregon have tried such intergenerational classes and found them stimulating. Such classes have usually lasted from six to nine weeks.

There may be merit, too, in having younger and older persons teach some Sunday School or First Day School classes as a team, with the younger person helping to select his or her partner in order to insure helpful cooperation.

Quarterly Meetings, Yearly Meetings, and national gatherings or conferences of Quaker groups also can be occasions for worthwhile study of questions relating to the aging. In such groups in various parts of the United States the following sample topics have been examined: Memory, Mind, and Maturity; Wholistic Health, Spiritual Well-Being, and Aging; Grandparenting–Positives and Negatives.

Another place for adult learning on aging issues is through Elderhostel programs sponsored by a Quaker group or college. Individuals connected with the Tilikum Retreat Center of George Fox College have found considerable interest in Quaker distinctives and lifestyles among the nation's elderly who have enrolled in the Elderhostel program carried on there since 1981.

One wonders, too, if there is not a need for Quaker colleges or Quaker-related groups to help train Friends as professionals to serve the growing number of elderly people in our country. Possibly there could be a Quaker College Consortium on Aging or a Quaker Gerontology Center in the foreseeable future. Something akin to that has been developed in Pennsylvania recently under the leadership of Lloyd Lewis, the Quaker who directs the Kendal-Crosslands retirement communities. There, Kendal Management Services trains professionals for Quaker boarding homes and retirement communities. Under the leadership of Lloyd Lewis, a geriatric center is underway in which Kendal-Crosslands, the Bryn Mawr Graduate School of Social Work and Social Research, the Crozer-Chester Medical Center, and the Thomas Jefferson and Widener Universities cooperate.

Some elementary research regarding the aged and their needs, as well as the contributions they can make, has been carried on by some local

Quaker Meetings and Friends Churches, by the committees on the aged of various Yearly Meetings, and by such national groups as Evangelical Friends Alliance, Friends General Conference, and Friends United Meeting. Much more research and research in greater depth needs to be carried on in the foreseeable future. Perhaps that need can be fulfilled in part by qualified professors in Quaker colleges as well as by trained Friends in other positions.

A start has been made, also, on Friends publications either about elderly Quakers or for them. Some of those publications have been developed by the Commission on Creative Aging of Friends United Meeting; several others have been published in the well-known pamphlet series of Pendle Hill, the adult Quaker study center outside Philadelphia. Several of these publications are listed in the bibliography at the end of this chapter. Excerpts from two of them should reveal the rich lode of wisdom contained in each of them.

The first is mined from a Pendle Hill pamphlet by Norma Jacob entitled *Growing Old: A View from Within*. Among the many assets of old age that she mentions are liberation, slowing down, making things last longer instead of encouraging them to wear out, emotion recollected in tranquility, discovering the younger generation, cherishing older friends, finding other things (not only people) much more precious, learning to live in the present, making an opening for new things, and being lazy and enjoying it.

In a lengthy volume on *Older and Wiser: Wit, Wisdom, and Spirited Advice from the Older Generation*, Eric Johnson includes Ten Commandments for Those with Elders in Their Lives:

1. Remember that elders are unique individuals. Do not lump them together as a class.
2. Never qualify a compliment by adding "at your age."
3. Encourage elders, but do not say, "You can," when in fact they can't.
4. Enjoy elders for all the extra life they have to give— deep and often sparkling.
5. Call elders in "for consultation" because those years of experiences can sometimes produce wisdom.
6. By love and affection overcome the frustrations of caring for those elders who seem stubborn, difficult, mournful, empty, or boring.
7. Remember that behind an age-dulled or age-prickled exterior hides a bright, warm soul and an eager intelligence waiting to be met and recognized.
8. Ask elders how they are and listen to the answer, for sometimes they need to tell.

9. Speak so that you can be heard—slowly, distinctly—but do not shout.
10. Stay close to the dying for they are venturing into new territory and need to go in touch with love.

A MATTER OF HONOR AND PROVOCATION

A basic thread in the social and spiritual fabric of the Quaker family always has been the admonition for children to honor their fathers and mothers (Eph. 6:2).

But by a curious twist in circumstances in American society today, eighty percent of those over sixty-five have living adult "children." In fact, ten percent of the parents today have "senior citizen children" over the age of sixty-five. So what does it mean today to honor your father and mother when they are seventy, eighty, ninety, or more and you may be a forty, fifty, sixty-year-old "child"?

Such a query is becoming of increasing concern for middle age and older "children" who wish to honor their parents by demonstrating respect and consideration through various social, emotional, and physical support efforts. However, such efforts to assist parents may be complicated by the stigma of age and increasing dependency in our society. How and when does a "child" express love and concern for his or her elderly parents without stigmatizing those parents with the label, "old"? How may there be the provision of assistance without reducing the human dignity, hope, and continued effort to be self-sufficient by a respected parent? Too often the efforts to assist result in the older adult having fears of a "take-over" and role reversal by "children." Such concerns are well stated in the prayer, "My Children Are Coming Today," by Elsie Maclay:

My children are coming today. They mean well but they worry. They think I should have a railing in the hall...a telephone in the kitchen. They want someone to come in when I take a bath...They really don't like my living alone. Help me to be grateful for this concern...and help them to understand that I have to do what I can, as long as I can!

They're right when they say there are risks...I might fall...I might leave the stove on, but there is no challenge, no possibility of triumph, no real aliveness without risk.

When they were young and climbed trees, rode bicycles and went away to camp...I was terrified, but I let them go, because to hold them would have hurt them.

> Now our roles are reversed. Help them see. Keep me from
> becoming grim or stubborn about it. But don't let them
> smother me.

The aesthetics of scriptural relationships is the mutual responsibility and sense of justice that is required between members in the relationship. Whether it is master-servant, husband-wife, or parent-child, both parties are accountable to one another. Thus, as children are to honor their parents, parents are not to *provoke* their children to anger (Eph. 6:4).

How could a parent in retirement years provoke a well-meaning adult "child" trying to honor his or her parents? When parents in this age group refuse assistance or emphasize the viewpoint that they desire not to be a burden to their children, the adult "children" may sense a lack of trust or respect for their efforts to assist. Thus the growth process in aging is not only to learn how to cope with gradually increasing physical and social dependence, but to learn how to receive from "children" and allow them to reciprocate their love to their parents. The two generations must make every effort to increase meaningful discussions on the "what if" circumstances in life with growing *inter*dependency rather than dependent/independent relationships. Such an interdependent relationship grows through the adult "child's" learning to listen for the needs of his or her parents and the parents increasingly perceiving their adult "children" as mature and dependable individuals whom they may trust.

POSSIBLE FAMILY AGING PROGRAMS

Just as there has been a national movement to strengthen the bond of marriage through Quaker Marriage Encounter Seminars, there is a need for Quaker-supported Generation Encounter Seminars. Such seminars would have at least three purposes:
1. To facilitate the strengthening of the family as a natural support system.
2. To integrate the need of resources by both generations for current and future "what if" situations.
3. To reduce conflict and to increase the sense of peace within family relationships

Such seminars have occurred recently in Northwest Yearly Meeting, as a quarterly topic in adult Sunday School classes in three Meetings, as the theme of annual family and adult camps, and as a part of the Elderhostel program at Camp Tilikum. Such an approach is recommended to many Quaker groups across the United States.

EUTHANASIA AND THE ETHICS OF AGING

Does a person have the right to die? Already people are examining several ethical questions arising from the prolongation of lives. Among them are such issues as artificial life support, care of the terminally ill, death with dignity, living wills, and euthanasia.

That term euthanasia comes form the Greek and means "a good death." Its proponents usually distinguish between active and passive euthanasia. Passive euthanasia is usually identified as the practice of not introducing any life support or extraordinary medical support (such as intravenous feeding, use of a respirator, or heart massage) when a person is terminally ill or dying without hope of healing. Many of those who support passive euthanasia believe such a practice should be a moral and legal option as long as medical technology is only prolonging the dying process rather than the living process. Active euthanasia is the practice of actually withdrawing life support systems (commonly called "pulling the plug") already serving individuals.

Recently there have been changes in our legal system that have allowed individuals (who may be healthy or ill) to give directions to their families and to medical personnel should that person's health fail or their condition become terminal. These are usually called Living Wills and must be prepared while the individual is mentally competent and not under coercion. Those wills are then notarized and copies given to the individuals concerned and are not binding should the individual change his or her mind in the face of an illness. They are not legally binding on representatives of the medical profession.

Conservative evangelical theologians such as Francis Schaeffer do not recognize the distinction between active and passive euthanasia (see his *Whatever Has Happened to the Human Race?*). Instead, he refutes the right of Christians to enter euthanasia practices on the basis that people are thereby acting as God by taking lives. He believes euthanasia should not become the pragmatic means of ending life to reduce health care costs or suffering. Schaeffer fears euthanasia may become a practice in the future which will reduce the dignity of life through wholesale murder of the older members of society.

So, what is the Quaker response to euthanasia and Living Wills? Certainly Friends are firm in their belief in the dignity and worth of every human being as a child of God. But does that belief require support for the prolongation the dying process with its attendant pain and suffering? Or, is passive euthanasia an option?

This is a profound and far-reaching question for all Quaker groups today. One answer comes from the practice of Friendsview Manor, a retirement home with lifelong health and social service care, administered by Northwest Yearly Meeting, in Newberg, Oregon. It does make a Living Will available upon request. Also, in consultation with the resident, the resident's family, and the attending physician, passive euthanasia is practiced if there is consensus among these various parties.

CONCLUSION

In summary, we strongly hope that Friends in the foreseeable future will give a great deal of thought and planning to ministering *with* the older members of Quaker Meetings and Friends Churches. Such planning should reduce hastily formulated decisions, programs, and ministries and promote a sense of peace and well-being in the lives of older people and their families. We hope, too, that Quaker groups will avoid the negative stereotypes which devalue and lower respect for older persons. Above all, we trust that Quaker groups will increasingly become strong support groups for older persons, giving them motivation, inspiration, aid, and love—and receiving from them in return—all as an important ministry to Christ's glory.

SOME SUGGESTED READINGS ON OLD AGE (GENERAL)

Butler, Robert M. *Why Survive? Being Old in America.* New York: Harper and Row, 1975.

Gray, Robert and Moberg, David. *The Church and the Older Person.* Grand Rapids, MI: Eerdmans, 1977.

Maclay, Elsie *Green Winter: The Celebration of Old Age.* New York: Reader's Digest Press, 1977.

Schaeffer, Francis. and Koop, C. Everett *Whatever Happened to the Human Race?* Old Tappan, NJ: Revell, 1979.

SOME SUGGESTED READINGS ON OLD AGE (QUAKER AUTHORS)

Allman, Wayne and Tollefson, Harold (Eds.) *Guides to Creative Living.* Richmond, IN: Friends United Press, 1978.

Andrews, Elsie M. *Facing and Fulfilling the Later Years.* Wallingford, PA: Pendle Hill Publications, 1968.

Creative Aging Committee of the Friends United Meeting, *Directory: Friends Retirement Facilities in the U.S.A.* Richmond, IN: Friends United Press, 1984.

Jacob, Norma *Growing Old: A View From Within.* Wallingford, PA, Pendle Hill Publications, 1981.

Johnson, Eric C., *Older and Wiser: Wit, Wisdom, and Spirited Advice from the Older Generation.* New York: Walker and Company, 1986.

Kenworthy, Leonard S. *Meditations for Older People.* Kennett Square, PA: Quaker Publications, 1986.

Murphy, Carol R. *The Valley of the Shadow.* Wallingford, PA: Pendle Hill Publications, 1972.

Smith, Bradford *Dear Gift of Life: A Man's Encounter with Death.* Wallingford, PA: Pendle Hill Publications, 1965.

SOME QUESTIONS FOR DISCUSSION

1. How do you interpret the author's title for this chapter?
2. Has your Meeting made a survey of the needs and contributions of older members recently?
3. Has your Yearly Meeting made a survey of the needs and contributions of its older members recently?
4. How is your Meeting a supporter or a detractor to older members? How could this situation be improved in the foreseeable future?
5. What special housing arrangements are provided for the elderly by your Meeting, Quarterly Meeting, and/or Yearly Meeting? Are there other measures which should be taken?
6. What special training do members of your Quaker group locally or regionally have in care of the elderly? What else might be done to encourage specialized training?
7. What assistance do you recall in your life from older people? How might their talents be better used in the future?
8. What difficulties have you encountered in dealing with older people? What suggestions do you have to solve or alleviate such difficulties?
9. What are the views of your local Quaker group on active and/or passive euthanasia? Of your Yearly Meeting?

ABOUT THE AUTHOR

Michael Allen has served as a professor of sociology at George Fox College in Newberg, Oregon since 1974. Since 1965 he has served on various community and national committees concerned with aging, such as the Arizona Governor's Commission on Aging, the White House Conference on Aging (1981), and the Mid-Willamette Valley Senior Services Agency. He has conducted research on aging in China, the aging of Native Americans in Arizona, and spiritual well-being and aging. He is a member of Northwest Yearly Meeting of Evangelical Friends Alliance.

Chapter 20

The Boundaries of Life: Is a Quaker Position Possible?

Dean C.T. Bratis

> We utterly deny...all outward wars and strife, and fighting with outward weapons, for any end, or under any pretense whatsoever; this is our testimony to the whole world.—Declaration to Charles II. November 21, 1660.

For the past three hundred years the Religious Society of Friends has struggled to live up to this expression of faith. Our belief in and commitment to peace is legendary. We can be proud of this legacy for it is one way to manifest our belief in the sanctity of life and in that of God in everyone.

I suppose it is because our history is so rich with the kind of courage needed to live this ideal that the current void is so obvious. It troubles me that we who so beautifully express our belief in the "light within" with such an explicit peace testimony, have not been able to crystallize our position on the boundaries of life. We have not wrestled with the substantive problems surrounding abortion, suicide, euthanasia, and the new reproductive engineering.

In the following pages I hope to present some information and pose some questions. I hope that these will be put into our collective cauldron and may in some small measure contribute to crystallizing our corporate position on this matter. Surely the issues are complex and a challenge to our belief in simplicity.

WHEN DOES HUMAN LIFE BEGIN?

There are many problems surrounding the question of life's boundaries, perhaps the most fundamental being to determine when life begins. We suggest, as a society, that life begins at birth. According to our birth certificates, we exist the moment we are born. But what of the moment before that or the one before that? What of premature babies? How do they fit into this definition?

Some would have us believe that human life begins when we are able to sustain it independently outside the womb. But on further examination such a definition is too shallow. We are, by our nature, dependent beings. An infant or toddler or even an adult cannot survive independently. Perhaps what we are saying with such a definition is that life begins when the fetus is viable outside the womb. What we mean by this is the earliest age at which our "machine" can sustain life. But does human life begin when our medical equipment says so? That time of viability will change as our medical equipment becomes more sophisticated. But beyond that flux, we are allowing our technology to dictate the answer to this key question.

Our "machines" have been telling us, for years now, when life ends. Many physicians agree that human life ends when we cannot sustain it without extraordinary means. But here again, what is viewed as extraordinary today may become routine medical procedure in the near future. Like the fetal viability reasoning, we are once again allowing our technology to make moral decisions.

It is not surprising that we are so dependent on our machines. A few short years ago we were told by our Supreme Court that life itself is a "machine." General Electric was given a patent for a bacterium they produced in their laboratory. The justification of that decision was an old Jefferson Patent Law. This law says that a patent may be given for the invention of a new machine or the improvement of an already existing one. So this living cell was seen by our highest court to be "a machine."

In April 1981, the Senate conducted hearings to address this vital question of when life begins. The consensus among the scientists and philosophers was that life begins at conception. A strong case can be made to support this, especially from a genetic view. A sperm cell or an egg cell has only half the number of chromosomes necessary to make a human being. No matter how we care for them, they can never be more than an egg or sperm; they live a few days and then die. A zygote (fertilized egg), however, has all the genes present that we will ever possess. It then becomes a matter of those genes interacting with the environment throughout our lifetime to produce the kind of person we will become.

It is this definition for the beginning of life, more than any other, that is the central focus and philosophical base for groups that oppose abortion. If life begins at conception, then abortion is ending a life by murder. Although I tend to lean heavily toward this definition of life's beginning, I cannot embrace it with the thunder and finality shown by my friends of other faiths.

The question for some is not when life begins, but rather when "humanness" begins. There are many markers used to identify that *"in utero"* moment: ranging from the first heartbeats to the development of the fingerprint whirls that mark our uniqueness. The one that intrigues me the most, and one on which I should like to concentrate here, has to do with our intelligence.

Some would have us believe that "humanness" begins when the brain becomes human. There are times in our embryotic development that we could point to and say that this cerebral development delineates us from other animals. But that does not address the question of when a brain becomes human. The answer to that question, I hope, is "never." Astronomers, for example, cannot hope to reach their full potential until forty or fifty years of age. Poets or musicians usually do not begin to attain their full potential until their life has unfolded. Carl Sandburg once paraphrased the Japanese artist Hokusai, who at the age of eighty-nine said, "If God had let me live five years longer, I should have been a writer." Certainly we who believe in continuing revelation cannot conceive of a time when we have attained our full human potential.

If it is our intellect that makes us human, then the brilliant would be far more human than the slow of tongue. This view would have us talking in terms of degrees of humanness; with adults being more human than children, by virtue of their knowledge. Beyond that, we would be forced to make value judgments. A retarded child in this scenario would be less valuable than one of normal intellect. Do children become more human and therefore more valuable as they become more intelligent? And, finally, what is the bare performance minimum to be reached before we say a person is now within the range of human intellect?

In many ways I question the merit of giving intelligence such a prominent role in determining our humanness. I submit that to see intelligence as the principal marker of our humanness is too narrow a view, for intelligence without soul is hollow. And, finally, the verdict is not in on the value of this intellect, at least not to the extent that we have used it thus far.

There are, of course, those who believe that abortion should be performed on demand. For many of these people the central focus is that a woman has the right to do what she chooses with her body. But do our bodies belong only to us? Are they shared by all those who love us? Are they even shared by those we scarcely know? Surely we have some rights over our bodies, but are they this absolute?

Another consideration is the role of the prospective father. To what extent should he be involved in this decision? How would that involvement obligate him after the baby is born? Should a man be allowed to insist that the woman continue the pregnancy if he is willing to participate actively in the care of that baby?

Finally, a case can be made for the woman's body changing so dramatically during a pregnancy that it is no longer hers. The fetus has suppressed her immunogenic system, altered her hormonal balance, and changed her behavior patterns to such an extent that she is scarcely recognizable to herself.

Perhaps the pro-choice position on abortion is saying that individual choice is the most important value. Even if it becomes universally accepted that life begins at conception, in other words, that life pales by comparison to the value given individual choice.

ZERO POINTS

Whether we support the pro or anti abortion view, we may not subscribe to either absolutely. If abortion is allowed, does that mean it should be allowed simply because the fetus is not the desired sex? If not, how do we justify this as an excuse, yet allow for other kinds of abortions?

If we are opposed to abortion, are we always opposed to it? What if the pregnancy endangers the life of the mother? If we allow abortion here, then aren't we making a value judgment that is at odds with our anti-abortion view?

The point to be made by these questions is that there are zero points for all of us. We have gradations of acceptability on either side of this issue. The zero point (or bottom line) varies from person to person and generation to generation. Consider, for example, former and current views on artificial insemination. To add to this dilemma is the prospect that zero points change in the course of an individual's lifetime. Is a corporate view possible given this kind of fluctuating ethic? Can we, perhaps, describe a range of acceptable alternatives? This is a compelling question that merits more discussion.

SUICIDE

A second extension of the boundaries of life question involves the problem of suicide. Those who support a person's right to commit suicide might again involve the idea of individual choice. Suicide, following this premise, is our ultimate choice of what we want to do with our bodies.

Traditional (often religious) opposition to suicide would be based on the idea that our bodies belong to God as well as to us. In addition, some traditional views have seen life as a preparation for entrance into another dimension of existence, which I shall call heaven. (I know full well the kind of images that word may conjure up). From this point of view, suicide might be seen as a sin against God. It might also give us a slow start in heaven—much like a deformed baby might get a slow start on life here on earth.

Before we turn our collective noses up at such a notion, perhaps it would do some good to consider any evidence in support of such a view. The most compelling work done in recent years on death and dying has been done by Moody and Kubler-Ross. Those investigators interviewed people who had been pronounced dead by their physicians. The large majority report it to be a pleasant experience and often did not want to come back. One common element in the accounts reported was an encounter with a "being of light." The love radiating from this being was beyond description. Additionally, Moody reports:

> According to these new views, development of the soul...does not stop upon death. Rather, it continues on the other side, perhaps eternally, but certainly for a period of time and to a depth which can only be glimpsed, while we are still in physical bodies, "through a glass darkly...."

The one striking exception to the near universality of such bucolic accounts of death comes from those who have attempted suicide!

Another objection to suicide can be mustered from a less traditional vantage point. Some would say that life should be devoted to growth and learning. The Quaker community might call this seeking or continuous revelation. Life from this viewpoint involves growth and learning not only in joys but also in the sorrows presented to us at each moment of our lives. One man says as a result of his near-death experience: "No matter how old you are, don't stop learning. For this process, I gather, goes on for eternity." Suicide would take away that opportunity.

None of the issues discussed in this chapter, however, take on their full meaning until we are faced with them in our own lives. What would we do, for example, about a suicidal *person* in our lives? Would we encouraged that individual to live on? If we did, how much of that person's burden are we then willing to share? Are we obligated to share that burden? Would we be more likely to support them in their successes and console them in their failures?

EUTHANASIA

Yet the burden of ending a life or at least allowing it to end without direct intervention is another aspect of the question of the boundaries of life. Euthanasia has been defined as "putting a person to death painlessly." A logical extension of this "active" euthanasia is that of "passive" euthanasia. Passive euthanasia involves withholding measures that would sustain life, and thereby letting nature take it course. Passive euthanasia is an idea with which many physicians feel more comfortable, since it may not fly in the face of their commitment to save lives quite as badly as active euthanasia does.

Two plaguing questions involved here are: who should make the decision and what criteria should be used? Often the decision is one reached by the family, the physician, and the patient, although there are cases when the patient wanted to die but was overruled by the courts.

What if the patient is incapable of making such a decision? This has led many people to the "living will." In such a document, legally used in fourteen states and the District of Columbia, we can specify how we want to be treated if we become terminally ill.

The question of what criteria to use was recently addressed by Jacob Javits in an article on what it means to be terminally ill. Javits suffered from amyotrophic lateral sclerosis (Lou Gehrig's disease). This infirmity results in an incurable disabling of the nerves that control movement. He sees a need to establish a test to determine who should live and who should die. Furthermore he suggests that it should depend on "whether the brain is functioning and whether there is any expectation that the patient will continue to enjoy what is truly life."

Although Javits and people like him are an inspiration to all of us, I question the validity of such criteria. Brain functioning covers a broad spectrum and, further, compels us to tie the value of life to levels of intellectual functioning. Does this, for example, mean vegetative functioning? Or must it be cerebral? If so, at what level do we consider the cerebrum functioning? Is it trial and error learning, conditioning, reasoning, insight, or any number of other types of learning?

Javits' concept of a life being "truly" a life must also give us pause. As we age we find that what was "truly" life for us in the past may pale by comparison to the stage of life we are in now. The vigor of youth, for example, may be replaced by a richness of inner peace and security. Which of these is truly life? Do not we all need to adjust to life's changing challenges?

Finally, the word "any" marks Javits as an optimist. But it would not provide us with enormous guidance in a decision regarding a terminally ill person.

DEATH

Our attempts at defining the moment of death have varied throughout human history and have included respiratory rate and heartbeat, among others. Many physicians now consider loss of cerebral function as the marker. Some thirty-one states and the District of Columbia now have "brain death" statutes. Yet it can be argued that we really do not know when life ends. After all, many patients return from what we call "clinical death" to tell the kinds of stories reported by Moody and Kubler-Ross. Were these people really dead, or was it simply our inadequacy at determining that moment?

Perhaps the questions of when life begins and when it ends are not opposite views of the same question at all. Perhaps they are so qualitatively different that to apply the same criteria to them is meaningless. Most people with a terminal illness have, after all, lived out the bulk of their lives. That alone is a marked difference that might impact on the criteria we use.

We are, in many ways, prepared for death by the process of aging. That, of course, is not true of the unborn. I can still hear the words, incomprehensible to my young ears, spoken by my grandmother. She told me how "tired she was and how she was ready for the peace and new horizons that death would bring." That was not to denigrate living, for she was an active woman until the end. It was only that she was ready. There is such a delicate balance between the sacredness of life and the comfort of knowing when to give it up.

I have witnessed two natural deaths in my lifetime. In both cases there was a marked change on what was to be each one's final day. Perhaps those last moments before death are necessary in order to finally give it up. Maybe it is another example of how each moment presented to us in our lives is an opportunity for growth. Do we have the right to take away that time of preparation?

There enters into this philosophical discussion the problem of pain. Should a person be allowed to die if the pain is unbearable? Death, of course, may not be the best answer. Were I in that kind of pain, I am not sure I would want at that moment to live on. But then, again, I almost feel that way with a bad cold. Is not that kind of reaction to be expected when a person is in pain? There may be other alternatives to this pain. It is possible, for example, to administer small dosages of pain killers in anticipation of pain. This can effectively control pain and is practiced by many people in our society. There are, also, natural pain killers produced by the body. And, finally, many people can bear the pain. It is difficult to know whether this tolerance is available until it happens. Suppose that we have included in our "living will" a stipulation to practice euthanasia if we are in pain. Then when the time comes, we find that we are much better able to bear it than we had expected, but we are not able to tell anyone this. That is surely one of the hazards of trying to anticipate our own deaths.

Is the idea of a painless death an extension of the idea of a painless life? Is pain a part of what Javits calls "truly" being alive?

REPRODUCTIVE ENGINEERING

Reproductive engineering, also called artificial or alternative reproduction, has added a new and confusing twist to the problems surrounding the question of life's boundaries. Recent developments in the area of test tube babies, frozen embryos, and the like, threaten to tax further our already strained adherence to the Quaker precept of simplicity.

There now exist approximately two hundred clinics, worldwide, capable of performing *in vitro* fertilizations and implantations. This technique, first made public by Steptoe and Edwards in England, is designed to help couples with fertility problems. The egg is extracted from the mother and fertilized in the laboratory *(in vitro)*, grown for a few days, and then implanted into the mother's womb. The success rate may be as high as thirty-three percent but averages approximately twenty percent. Another way to express this is to say that eight out of ten attempts are not successful and result in abortions. If life begins at conception, then we are knowingly destroying human life. Should we continue this experimental research on human embryos?

The problem has recently escalated to frozen embryos. In a case in Australia, a wealthy couple had the wife's eggs fertilized by a donor's sperm, since the husband's was not viable. The subsequent embryos were frozen, awaiting implantation. The couple, however, were killed in an airplane accident. The question became what to do with those embryos. Should the government be allowed to make such a decision? Should it be a decision considered only from the legal point of view? Would such a case establish precedent for any subsequent cases?

The problem will surely escalate. In the not too distant future artificial wombs could become a reality. Coupled with improving techniques in genetic manipulation, the possibility of producing "tailor-made" babies may become a reality.

Addressing the question of life's boundaries is long overdue. I am not suggesting that we dictate morality, only that extensive consideration of this matter would surely produce a wide spectrum of possibilities for all of us.

QUAKERS AS RECONCILERS

Given the belief system we adhere to, is a Quaker position on the boundaries of life possible? I am not sure it is. However, it must be quickly added that the same kind of question might have been posed regarding the peace testimony at an earlier part of our history. This is, certainly, not an easy question. But it is one to which we need to bring our best thinking. Something which, in my view, we have yet to do.

We sometimes use as a reason for not stating a corporate position that we do not want to impose our views on others. Could not that same reasoning be applied equally well to other problems for which we have taken such a position? As I pose this question, I am reminded of something that Arthur Eddington, the eminent Quaker scientist, once said: "We understand the true meaning of neither science nor religion unless seeking is placed in the forefront." Such an idea from a prominent Quaker might suggest that we play the role of reconcilers. Surely such a position is one with which we are already familiar.

Our belief in that of God in everyone almost forces us into such a position. The light of Christ within would apply equally well to the mother and the fetus, the suicide victim and the loved ones, and to those in need of care and the care-givers.

We can be reconcilers if we have a mind to do so. A suggestion, for example, on the issue of abortion was made by Chuck Fager in the February 15, 1985 issue of the *Friends Journal*. He suggested what he calls the "St. Louis Proposal." That is a legal recognition of fetal humanity but the exclusion of criminal sanctions against abortion as a way of protecting that humanity. Clearly here is a reconciler's view that might open the way to the protection of that humanity.

Rather than taking sides and debating, perhaps we need to admit what truth there is on either side. Then we can work to open the way for alternatives. That does not, however, prevent us from taking a position on the matter of the boundaries of life any more than it would prevent us from taking a position on war and peace.

We have taken clear, corporate positions on matters of peace, prejudice, and imprisonment. But we have done it without being judgmental. We have done it by having equal compassion for both the soldier and the pacifist. We have presented alternatives that care for their humanness and for that of God in each of them.

RELYING ON THE SPIRIT

I am not sure what direction we will take in the future on this matter. If we remain true to our heritage, however, whatever emerges will be an expression of our allegiance to the law of God and not of man. For as we are reminded by the Elders of Balby, Yorkshire (1656), it is: "...not from the letter, for the letter killeth, but the Spirit giveth life."

SOME SUGGESTED READINGS

Brandt, Richard B. *The Morality and Rationality of Suicide: A Handbook for the Study of Suicide.* London: Oxford University Press, 1975.

Fager, Chuck. "The Abortion Impasse: A Way Out." *Friends Journal.* (February 12, 1978).

Javits, Jacob. "When Should Doctors Let a Patient Die?" *Discover.* (August 1984).

Moody, Raymond. *Life After Life.* Harrisburg, PA: Stackpole Books, 1976.

Taylor, Phyllis. "The Journey." *Friends Journal.* (February 15, 1978).

Tifft, Susan. "Debate on the Boundaries of Life." *Time.* (April 11, 1982).

Wallis, Claudia. "Making Babies: The New Science of Conception." *Time.* (September 10, 1984).

SOME QUESTIONS FOR DISCUSSION

1. What opportunities present themselves from time to time to witness to your views on abortion, euthanasia, or suicide? What problems have you encountered? How have you tried to overcome these obstacles?
2. Discuss instances of people growing from the difficulties of wrestling with the boundaries of life.
3. What are some implications of the St. Louis Proposal?
4. Is there a need for a Quaker position on the issues discussed in this chapter? What are some stumbling blocks to such a position?

248

5. What role should the federal government play in each of the following areas: abortion, euthanasia, suicide, test tube babies and frozen embryos?
6. How do you feel about this 1980 Vatican declaration: "The Roman Catholic Church says that treatment could be stopped on a terminal patient if its continued use could only secure a precarious and burdensome prolongation of life"?

ABOUT THE AUTHOR

Dean C. T. Bratis is a graduate of the Trenton State College in chemistry, with an advanced degree in biology from the University of Pennsylvania. He has taught college-level biological sciences for twenty years. He has also taught a course entitled Science and Society for the past six years. He has authored several articles in scientific, educational, and religious journals. His most recent book is a laboratory manual in *Human Genetics*. He is currently working on a human genetics textbook. He would welcome letters from readers who want to share their views on the boundaries of life with him. He can be reached at Route 2, Box 32, Glenmoore, Pennsylvania 19343.